Autism: The Big Book Set of HELP!

Book One: Autism and Diagnosis

By Heather L. E. McKay

Acknowledgements

My sincerest thanks and gratitude go to:

My sister Lauren, for always being there for me, giving me the confidence and backing to become an inventor, and looking after the kids long enough for me to be able to complete this book. You are my best friend, my mentor, my hero, and my confidant, I love you.

To my boys, the loves of my life; the reason I keep going, and the reason this book exists. You both light up my life and create so much joy; you are best things that ever happened to me.

To my whole family for supporting me through the good times and the bad. To my parents for always supporting and loving me as I am and giving me the space to grow and develop in my own unique way.

To my friend and publisher Clare, that buoyed me up when I most needed it and put me on the right path. And to my publisher Cat who was very patient, and extremely helpful in getting my book out there.

To all the autistic advocates, writers, bloggers, and artists (and the autistic community as a whole) that constantly face adversity while daily dealing with their own struggles; but still manage to be there for complete strangers. You manage to create safe spaces for us to connect and learn, and continually strive for the improvement of disabled people the world over. I have added a list (at the end of book five) of those of you I have been admiring for some time – I think you deserve more credit, thanks, and acknowledgement than you get. Truly – thank you – and please keep up the wonderful work (if you feel you can).

To John Greally for graciously allowing me to quote him and learn from his experience and wisdom. One of his greats quotes was written on 22/09/2023 "Autism, like Womenism and Gayism, does not exist. But Autistics, like Women and Gays do exist. That is where endless confusion seeps in. It is not a defect or disorder. It is a way of being".

To my therapist, medical and support group (in no particular order): Kimberley & Hannah, Fiona, Lydelle, Bianca & Rani,

Michael, Nicole, Lucy, LeighAnne, John, Bonnie and Robyn, Sari, Alex and Jodie; thank you all for your continued patience with me and help with my children, without your support I'd hate to think where we'd be.

And finally, to my friends; Cindy and Jen. You two have been stable steady rocks for me, and I appreciate you being there for me, no matter how close or how far away you live, thank you.

Foreword

Do you have a loved one who is suspected of being neurodivergent, has been diagnosed as autistic, or is wondering about their neurology?

Do you struggle as a parent to understand your neurodivergent child?

Are you a teacher or therapist who needs or wants more information about being neurodivergent and better ways to help?

Are you a late diagnosed autistic, or an autistic who is struggling and needing ideas to cope in a neurotypical world, or just needs a little support, or help, or additional information?

Congratulations, you've come to right place, and you've taken the first step.

What's different about this set of books? It's a set of references books, that's all about autism. But this is different because it's written by an autistic person; for parents, teachers, employers, autistics, and therapists that love, teach and help autistic people. It was an extremely big book, so I broke it into 5 books to help you manage it better, because there's a lot to know about autism and how to help, hence the name: The **Big** Book Set of Help!

These books are here to help.

The inception of these books came about from my need for more information... and the **right** information. Like many parents before me, when my kids were diagnosed; I asked myself and everyone around me:

"Where do I start?"

"Where do I find information?"

"How do I get help?"

"How do I help my kids?"

"How do I know this will even work, or help?"

"Why isn't XYZ working?"

Why are my kids diagnosed, but I'm the same as them and not diagnosed?

Could I also be autistic?

Do I need the same supports?

What could help me and the kids as a whole family?

I couldn't find the answers. The doctors were telling me to take my children to a bunch of different therapies. But how? How much will it cost? Who? Where? Why? What do they do? What next? How does any of this help?

These books are for anyone who has asked these questions. Anyone who wants to learn more, know more, and help more, just like any parent or good therapist.

Read them like any reference book – if you need help on a specific topic; look it up in the contents – and go straight to that section. We are busy people, that face many daily challenges, and we sometimes need access to information immediately, or perhaps later on down the track. Finding it at the right time is extremely hard. I hope these books are comprehensive enough to help you find the right answers and to guide you to where to get more information, if you need it.

My writing style and way of talking can be very direct – please do not read into my writing as having a 'tone' or having more meaning than it does. I'm extremely factual, I'm direct, I like to speak my mind, (and sometimes I don't have a filter), I do not say things to offend or to have additional tone or meaning – take me as I am, at face value – I'm autistic.

Some of the topics you will not need to know anything about –
as they will not apply to your individual child, student, client, or
yourself. Skip over those sections until you need them. I wish
you luck on your journey getting to know your wonderful child/
ren/loved one or self; for the unique miracles they/you are. You
will begin to realise that your neurodivergent loved one just
thinks differently, and just needs your love and support.

Don't panic, don't stress – you've got this! All you need is
information – and I hope these books will fill the gaps that have
been missing – **if** any has been missing.

Contents

The layout of these books

These books are designed to be used like one whole reference book. They have been broken into separate books, for easy access and to easily identify different topics and needs for each individual or family. Pick up Book One if you need general information on autism and diagnosis. Pick up Book Two if you need more information on the co-occurring disabilities that may be causing you to struggle, or you need to know where to get more help. Book Three is all about therapies and ways to help, **and** what not to do. Book Four gives you more information about tools and ideas on extra subjects you may need to know about to support your autistic loved one, student, or client. The start of Book Five is mostly about schools, learning, homeschooling, and where to after school ends. The second part of Book Five is about adult lives and studying at university, working life and the future for autistics, and may be beneficial for autistics themselves.

To use these books: go to the section that you need information on, and skip the rest, or read them cover to cover if you have the spoons (check out SpoonTheory for more information). I know the size is daunting, but once it is broken down into subject matter, it is easier to read and understand. You do not need to read all of these books, but you can, if you want a more thorough background and understanding. I have gathered all the information, so it is readily accessible to you; there is an awful lot to learn about autism and neurodiversity – but not everyone needs to know everything. But when you do need to know something, hopefully you will find it here.

I have spaced out the paragraphs, because that's how many neurodivergent people prefer and need their reading material spaced. I have printed these books in a font that hopefully meet the needs of the majority (it is from the sans family); with less embellishments and more gaps and no italics (for Dyslexics and people with stigmatisms and other vision issues). I'm sorry it's printed on white paper, for those of you who find it polarising, I only had a choice of white or cream. I do suggest you read the section on Irlen's Syndrome to find overlays that may help with toning down the colour of the pages. You don't need to have Irlen's for a coloured overlay to help with your individual needs.

Take your time and remember to take care of yourself. Learning anything new can be overwhelming, take it one subject at a time – preferably the subject which is causing you the most stress or the most confusion.

What will you learn from these books?

- Each book has been broken into segments of information. Categories like ARFID, Elopement, Regulation, Schooling, Toileting (incontinence) and Co-occurring Disabilities; the topics that people often need help with the most. And other general information and more in-depth explanations about things like ABA, autism, tools, and products, and neuroaffirming ways to help your child.

- You will see that many sections have links to more information, tools, and resources. If you have a digital version of these books, you will be able to click on the links. But if you are like me and prefer printed books, this may be a pain – I'm sorry. You don't need to click on the links, as I've tried to summarise some of the information contained therein, to simplify for more tactile people who like reading from physical pages.

- The books are full of interesting information, tips and advice about how to deal with different situations; taken from my actual lived experiences. There is also a list of tools of the trade: these are products/ toys, therapy tools and equipment that can help your child to learn a new concept, develop a certain skill or how to use products to self-regulate emotions and deal with stressful situations, advocate for themselves, or overcome a particular problem.

- There is also information about some other divergences or some disabilities that your child may or may not have, with links and information about where to go from here. Eg: ADHD and executive functioning, PDA, or a learning disability.

I hope these books will inspire and help, but also encourage people to learn about inclusivity for neurodivergents, and change thinking. I know it won't suit some, as "you can't please all of the people, all of the time". But I hope it will be a set of books that can help people out there like me; parents, teachers and even neuro-divergents who perhaps are struggling, but not understanding why. People who are doing everything that the parenting books and universities have taught us about parenting, teaching and autism, but it's not working. The children are still having meltdowns, and everyone seems to be at odds, or perhaps mental health issues seem to becoming more of an issue, and you don't know what to do.

I thought I was right, and doing all the right things, but when I allowed myself to listen and learn, I will freely admit – I was wrong! (my mum will faint when she reads these three words). Admitting that I was wrong was my first step. Changing, accepting, learning, (from autistic people) and figuring out what to do now and in the future was my second step, and especially what will and does matter most to my children!

I will also freely admit that I was ableist, I had no idea that I had (and probably still have) some internalised ableism that was getting in the way of me truly understanding and helping my children. I was doing everything according to social norms and expectations – and it was wrong! I was actually hindering my children's development, and I was causing more stress, more anxiety and more masking. Once I asked myself why I was doing those things – (and then chucked them out the window along with some of the advice I'd been given) and changed my mindset from the medical view of autism to a neuro-affirming view (social model of disability) – everything calmed, everyone calmed, and everything became very clear and, generally, fairly simple.

I began to question everything I'd ever done, and why I'd done it that way. Ask yourself the question "WHY?" to everything you do in your life. If the answer is because someone at some stage said, "because I said so" – or because "that's the way we've always done it", or "because society expects that", or because of some other inane or arbitrary answer that doesn't truly justify **why**. Then find a new way, one that makes sense for; your child, your patient/client, your student, or yourself.

Please read this book with an open mind and try to look at whatever you do with a fresh perspective and ask "Why?" to everything. I guarantee you will start to see your child and the world around you in a more positive and helpful way. A way that will help your child, student, or client to succeed -not as society demands, but as **they** need and want to succeed, in their own natural and beautiful ways.

About me and these books

I'm a single mum of two adorable boys, they are both neurodivergent just like me. I didn't know I was autistic or ADHD until we undertook the diagnosis journey for my boys. I knew my boys seemed to require more from me than other children needed from their parents, but I never understood why. I thought it was all down to me being socially awkward or being a bad parent. I had never really been around children as we are a tiny family. I had a limited knowledge of children and their developmental milestones, and I blamed myself for being a terrible parent and not knowing how to help kids, use boundaries, or get them to eat vegetables. As it turned out, it was not my fault, and it was not my children's fault. I wasn't a bad parent; I didn't need more, or any 'discipline', and my kids didn't have to eat vegetables; I just didn't have all the information I needed to be the great parent my unique kids needed me to be.

I needed to understand that my children's brains, and even my own brain works differently to others. I needed information about how to understand them and myself, and how to help them and guide them in a way that made sense to **them**, that helped them according to **their** needs and preferences.

I needed to unlearn my self-imposed 'normal' (or typical) social expectations; that children should act a certain way, have to be disciplined, taught, fed, toilet trained using behaviouralism, raised and schooled the same way that all the other parents were doing with their children (and achieving brilliantly – I was jealous). Once I accepted that my parenting method wasn't working because we were having a communication and understanding breakdown, and some of the things I was doing, was causing trauma and felt abusive to my kids; we turned it around. I changed the way I thought, I changed my expectations, and I changed the way we did every little single thing – and I said to myself "screw everyone and their judgement" I'll do what makes my kids happy.

This took a major lens shift to achieve, and the unmasking of my 40+ years on earth. I took a weekend of respite away from my boys. I cried about how silly I had been, and how lost I'd become. I never cried **for**, or **about** my boys – because there was nothing wrong with them – I was the problem!

I started to look at my boys in a different light. I compared them to me. I thought about my own childhood, my own struggles, my own strengths, weaknesses, opportunities, and threats. Yes! I did a SWOT analysis on myself – because that was how my brain worked. I wanted to analyse and deconstruct everything – then rebuild it. And I had my "AHA" moment. I realised that every single thing that my kids struggled with, was what I struggled with as a kid and even now as an adult. But I had been taught, instructed, brow beaten and self-taught into masking all of my problems, and taught that there was only one way to do things – the neurotypical way, but that hadn't worked for me, and wasn't working for my kids – but **why**? I had been hiding everything about myself for 40+ years. I had learnt from society that I was supposed to think a certain way, learn a certain way, teach a certain way, manage a certain way, parent, and live a certain way, and even laugh, eat, and be depressed a certain way – and none of it had felt natural or 'right' my whole life.

I was autistic!!!! I am autistic!!!! And I am also ADHD. I saw a psychologist and received my autism diagnosis, but I forgot to ask about ADHD. I consider myself a self-identified ADHD'er. I forgot to ask about ADHD because that's a part of also possibly being ADHD, I forget things, or I become distracted or focused on something else entirely, and because autism and ADHD have so many cross over traits that I thought it was redundant. I will not be telling everyone what 'level' the psych gave me. Not because I'm ashamed of it, but because levels are discriminatory (they are effectively functioning labelling which hurts us) and these levels act as barriers to being seen as competent or alternatively, they are used for denying supports.

Please don't think or say that I'm not autistic **enough** to talk about autism either. Or that I'm too white, or too privileged, or too straight etc. That train of thought is what leads to segregation of our community, and to white and/or privilege, racial, sexual, disability, or any biased shaming (yes, I've been shamed in my own community for being too 'white', or not disabled 'enough' and not intersectionalled enough), and it causes bigotry against anyone and everyone. Every autistic person deserves to be heard and respected as autistic individuals, no matter their background, or intersectionality, where they live or their family dynamic (see the section on **Minorities within Minorities**). My assigned 'level' (of autism) is my business, and because it changes daily and weekly, it is also obsolete (more about that later). I'm **not** less autistic just because I'm not like your child.

If you think I am not autistic **enough**, it might be because you are comparing me to your child. But I'm not your child, no one is. But you have to remember that autistic adults exist, and your child will one day be one of us. We learn and grow, like any human. Your child will learn and grow too, but it's hard to picture children as adults, and it's hard to picture a disabled child in the future, either because we are fearful of the future, or because we are not presuming competence, or know nothing about autism and co-occurring disabilities. We want everything in the world for our children, but we don't want to project unfair expectations on them – no matter what their neurotype. But we also don't want to hold them back with unfair assumptions that they will always be like they are now. I guarantee you, that they will **never** be the same as they are now – because no child remains a child forever.

I had delays like not walking until quite late for a toddler, and I didn't speak (use mouth words) until I was at school for a while (around 7 years old), and even then, I was delayed for quite some time, people thought I was shy and would 'grow out of it'. As it happened, I did. But I wasn't growing out of it, I was growing **into** myself. And no – it **wasn't** school that helped, it was **time**. I had been in daycare, fulltime, from 6 months old, so I had had plenty of time for 'social' practice and opportunities to learn language from many different people and sources. I wasn't put in therapy as no one knew much about autism back then, so I was allowed to grow up naturally, in my own time and in my own way. And when I reached about 10 years old, no-one could shut me up. Every autistic is different, that's why the phrase "you are not like my child" is quite true, but it is also extremely offensive and shouldn't be used to invalidate autistic adults. Yes, I **was** like some of your children, as I couldn't use mouth words, but I'm not like them now, because now I can. My experience and life take nothing away from your children, but my experiences and knowledge **could** help some of you who have children who are experiencing what I went through.

Not all autistics experience the same childhood, or upbringing, the same co-occurring disabilities, or the same delays, in fact some don't have any delays at all, and some have co-occurring disabilities that make not using mouth words a lifetime occurrence. It doesn't make them less, or better or anything else. They are still autistic and disabled by society because society is what disables us. I couldn't make friends or understand social situations or expectations. I hated school and was bullied. I didn't 'play' like other kids, and I never learnt to do cartwheels, use skates or swim. I watched the same movies on repeat; when my family eventually bought a VHS player in the late 1980's. I listened to the same music on repeat until my parents wanted to scream.

I was attached to my mother's hip, but everyone said I was shy or 'a mummy's girl'. I had ARFID my whole life, but it wasn't called ARFID in those days. I was called an undisciplined picky eater and a 'spoilt brat', and I had a bottle till I was 7. I had many co-occurring disabilities, but we didn't know that until I was older. I had meltdowns, and looking back now, I realised my fainting episodes were manifestations of meltdowns and shutdowns. I was agoraphobic and never left the house and refused to wear anything except one blue and white striped jumper – even in the summer in Australia. I was unco-ordinated when eating and constantly dropped food on my clothes (I found out later that I had fine motor skill problems but was great at gross motor skills), hated sport of all kinds and couldn't concentrate in school. I hated books and reading, I was intelligent but just couldn't 'apply' myself. I was called a bitch, and bad-tempered little girl. I was suicidal as a teen and I was eventually told that the people in my year level at school "were scared of me", I had no idea that they all thought I was constantly mad.

When I grew up, I couldn't hold down a job, or keep friends, or relationships, and I found solace in many bottles of Jim Beam.

I still have some of the same struggles that I had as a child and as a teen; but I have learnt to hide them, to mask them. Some of them went away with leaving school, as many of my problems were due to the mainstream schooling system. I still can't hold down a job, and have been long term unemployed for some years now. I'm still agoraphobic and still have meltdowns and sensory issues and ARFID, and many co-occurring disabilities. So, in some ways, yes, I'm still like the autistic child that I was, but now I can walk, talk, read, and write, and I now have my own children. Every autistic person is different, and one is not more or less autistic than the next. Do not devalue me or your child by saying I'm not autistic enough to talk about autism, or understand some things about your child, or understand about autism. My experience is my experience, your autistic child's experience is their experience, and they **will** grow, develop, and learn – in their own way, and they will become autistic adults, children do not remain children forever.

When I realised all this information about myself and about my children, I started to research more about autism and ADHD. But the books and literature I found about autism were all written by neurotypicals or allistics, and I realised that none of their information was right, and some of it was downright offensive. With every new piece of information I found, I realised I didn't feel like it applied to me or my children. It didn't gel. It felt wrong and incongruent to everything I felt and knew growing up and now. Even some of the therapists (that I eventually fired) were saying and doing things that made everything worse, and yet they were supposedly the experts on autism. Some of them even made me feel physically ill with their suggestions of what to do and how to help my children. It turned out that they were using behaviouralism, and that's why I found it to be so abusive and harmful.

There had to be better information available. I searched the internet and support groups, but they were all still filled with misinformation and advice that was abhorrent and hurting my children. I finally found organisations and support groups that were run by autistic adults. And I had my second 'AHA' moment. I was already doing some of the things that they were suggesting to other parents, things that I knew were already working with my children. So, I read more, I even tried out a couple of their suggestions and followed some of their advice – and those worked too. Could it be that autistic adults really do have some sort of secret magic? No! It's just that autistic adults used to be autistic children, and they know what works for them, so their suggestions also often work for other autistics and neuro-divergents that are experiencing similar issues. It's not rocket science, just common sense.

If you want to learn how to play golf like a pro, you ask a pro golfer their habits, tricks, tips and how they deal with certain issues. You don't go to the therapist of the golfer for help – you go to the golfer. Yes, the therapist can help you with your individual issues, but they can't help with generalised golfing problems, and how to play golf better, or become an expert on it, unless they are golfers themselves. You might be surprised to learn that autistic adults love helping allistic parents how to help their autistic children. Because these autistic adults want all autistic children to be supported, loved, and helped. They want these children to have better lives than they had, easier lives, accepted lives, inclusive lives! And so do I! I wanted to help other parents, teachers, and therapists; the way autistic adults helped me.

I had been researching for a few years and had gathered a lot of information. But that doesn't help other parents, it only helped me. So, I joined allistic run groups, and started replying to parents questions and appeals for help. But that only helped one or two parents – not teachers, and not therapists. What I needed was a book, a reference book that people could look up and get help from immediately. But I needed one that was written by an autistic, that understood what it was like to be autistic. One that didn't suggest toxic methods or use offensive language that triggered ND's that might be reading it. And one that combined information from neuro-affirming sources and neurodivergent voices. So, I wrote this book, in hopes that it might fill some gaps.

I gathered the information in this book from autistic sources that had 'been there, trialled that'. I cross referenced it against all the autistic groups/bloggers/writers and companies run by autistics that I could find; to make sure that the information contained herein was a good representation of what autistic preferred and what autistics would approve of. I wanted to make sure that the advice I was receiving was not just one person's opinion – but the combined opinion of the autistic community.

Disclaimer

This book is not intended to be a scientific research book, it is the combined information of a community that has been suppressed and misunderstood for generations. I've written it from the perspective of an actually autistic person with autistic kids – because I am! It is a 'help' book, you can use the information contained in the way you feel best. It is not intended to be offensive to anyone or any group, or to tell you that you have to do it my way, or the autistic way; it has been written in the hopes that someone out there may benefit in some way, from even one piece of information I have gathered over the years.

These books are not intended to tell anyone they are doing anything wrong or to tell them they must do it in any specific way – do it your way! It is intended to get people to think about their life, or their child's life, or the way we work, learn, and live, and hopefully make changes for the better – for everyone involved. The suggestions are just that! – Suggestions! There are tools, links, and tips that I have trialled myself or have found suggested by multiple autistics across multiple platforms – none of the suggestions in this book are from just one autistic person or one specific autistic group. You will see that I also back up most of the suggestions with articles and research - as I have an analytical mind and never rely on opinion alone – I love facts and research.

I believe strongly in questioning everything; and a pet hate of mine, is when people state "that's the way we've always done it". Just because that's the way it has always been done – does not mean it is the best way, or that it could not be improved upon, or that it is not harmful to an individual or a group of people. I also hate 'change for the sake of change' – If something is working for you and your whole family – do it, but make sure you are fully informed about the possible consequences and outcomes, and make sure you are doing whatever it is for the benefit of all, and mostly for your autistic loved one (whether that's your child, or yourself) – it has to be their decision and their want and need – not the need or want of the parent, teacher or therapist.

I did not write this from the position of a professional psychologist or therapist, I've written this as a parent and as a personal neurodivergent perspective. I hope it can help to explain some of the issues and problems that we as parents, and as ND people face every day.

I'm not asking you to change yourself or your family to be more neurodivergent, or the neurodivergent in the family to become more neurotypical. I'm asking that we meet each other halfway. The only change that may be needed is understanding and compassion, love and kindness. The information is here, so you can get a little glimpse into our lives and our neurodifferences. We sometimes do the same thing, but in reverse to NTs. We study NTs like a national geographic documentary, so we can understand how to navigate your world and society, and cope living within it. If you do the same, and study us by learning **from** us (instead of from 'experts' who only guess as to our reasons, behaviours, feelings and thoughts), you can quickly learn how to **help** us and live **with** us. It is unfair to ask anyone to change to be more like the other group – as it's unnatural and you will likely give up and return to your natural state anyway. But if we understand each other, we have a better chance of all neurotypes not only surviving, but co-existing happily in our own natural states. Neither neurotype is superior nor inferior, we are just different and could definitely benefit from listening to each other more.

Please use these books as a chance to listen. What you do with what you hear is up to you, I cannot force anyone to understand, to be anything, or to do anything. I only hope that you will feel more confident and aware of the differences (and why they are a positive thing), and hopefully become more understanding and embrace all neurotypes into a more inclusive world.

- The author provides this book and its contents on an "as is" basis and make no representations or warranties of any kind with respect to this book and/or its contents. Although the author has made every effort to ensure any information contained herein was correct at the time of publication, the publisher and the author assume no responsibility for errors, inaccuracies, omissions, or any other inconsistencies contained herein. The author and publisher disclaim any liability to any party for loss or damage, including consequential loss, caused by any errors or omissions, which you may suffer as a result of your reliance on this book.

The contents of this book are for informational purposes and not intended to diagnose, treat, cure or prevent any condition or disease. You understand that this book is not intended to substitute for medical advice or a consultation with a licensed medical practitioner. You should always seek the advice of a doctor, psychologist or other qualified medical professional regarding a specific medical condition or treatment.

The publisher and the author disclaim all representations and warranties, including but not limited to warranties in regard to medical diagnosis or treatment for a particular purpose. The testimonials and examples contained within this work are derived from the lived experiences of the author and are not intended to represented or guarantee that you will achieve the same or similar results.

Any opinions expressed within the book represent the personal views and opinions of the author derived from their personal experiences and reflect the authors recollections of those experiences over time. This book may contain references to organisations and natural persons, living or dead. The author and publisher does not assume responsibility for any third-party materials or opinions referred to in this book. Neither the author, the publisher nor any associated parties shall be liable for any loss or damages arising from the opinions or interpretations expressed within. The author and the publisher are not responsible for any consequences resulting from misinterpretation or misuse of the opinions, interpretations or material presented in this book.

NOTE: As I am in Australia, I have written these books from the Australian angle – eg: where to find certain tools and products in Australia, but also abroad or online. It can be used by people who live anywhere, I've tried to make it as universal as I could (I have added some extra information in places; for people who live in other countries). Most of the information is universal – as autism is universal, eg: somewhere on earth at this exact moment, some parent is probably cooking chicken nuggets for their autistic child. Some of the products are listed by brand names, and that name might be foreign to you, so I've given a picture and description of the item, so you can find a similar tool in your home country, most of the products are available worldwide by different companies. I just don't have the space in these books to mention every brand name in the world – but if you do an online search for what the product does (by reading my descriptions and looking at the pictures), you will be able to find a similar product. I hope to have an App up and running soon, one that is constantly updated and amended for new information and new products.

Affiliations: Please note that I am not affiliated with or sponsored by any group or individual. Any opinions or affiliations of any of the researchers or articles that are mentioned in these books are those of the individuals and do not represent my views or opinions.

I'm not responsible for the thoughts, writings, and future progression of any of the bloggers, journalists, writers, Facebook Groups or social media groups, companies etc mentioned or linked in this book. I have no control over what they write about, think or display, in the future or past. I have linked articles and books in this book; because they can be of use to help you, to help your autistic family member, client, or student. If I follow a certain group or writer on Facebook, Twitter etc- it is for research and understanding of other people's points of view, opinions, and research; it does not mean I agree or disagree with anything that is said or done in those groups/forums.

A NOTE about Anonymity: Many autistics will advocate for not revealing your child's diagnoses to anyone; other than health care professionals that are on a need-to-know basis. This is due to the fact that a person's diagnoses are their own personal business and theirs alone. It is their right to keep it a secret, or to scream it from the rafters. I originally wanted to write this book as an Anonymous entity, for this very reason to keep my children's diagnoses private, but soon found it to be impossible. I wanted to keep my children's disabilities a secret and leave it up to them as adults and individuals to decide for themselves.

I have been having a lot of inner turmoil over this issue, and over my decisions, and how they affect my children. This has not been an easy decision. I'm proud of being autistic, and I want that for my children, and their children (if they ever decide to have children). I want the world to see us as proud, and not hiding. I didn't want the world to think, that by publishing a book anonymously, that I was acting out of shame or embarrassment for myself, or ashamed of my children or their neurodivergences. So, I'm publishing it under my name, I'm trying to set an example for my children, and for others – that it's alright to be out and proud; to Neuroqueer.

Some will say I'm robbing my children of the right to speak for themselves on this matter. I have talked to them about it, and they have agreed to allow me to say they are autistic and neurodivergent; as this is just a different way of experiencing and thinking about the world – it's nothing to be embarrassed about, or shameful of. It's still my children's decision how they identify and if they ever reveal anything to anyone. For the purposes of this book, to explain that I have experience in raising ND kids – I cannot deny their neurodivergences, as that would negate my experience as a mother to neurodivergents. I'm proud of them and of who they are. So, I'm going to make the statement of fact that **we** are an autistic family, we are neurodivergent - and proud of it.

There it's been said, it's out there. I realise that some will argue this, and some will see it as making my children targets or vulnerable members of society. But to prove that I have experience with raising autistic children, I'm not sure how else to do this. I'm taking precautions with my kids; I explain everything to them, and I make sure they understand the risks by explaining dangers and teaching them how to remain safe in a society that is not built for them.

I'm sorry to those who argue that I shouldn't have 'outed' them – and I totally agree with your argument, that's why I've argued this point with myself and others for the better part of two years now. But I also believe it's time for us to come out of the shadows. We can't change society and create awareness or acceptance if we are hiding. When we hide, other people start talking for us and about us. They talk over us because sometimes they don't even believe we exist, or they believe that we cannot speak for ourselves. It makes me feel dirty and ashamed if I hide it, so I'm not going to. I feel like I'm perpetuating societies myth that autism is bad if I hide it and make my kids feel ashamed of themselves if I make them hide it too. What makes them unique and wonderful quirky people is their neurodivergences. I know this is a privilege that me and my children have, that other people do not have. And if I am privileged, I also feel obligated to use that privilege to help others.

This whole process has opened my eyes. It has made me analyse my whole life, my family, my friendships, my schooling and my working life. I'm happy to say that I now feel free, like a weight has lifted; that I can finally make sense of myself and those around me, better than ever before. I am still at the beginning of my journey and I'm trying to help others, including my own children to become confident, proud and possibly great advocates for themselves; they cannot begin to advocate for themselves unless they have the self-belief, self-worth and trust in themselves as neurodivergent people to openly say that they are disabled and need support. If they remain silent about themselves and their struggles, no-one will ever know how to support or help them or understand why or how they are wrestling with certain things.

Kids are labelled with many things; lazy, fidgeters, loud, obnoxious, badly behaved and many others. A 'label' of autism, or neurodivergent is not a label at all, they are diagnoses that helps us to access supports and understand our brains or nervous systems better. Don't be scared to use the words disabled, neurodivergent, autism or ADHD etc; they can only help us to find the right accommodations and help others to understand that we do truly need them. Some people will use them against us, but those people don't deserve our respect, our time or our emotions. This book will hopefully help those misguided people to change their minds and learn to help instead of hinder us. But I cannot help my children or myself by staying in the shadows. I obviously won't be sharing anything embarrassing about my children – (only about myself), as that is their business to share if they ever want to, and my obligation to protect.

Important Trigger Warning
NOTE: These books are written by a white woman who is able to use mouth words and I acknowledge my privilege. I mean no offence to any race or minority group with anything that is

written. But I also realise that I speak from a place of privilege and that some of the things written in these books may be triggering to certain minorities or individuals. For example, there is a section about ABA and another section about Masking. These topics are very triggering to some people, and I've tried to make it holistic and not leave out any minority group within the autistic community, but I am privileged and freely recognise that.

TW: in the above-mentioned sections I talk about ABA and Masking being harmful to an autistic person's mental health. But I fully recognise that some minority groups do not have the privilege to not mask; as masking will literally save their life in a situation where they are being abused, bullied, attacked, shot at, accosted, gender and/ or racially profiled, or condemned by police in some countries etc – the list goes on and on and on. I will never be in a place of understanding what these people go through on a daily basis. Obviously, everyone has to do what is right for their family and their situation; I would **never** tell you that you **have** to do any of the things in these books. These books only give you information about why certain things are deemed harmful to autistics. I recommend you read the section on Minorities within Minorities, or AAC; for links to groups, blogs, writers etc that can truly speak from the BIPOC/ BAME, non-speaking and/or LGBTQI+ perspective, so you can follow these other great websites, writers, advocates and bloggers etc - who may be able to help you address/understand things such as 'masking to save your life' and other very personal and important issues.

Examples given with the book:

I have given personal experience stories within this book as examples of what works for my family. Not everything that we do will work for your family, and what works for me or one of my kids, may cause harm or simply not be right for your child. This book is not about copying what I do, or what others do – you need to find your own rhythm, your own way of doing things and find what works for you and your family.

As an example: I don't use screen time; we don't limit our children's time on screens in any way. We co-sleep and we use radical acceptance in everything we do, and we avoid tight routines or schedules as they cause us pain. This works for my family, but for some; not being heavily scheduled can also cause pain, or a feeling of lack of control or causes dysregulation. If this is the case, do what you need to do, follow your gut. Every individual will have different needs – you need to discover what those needs are and meet them. I do not advise adding boundaries or rules to any individual, if those boundaries would cause anyone to be unfairly disadvantaged, treated or debilitated by the boundary.

I recently came across advice about bedtime boundaries set by parents because they need sleep and want their children asleep by a certain time. Some of the advice was to seek out sleep disorders and do proprioception activities before bed, or reading, white or brown noise, or co-sleeping or many other things that I've suggested in these books. But one person offered great advice about setting a boundary; that only a certain number of minutes were allocated to talking before the child was expected to be silent and try to sleep. For some households, this is a great boundary, and can teach kids the importance of winding down before sleep. But in my household, this would cause trauma, masking, depression, self-doubt issues, distrust, and possible hatred for me.

One of my kids only feels safe when they are in bed, late at night, with the lights off, when there's complete silence and no one can look at him or judge him or interrupt him. This is his time to talk, to unload and to regulate and make sense of his day. If I limited him to a set time (eg: 5 to 10 minutes for talking), I would be limiting his regulation time and tool,

I'd be invalidating him and his needs, I would be causing dysregulation, he wouldn't be able to unload his thoughts and he would resent me. He would also have nightmares, or not be able to get to sleep in the first place – because his thoughts would still be stuck in a loop – circling in his brain, causing insomnia. This would be a boundary that may help me to get more sleep or time alone, or for self-care – but because it would severely detriment and harm my child, it's not one that is available to me or my family.

For some families, setting a bedtime routine is for the sanity of all, for others – they need to follow the child's lead, and for others, it is about looking after the parent, and making sure the parent is caring for themselves as well as their children. Boundaries are important, as well as body autonomy and consent. But boundaries need to be seen from both sides. When you set them – look at it from both sides. What does each party get out of it, that is positive and negative on both sides? If one side is disadvantaged, then it's not a good boundary and will need adjusting or tweaking.

This book is more about supplying options that may help, and offering reasons for why some things might be good or bad for some ND people. This information and examples are given to help you to understand and investigate what might be going on for your child, student, client or loved one. I am a full supporter of trialling things, and if it doesn't work; adapt it to your needs or throw it away. We are all unique and need different things. Parents need self-care and they need their own boundaries to be able to cope and live a great life. But make sure those boundaries, tools, strategies, rules, and choices are of benefit to everyone, not just one person.

Parents – please take care of yourselves. You can't help your child if you are overwhelmed or dysregulated. But you will be stuck in a trauma loop if the boundaries you set dysregulate either your child or yourself. Co-operation and collaboration are key to a happy home, when the balance tips, often the happiness tips as well. I hope you enjoy the books and find lots of useful tips and tools – that you can adapt to meet your needs.

The problem with Autism

The problem with autism, is **not** autism. It is how the world thinks about and views autism, and how it treats autistic people - that is the problem!

How the world views us is a direct result of the way people talk about us, and how we talk about ourselves. Language matters! If you talk about yourself using negative words – then other people will see you as negative, deficient, wrong, or unworthy. It is the same with autism. If you use Person First Language (PFL: 'with' autism, 'has' autism) to talk about autism; you are telling society, that all autistics 'have' something. You may think – 'so what?' or – that's how people say it, that's the medical language – 'who cares?' I can tell you that the autistic community care – **a lot**! And using negative language to talk about us – hurts all of us, not just the one individual you are referring to when using these words.

During the height of the covid pandemic there was (unfortunately) a lot of incidents of ableism occurring in hospitals, and especially emergency departments. There have been many reports of doctors putting DNR's (Do Not Resuscitate orders) into patient files; without discussing this with the patients, or the patient's family (see later in the book for more information and linked articles on this). Why did they do this? Because, the patient or the patients file, or the patient's family: mentioned that the patient was autistic!

This is of course revolting behaviour, and those doctors and hospitals are being investigated for effectively signing the death warrant of disabled people, just because they have a 'label' of autism or disabled. A home for autistics even received a stack of DNR's to sign (from a hospital) – just because all the people living there were autistic. What gives any one the right, or the wrong information that autistic people should die, or not have the same rights to live as other people? I say, it is because of the education about autism, and the language people use to describe us.

This is a huge problem in our society. People hear the words autism, ASD, on the spectrum etc and can have a negative reaction, or negative view. They misinterpret, misunderstand, and sometimes even purposely use the label to discriminate against us. Some of us even die or are killed because of that label, misunderstanding and poor education.

Sometimes, within our own community, people will say that the language we use is less important than things that kill us, like our co-occurring disabilities, eg; epilepsy, diabetes, asthma, and other things that kill us like the high incidence of filicide or some autistics propensity for eloping or suicide ideology. I agree that those things are extremely important. But what is happening is an endless discrimination and negativity loop.

A person describes us as low or high functioning, level 1, 2 or 3, disordered or spectrumed. These all have negative connotations attached to them. They then use these words to talk to others about us, for us and over us. These people then perpetuate the negativity around autism, they use negative words to describe us and our struggles, and then find even more negative things to help us, or even ignore that we need help at all. We then struggle more, because we aren't being helped or supported – because we are seen as 'disordered' or unable to be helped.

More people jump on the band wagon of negativity surrounding us and sometimes even stop seeing us as human, they use filicide, they use ABA, they take minority indigenous children away from their families and place them in foster care (under the guise of 'helping'; please follow Jules Edwards of Autistic, Typing www.autistictyping.com for more information about indigenous issues in the States). People continue to use negative and offensive language about us. We start to see these things in ourselves, we start to believe the rubbish bandied about, we become depressed and even suicidal. We give up trying to treat our co-occurring disabilities, and so do the doctors; because all they see is the negative words, and they stop seeing anything beyond it. Sometimes it ends in tragedy. And all because no one is willing to support a minority group to change the way we are viewed, talked about, treated and respected. All because of language, education, and the willingness to see anything passed the word 'disordered', or ASD.

Many of our co-occurring disabilities also have the label of disordered or deficient. They all need to be changed. Being ADHD is not disordered. Having a different sensory profile (SPD) does not make us disordered. Having a different need for different ways of learning (dyslexia, dysgraphia etc) is not disordered or wrong, it is just different. They are all just a different way of being, learning, feeling, emoting, behaving. But instead of being respected, helped, and accorded equal respect to decide we do not want to be called negative names, and bullied by the medical profession and general population that use these words. We are told we are wrong, disordered, deficient, broken and don't have to right to change the narrative around how we are spoken about, and to. About how our own brains work, and how we interpret and experience the world. We are gaslit by neurotypicals and even our own kin who perpetuate this negative narrative to the detriment of all.

How do we get people to look at our co-occurring disabilities and the things we need help with, when they never get passed the label of 'disordered' or 'autism'.

- ▶ Caution: Yes, we are disabled because society disables us. Just because we want people to start using positive language and IFL – does not mean we are not disabled. We just want respect. There has been some businesses and countries around the world that have listened to our narrative about using better language and then used that to remove autism from the list of disabilities they are willing to help, support or call a disability. Because they assume that it is just our co-occurring disabilities that cause our disabilities. I want to make it clear here – that YES! Our co-occurring disabilities do cause an awful lot of trouble for some of us, but autism in itself is still disabling. Because of our communication style, our body language, our interests, our sensory differences, our experiences and the Uncanny Valley and the Double Empathy Problem etc. The majority of the world sees us as disabled and treats us as such. But also, we can be completely disabled by these things. They can prevent us from getting or keeping jobs, finding friends, accessing the community, and simply living day to day. Changing our language won't change that we are disabled or that we need support and help. And removing autism from being a disability is ableist and shows no understanding of autism or disability. Please treat us with respect, respect our preference for IFL, and continue to support our needs for disability specific help.

People see the label of 'ASD' and want to 'treat' the autism, or (like in the aforementioned DNR's during covid) they just wanted us gone – eradicated and out of the way. These people see the label, the Person First Language; they see a stigmatism, and the medical model of autism and they look no further. They often don't want to look at or help with the co-occurring disabilities and things that cause our struggles, our incapacities and even our deaths. They often see us as what PFL implies: conditioned, disordered and spectrumed. It does not see the person – the autistic person and what that truly means.

Language **does** matter, if you think it doesn't, I think you might be in denial. With the example of the DNR's, society has proven that the label, the language, and how we are seen: directly resulted in how they treated us, and how they tried to hasten our deaths ahead of neurotypical people. If those doctors had been taught about autism, and to use positive language, and see autistics as they truly are - as people with different neurowiring. As people who have equal value in society. As human with the exact same human rights as neurotypical people; there might've been a better outcome for some of those poor innocent DNR patients. This change in attitude and of viewing disabled people; starts with education and with the language we use.

If you use the word 'have or has'; what do you picture in your brain? Say it in a sentence and exchange autism for another word. Do you liken it to 'having' a medical 'condition' that can be cured or defeated? Or do you think about carrying something 'with' you – like a handbag, or a phone or a wallet?

Something you stand on, like 'on' the spectrum. Or even eating something like "I had a banana". Autism is not a disease, it is not curable, and it is not an accessory to be carried around, and you definitely can't consume it. Even though this is the imagery that PFL invokes, this is not the biggest problem with PFL. Please see the fantastic infographic titled "Neurology Is Not An Accessory" by Identity First Autistic (www.identityfirstautistic. org) that has spread like wildfire across the autistic community to explain why PFL is so harmful; in a simple drawing format. Unfortunately it's very hard to find on their website, but you can find it by searching through google.

PFL is the deficit language people use to describe our worst traits, our struggles, and our diagnoses. It was originally brought about because medical professionals wanted to separate the person from the diagnoses; and they still do. And that is appropriate for some conditions or diagnoses; because a person is not their cancer, or their tumour. Medical people usually only study how to cure and treat people. They are not taught that conditions and diagnoses can be a good thing, that certain things **can't be**, don't **want** to be, and don't **need** to be cured. They are not taught the social model of disability. They are not taught that society disables people, not always their conditions. Medical professionals thought it would be nice to use PFL to see the person first, and the condition second – or separate, or cure us. They wanted the person to feel that they were not their disease, or their condition. But autism is neither a condition or a disease; it is a neuro difference, a different way of seeing, experiencing, feeling and seeing the world, and you cannot separate us from our autism. And more importantly autistic people prefer Identity first language (IFL), and you should listen to a minority group when they tell you their preferences.

If you were to take the 'tism' out of the person – you'd be killing them. You cannot remove our nervous system, or our brain. Autism is a wiring of the **whole** person. To say that a person **has** autism; you may be trying to be kind and show that person that they are more than their autism, but unfortunately, it's belittling, rude, condescending, and it's a lie. The person is autistic and will always be autistic, and there's nothing wrong with being autistic.

If you speak about autism as being a thing that is separate from them; as being like a handbag, or something extra added to /or removed from their genes; you are saying that you know nothing about autism and don't understand what it's like to be autistic. If PFL is used to describe autism; it is by definition saying that you do not understand what autism is. That you don't understand that it is a wiring of the body-brain nervous system that controls and explains everything we think, do, feel and say. You are saying, by using the wrong words; that autism is something secondary to the person, a curable or removable condition or disease, and that you believe the person would be a better person without the autism. But since we are our autism, we can't be separated, and if you 'removed' it, we would die, but we would also no longer be recognised as anything like the person before you. To hate our autism, is to hate us, as individuals or as a community.

Autistics use Identity First Language (IFL) because we are trying to get people to see us as we are – not by being 'disordered'. Disordered is the word at the end of the diagnosis (Autism Spectrum "Disorder"- ASD), it is not who or what we are. This particular acronym (ASD) makes me cringe every time I see it or hear it. I know it's technically what we are diagnosed with – but to be constantly reminded that the world sees us as 'disordered' is soul crushing. Every time you say or write 'ASD' you are reminding us that neurotypicals, or allistics see autism as a negative thing, you are effectively telling us that there's something wrong with us – that we are disordered! We are not disordered – we just think differently to allistics. Using euphemisms for words only ever increases the stigmatism. If you use things like 'differently abled', 'special needs', 'handicapable', 'ASD', 'on the spectrum', 'has autism', 'tism', etc; you are avoiding using the right words, the ones that that community prefer. We prefer autistic and disabled. To use anything else is to be Autistiphobic, or ableist. 'Disabled' or autistic are not dirty words, but to avoid them, is to increase the stigma of using them.

The medical world sees us as disordered because they compare everyone to a perfect mould. If you do not fit into that mould perfectly – then you must be disordered. If this was taken literally – then everyone on the planet would have to be called 'disordered' – as NO ONE is perfect! But only autistics or other people diagnosed under an acronym that ends in D (eg: SPD, ASD, ADHD etc) are called 'disordered' – Do you see ableism or discrimination here? I do.

When people say someone 'suffers from autism'- it is saying that we are afflicted or damaged by our autism. We do not 'suffer' from autism, but we do suffer every time someone uses one of these language choices – as you are insulting us, and who we are. But you are also perpetuating the image in societies mind that we do "suffer, that we are "disordered", that we have a "condition", or we "have" something wrong with us. Sometimes we do suffer, but it is usually because our SPD heightens our sense of smell, taste or hearing to the point of pain, or because one of our co-occurring disabilities causes physical pain (like Fibromyalgia sending nerve pain shooting through our limbs), or because society has disabled us by not providing accommodations or supports.

People view us as a stereotype of either; non-speaking and 'severely' disabled, or brilliant and eccentric. Both are wrong, and discriminatory. The deficit model is directly taken from the DSM-5. Doctors see us as a patient through this medical, or deficit model; to 'treat' us. But we do not want the world to view us in this way. And we don't want to be "treated". We want you to see passed the initial autism label and help us cope and deal with our co-occurring disabilities, or with the things that hinder and stop us from being able. We want accommodations, support and love.

EXAMPLE:

> Children learn language at a very young age. Think about a classroom where children are learning the meaning of "have" or "has". Where do they next use these words? Is it to create a wonderful story or sentence about having

beautiful hair? Or is it used to pick on someone about "having cooties" or "having boy or girl germs" etc????? If their teacher, then says "Jimmy has Autism" … do you think the other children will view Jimmy in a positive or negative light? How do you think the children will treat Jimmy from now on? What visual connotation or connection do you think children make without further information? Or do you think that further information will be ignored – because all the children heard was the dreaded "HAS"????

Language matters! Be positive about your child, about your autistic loved one, about your autistic patient or student – it makes a huge difference to their self-esteem, their self-confidence, sense of belonging and being accepted by others. Language also affects our ongoing ability to cope in a world that already sees us as deficient. We don't need the people who are closest to us using this horrible negative language anymore. Give it up! For the sake of every autistic person, but also for yourself. When you stop talking about your loved one in terms of their deficits – you will realise that your opinions and thoughts about them change as well. You will think more positively, talk more positively, act more positively – and doesn't everyone need a little more positivity in their life?

Some autistic people will use PFL to talk about themselves, and that is their choice and their prerogative. And you can use their form of language to talk to, or about them – but please, when you are talking about other autistic people – use IFL, as that is what the majority of autistic people prefer. Some children will use PFL, but it is usually because that is the only language they have ever been told about or know about. And they are often never taught the harm it does to their psyche and that of the people around them. If you use negative words about yourself, others will see you this way.

The autistic community uses IFL, and yet it's obvious to us that we are not being listened to or accepted - we are ignored and argued with. Day in and day out we hear PFL, and negative language being thrown around. If autistics were truly accepted and listened to; everyone would adopt a positive way of talking to us and about us, everyone would be using IFL in reference to autism. It feels like a slap in the face and a personal insult every time I read or hear PFL, it feels like people are intentionally trying to gaslight me. I know it's not intentional, but once we tell you it's like being called the "R" word or other horrible slur – why do some people continue to argue with us, why do they continue to use PFL?!!! The answer is that they do not accept us, or listen to us. And are intentionally being discriminatory and rude.

If you asked me to stop calling you Dave, because your name is Judy, I would do it. And I would apologise for ever calling you Dave in the first place, because that would have been bullying and rude. Your name, and your named preference, is your choice and right – and you deserve to be respected. So, please respect us. Please use IFL.

Once we educate people about how to discuss and talk about autism, (and can prove that people are listening to us. ... by not having anyone use the deficit language anymore); we will be able to make real strides into making real change, and real acceptance in the world. The first step is to change the way people view us and talk about us. Because first impressions count. They are what stick in people's minds and what forms the basis of opinion for all things. Let's make the first impression of autism a positive one and build on it from there. Let's educate the world about autism in a positive way that makes people stop seeing us as people that require DNR's.

For more information on IFL- take a you look at the article by Dr Melanie Heyworth from **Reframing Autism**: "A Manifesto for Allies Adopting an Acceptance Approach to Autism" (https://reframingautism.org.au/a-manifesto-for-allies-adopting-an-acceptance-approach-to-autism/); you will see that approximately "80 – 90 % of Autistic Adults chose to be identified as 'Autistic'".

Or check out **Aucademy**: (25 November 2021) "Resources supporting preference, but importantly wellbeing properties, of identity-first language: we are Autistic". www.aucademy. co.uk/2021/11/25/resources-supporting-preference-but-importantly-wellbeing-properties-of-identity-first-language-we-are-autistic

Note about languages other than English. For those of you that English is your second language; PFL and IFL may make absolutely no sense to you, as the words don't translate in the same way. Try to think about your own language ... are there any words that portray a negative view of something, that you could slightly change to turn it into a positive? And if so; would you prefer to use those negative words to describe yourself or your child, or the positive ones??? I'm going to assume that you'd pick the positive ones, no matter what your country of origin, language, or dialect. Because positive words create positive thoughts, impressions, and treatment. Please choose words in your own language that talk about autism in a positive way that will make people see autism as a good thing, a positive thing. Just a difference in thinking and experiencing;

not as a negative in any way. I hope you weren't offended by this section about language, I was attempting to explain PFL to English speakers. There are autistic support groups in every language, and in every country, that may be able to help you with finding positive language in your own mother tongue or dialect.

Side Note: I will not be using the word Autist in this book, as I've been informed that many autistics also do not like this term. But I do realise it is the preferred term in some languages. Until there is a consensus for this word, I will continue to use autistic, not autist. I'm prepared to change to this word when there is a majority in favour of it. Thank you to autistics like Chris Bonello ("Autistic Not Weird") for conducting surveys that proved our preferred language is IFL. Check out the website: www. autisticnotweird.com/autismsurvey/ It's a fantastic, interesting read, I'd love to see an updated one in a few years, if Chris is willing.

Please be aware that some people with difficulty reading, or people with diagnosed eye, or eye to brain processing difficulties; also may find it difficult to distinguish between some words, autist and artist are two of these words that sometimes blend into one.

My Mistakes

One of my main mistakes when starting my journey learning about autism, was believing that if I researched on my own, I'd find all the correct answers. But what I didn't know, was that there's an awful lot of incorrect and skewed information out there about autism. I also didn't realise that there was an even better way to research. That I should've gotten my information from the source, from the real experts on autism. I had no idea that therapists and doctors were **not** the experts on autism. I realise now, that my naivete was embarrassing. But I'm glad to say that I learnt my mistake, and I am trying to make up for it, to myself, and to my kids.

I should've found autistic Voices, people who had been there, and done that. The support groups I had joined were for parents of autistic kids, (and don't get me wrong), I never would've gotten through some days without these people, they are amazing, resilient, people in my eyes. ... A true lifeline - and they are great for sympathy and support. But what I was missing, was actual knowledge about what autism was or is, and how to actually support both myself and my kids. Sympathy is great, but in the end; sympathy doesn't help to move you forward or to learn anything of real value. All it does is give you a sense of not being alone; a sense of being heard and perhaps pitied, but it wasn't helping me to grow or understand the needs and wants of my children. I was feeling supported, up to a point, but I was stagnating. And when I realised that I too was autistic, I realised that I was not just stagnating, I was going backwards.

I was starting to believe the negative language and things people said about their children. I was daily hearing parents bemoan their existence and their children's existences. This rhetoric was making me feel depressed and I started feeling sorry for the children, I was no longer feeling sympathy for the parents. I was feeling gaslit and ostracized. Who on earth wants to feel like this? To live like this? To think about their beloved children like this? So I said some words that I regret, and was kicked out of one of the groups. And I am sorry if I insulted anyone in that group. But I couldn't go on with that vein of thinking. I love my kids, I love life and I never want to think of my kids as burdens, controlling tyrants, or 'conditions', or any of the other hideous words that were being used.

Please learn from my mistakes, as soon as you find a group that is talking about autism in a negative way; do something. Walk away, take a breather, or even better – call it out. These types of groups cause depression and hatred of autism. Depression is hard to overcome, it helps no-one, especially not your wonderful children. Red flags are easier for me to spot now. As soon as I see a group that uses PFL, I know that it will make me depressed and sad about my children, so I walk away. I protect myself, and my children from negative rhetoric, and I ask my children's therapists to use IFL and use neuroaffirming techniques; ones that see the child as being competent, worthy, positive, able, and respected. Techniques that help my child do the things that they themselves choose to do – not what the therapist thinks they 'should' be able to do.

I joined groups that refused and banned the use of PFL, that were autistic led, and neuroaffirming. I followed autistic advocates and started reading only books and articles that were written by autistic people. Because I realised that they are the only true experts on autism. And I started to feel more positive, less depressed, I found people that truly understood my children (and myself) and how to best support and teach them, and how to make a happy home; for everyone. I went to the source.

Many parents of autistic kids are autistic themselves because autism is genetic. Just like ADHD and some other disabilities are also genetically passed on through the generations. And because autism and ADHD are thought to be under a similar neuro-umbrella, some parents might be Allistic, but they may be neurodivergent in other ways. Within my own family we have a good mixture of autistic and ADHD members scattered throughout history.

Many parents are like me and have not realised or been accepted, or officially diagnosed as autistic until well into adulthood; and have therefore not been through the same therapy and interventions that I was putting my children through. Children that are assumed to be neurotypical are not put through these therapies, so many late diagnosed autistics may not have experienced these therapies firsthand. I was one of these late diagnosed autistics that had not experienced therapy as a child.

I wanted, and needed to know from experienced autistics, what these therapies were, and how they help and /or harm. Autistics who were diagnosed as children were often put through these therapies. Just because they are now adults, does not mean they know nothing about current therapies. Most of these autistics have trialled the current and new therapies on their own children. Because autistic adults who were diagnosed as children have the benefit of foresight. They have not only, been there and done that, but they have the benefit of knowing that they are autistic, and that if they ever had children; the likelihood of their children also being autistic is very high. Therefore, they are often a little more prepared before the birth of their children and know that their children may benefit from certain therapies. They often know what therapies and tools did not work as a child, and which ones did help them. I think I know what would've helped me better as a child – but I do not have a time machine, so I can only guess and try things with my children, that I think might work. Autistic adults with or without their own children are the ones to ask and learn from.

I was recently told by an NT mum (when I suggested they ask their question again, but in an autistic led group): "that's not something we'd be willing to entertain". I can't tell you how insulting that is. Is it because they hate autistics like their kid – or just me? Or possibly their child? (I really dread to think it's the last one). They'd specifically said that they'd tried everything that the NT parents had suggested, and nothing had worked. But when I suggested to ask people who are the same as their kid – they told me it was anathema to them – something they could not even begin to think about trying or exploring. If you are truly willing to help your child – wouldn't you do anything? I know I would and have! I can only think that people like this hate disabled people and hate them so much that they are willing to deny their child help, instead of reaching out and interacting with us. I have been hurt many times in my lifetime, but this one is fresh and directly related to this book - and hurts my genuine want to **help** people. Having it thrown in my face, and especially thrown in the face of their child. … truly hurts.

Please think about why you wouldn't ask for help from people like your child. Do you presume us to be intellectually disabled, incompetent, etc? And is that how you see your child? Or do you hate us? Do you have internalised ableism? Or perhaps don't believe we exist? We want to help, we want the best life for you and your child – ask us – talk to us, I implore you – reach out and make a connection – for your child, but also for you.

The NT experience is totally different to the ND experience. When I want to know about the NT experience and how to interact with NT people, (and find out what an NT person meant by XYZ etc) – I ask NT people!!!! I do not assume that a ND person would know anything about the NT experience, or that the ND's information about NT people is correct or what I should believe or listen to. Because we are simply guessing what the NT's think, need, and know – we don't actually know! And yet NT therapists are constantly being held up as the experts on autism and ND – they are not! Only someone who is ND can be an expert on ND things! Only an NT can be an expert on NT things! Stop taking for granted that the NT 'experts' know what they're talking about – more often than not – they do not, and what they recommend can actually be harmful to the autistic or ND individual. That is why autistic advocates came up with the slogan "Nothing For Us – **Without** Us!"

I found that listening to thousands of autistic voices was giving me a little glimpse into the thoughts and feelings of my children. I've been to Uni, a few times, and I'm autistic myself – but no one ever stops learning, and no one ever knows it all. And I realised that I definitely do not know it all. I realised the very little information about neurodiversity I'd been taught at university (including in my teaching degree) was utterly and totally wrong! It took me a while to overcome my own ableism, and my own pride; to come to these realisations and to accept them. But I got there, and you will too. I had to be ready to put aside my preconceptions, my misconceptions, my ego, and totally unlearn society expectations and pressures. I had to be open to helping my child by doing what is best for the child – not what **I** thought was 'best' or what 'society' **deems** as 'best', but what was **actually** best for each of my unique babies.

NOTE: If you join an autistic led group, please read the rules of the group very carefully – and follow them to the letter. Those rules are there for the protection of the autistic members. In NT groups, autistics are gaslit, triggered and forced to obey rules that they sometimes don't agree with – but we do it anyway, because we respect you and the rules of the NT society. If you go into a new job with rules and regulations, you follow them – because you are the minority (the new person) and the rules are there for the protection of those already there. You do not ignore the rules and do whatever you want. You would also not go into another country and tell them they must learn English because you are the only English-speaking person. You would adapt to them and learn to be culturally sensitive as you are now the minority.

The same is for entering an autistic group, the NT person is now the minority and needs to be respectful of our ways, language, culture, and rules. We put up with NT societies unwritten laws and expectations our whole lives (every second of every day) I think the NT person could bear to stand a couple minutes of their life being respectful to a minorities way of doing something. Autistics in these groups are there to try and help you and your child, don't be disrespectful.

I recently came across a group of NT's calling autistic people rude, unempathetic, abrupt and unhelpful, because the autistics told the NTs that their use of words were insulting and offensive. The autistic people went into full detailed explanation as to why those words were offensive (we were educating them, after they explicitly asked why those words aren't to be used). But instead of the NT's stopping the use of those words, they retaliated with insults, and told us to stop being autistic.

They asked us to stop info dumping, to be 'polite' (to use NT words and phrases, so they didn't find our words offensive), to be 'kinder' and to educate and not insult them. We were educating the NT's, but they couldn't get passed their own internalised ableism and their own NT language barrier, to understand that autistics are not rude, unempathetic or disrespectful – we just have a different way of communicating.

Telling us to do these NT things is highly offensive, incredibly ableist and does not help us to want to help them. They came asking for help, but it turned into insulting a group of autistic people that were giving up their free time, out of the goodness of their hearts to help struggling parents. Nothing we said was offensive or disrespectful, or unempathetic – if anything, we were overly empathetic. NT's tend to read into our communication style things that aren't there, and aren't intended by us. This is where the Double Empathy problem enters (see more information on this later), and the communication breaks down. But it's also where we are the ones to take the blame for the miscommunication. This is unfair, ableist and wrong. We are not to blame, and neither are our NT counterparts; there was simply a breakdown. But unless both parties are willing to acknowledge this breakdown and stop being at loggerheads about it – we will continue to be the ones blamed, segregated and ostracised, and NTs will continue to misunderstand us and call us terrible insulting names.

Please be aware that if you enter an autistic led space, the language changes, the communication style changes, the writing and speech changes. Just like this book may be different to what you are used to; it's because it's written by an autistic person, with an autistic culture, background and language style.

Please: if you are a neurotypical parent, seek out groups that will expand your knowledge of autism and not just back up your own views and opinions. I know it's nice to have other parents out there that understand what you are going through, and like-minded people who are going to support you, and people you can vent to - in a safe space. And I'd suggest you belong to at least one of these groups – for your own support network, and mental health. But these sorts of 'support' groups will only be for support, they will not be able to see the same 'vented' situation as the way your autistic loved one sees it. You will continue to have the same outcomes (meltdowns, aggression, violence, misunderstandings, school can't etc) in an endless loop – until you can see it from your child's perspective. To do this, you will need actually autistic voices to help you breakdown the barriers and link you to our way of communicating and styles of language.

My Worries

As a parent of autistic children, I worry in the exact same way all parents worry. I worry about what would happen to my children if I was to die or became infirm. This is the main thing I hear from other parents as well; "What will become of my child?", "Who will look after them?", "Who will advocate for them?", "No-one understands them like me", "My children are dependent on me for everything".

I worry that if my children went into foster care or were eventually adopted; would the new parents be able to find the right information, would they listen to autistics like my children;

or would they continue my old mistakes and learn from neurotypicals about a neurology that they simply will **never** truly, fully understand. **I** will **never** understand neurotypicals, and I admit that- with no doubt or hatred in me, it's just a fact! I can learn about them by living with them and living in their world. But I will never fully understand what it's like to be neurotypical. I will never be able to change my inner workings, my thought processors and the way my neurons react to stimuli – it is just not possible, but I'm humble enough to admit it and accept it- and to ask NT's for translations and assistance to understand them and their culture. I will not talk over them or for them, because I am not them.

I want the same respect to be given to me and my neurodivergent children that I give to neurotypicals or allistics. That they know their own neurotype and experience, but they cannot and do not know mine.

My Hope

I hope this book will alleviate a tiny bit of these worries for some people. That in reading this, and having other people read it (and the books I've suggested throughout this book for everyone to read to learn more); that the world will gain a little more understanding and learn ways to help autistic people of all ages. So that if something is (cross my fingers it never does) to happen to a parent of an autistic child; that anyone would be able to pick up this book, (or any of the books mentioned within); and be able to learn how to help, teach the children how to self-advocate and learn how to accept them as they are; in a loving, nurturing, and neuro-supportive way.

I cannot banish all your worry, but hopefully some of the tools and information in this book will set you and your child up for as much success as possible for your unique family.

Terms

TW: This section may contain a lot of words used in PFL and the Medical model of disability, like 'Disorder' or 'Condition'. I do not approve of these words, but to explain an acronym, the use of these words is unavoidable.

ND   Neurodiverse, Neurodivergent, Neurodiversity, Neurominority.

There are many words, and they all mean slightly different things. If you want a very comprehensive and great explanation of all of them – you cannot get better than Dr Nick Walker "Neuroqueer Heresies" or any of her writing on the website www.Neuroqueer.com

Neurodivergent is usually what people are referring to when they use the acronym ND. This is the term used for an individual. **Neuro** means nerve not brain, as most people usually think it is. Judy Singer was credited with coining the term **Neurodiversity**, but there is now proof that the term and idea was around much earlier. To see this proof, check out the blog by Martijn

Dekker http://www.inlv.org/2023/07/13/neurodiversity-origin.html Dr Chloe Farahar on „Aucademy" has also researched this and has a good glossary of terms available at www.aucademy.co.uk/2021/05/11/glossary-of-autistic-terms/

Neurodivergence and **Neurodivergent** were coined by Kassiane Asasumasu in 2000. **Neurominority** (2004) was coined by Nick Walker, and **Neuroqueer** was also brought about by Nick Walker, Melanie Yergeau and Athena Lynn Michaels-Dillon (pen name Michael Scott Monje Jr)- in the late 2010's. Check out these authors for more information on Neuroqueering, including the book by Melanie Yergeau (2018) "Authoring Autism: On Rhetoric and Neurological Queerness".

These terms are meant to explain that humans diverge from the socially accepted typical expectations in terms of neurology and the way our body-brain wiring experiences and reacts to the world around us. We also differ in other ways, eg: skin colour, eye colour, culture, sex and even as Nick Walker puts it: "Body mind" experiences. **Neurodiversity** refers to the spectrum of very differing ways we feel, think, emote, express, and function. The autistic rights movement (started approx. 1990's) and the **Neurodiversity Movement** (started approx.

2000's) are movements to seek civil rights and justice for the neurominority/neurodivergent individuals.

Neurodivergent refers to the individual's that have mind/body's that diverge significantly from what society envisions as the typical (majority) way of thinking, behaving, feeling, emotions etc.

There are many ways to be neurodivergent, being autistic is just one, you can also be ND if you fall under any of the following: ADHD, Dyslexic, OCD, Down Syndrome, PTSD etc. If you fall into more than one of the ND categories, you are **Multiply Neurodivergent**, eg: ADHD and autistic, or Dyslexic and Tourette's. I honestly believe it's very hard to not be Multiply Neurodivergent; I also fit into many of the ND subheadings.

Neurominority is the group under the neuro umbrella that are usually discriminated against or oppressed. You can be neurodivergent and not be discriminated against, like Nick Walker says: Monks that have spent years meditating and have altered their neurology; are considered to be neurodivergent; but they are not usually prejudiced against, so they would not be considered part of the Neuro**minority**.

Neuro differences are neither positive or negative things. Our nervous system and brains work together in unique and interesting ways that have not properly been explored, understood, or explained, and probably never will be, because every single person is different and unique. Not one autistic person is exactly the same as the next. The way our systems work and interact within us, are why you cannot separate our autism from us. Autism or ADHD is built into everything we do, everything we are, everything we think, feel and experience. Our wiring may be different to the majority, but we are still human.

NT   Neurotypical.

NT does not mean allistic (or non-autistic), because you can be allistic and ND, eg: you can be dyslexic, which means you fit into the ND category, not NT category, and you can be dyslexic without being autistic; which means you are ND and allistic.

NT is also not a bad thing. It is just the word used to describe the majority of the population, but not in the sense you are thinking. It does not mean that there is a 'normal' brain, or 'normal' nervous system. NT refers to the majority of people that can fit into the social expectations of the world, or culture that they live in. Everyone's brains/nervous systems diverge – otherwise we wouldn't be unique, we'd all be clones.

So, if you think about it, no 'one' individual is actually NT. But we can see a group or society as being more 'typical' and following of a certain set of social rules or conventions. For example: Babies are all born differently, with unique everything. As they grow; you can see habits arise and change, preferences become known and personalities shine. They often copy or mimic the people around them (the argument for nurture vs nature). And they will stim (just like autistics), they may use a bottle or a dummy to stim with. As they grow, their parents remove these stimming opportunities/tools to make the child appear more typical or socially acceptable. They are removed so they will fit in with the majority and appear more 'typical'. The child will still be the same child, and have a need for comfort. Whether that child accepts the change or not is usually why they are labelled NT or ND.

If you read the book by Edith Sheffer, called "Aspergers Children" (which I highly recommend you do, as my explanation in no way does this great book justice); you will see that the diagnosis of 'autism' came about because psychiatrists and psychologists in the 1920's to about 1970's (but mainly during the second World War 1939-1945) were studying ways of grouping people. In Nazi Germany and Austria, they were finding ways of identifying people and groups of people that would fit into categories or groups that represented a threat to the German 'Germut' (or

'Volk'; German way of being/culture and society), or Nazi rule. If you did not fit in, you were categorised. Autistic individuals were identified as not fitting in and given the label (or death sentence) depending on 'severity' of not fitting in, and not being able to contribute to the Germut or Volk.

This was the social agenda of the time. But it meant that a new diagnosis arose. And now, we have 'neurodiversity' which is a nicer way of categorising people, but it's still a category. At least now, ND means something positive, it means that we differ from the majority; but not in a bad way, just different. The 'label' of ND is a great one, it lets us understand ourselves better and it helps us to seek support and accommodations to better meet our needs within that majority 'Typical' society.

Basically, if the individual is able to accept the social agenda pressed upon them, able to cope with NT pressures and fit the mould, fit societies expectations and fit in without pain and struggles; they are labelled as NT. If they cannot accept it, and they fight it, the more 'severely' ND they appear. This is why 'severely' or 'profoundly' is insulting, because we are ranked by social ability, and given therapy to align ourselves within the small narrow acceptable range and extreme bias of NT skills and behaviours. To quote Nick Walker (page 181, "Neuroqueer Heresies") "Neurotypicality is more a social phenomenon than a biological one".

NOTE on stimming and society rules of fitting in: I find it interesting that as adults, the majority of people now stim with bottles– not baby bottles, but water bottles. Because the majority of people have taken up this stim, it is now deemed as socially acceptable; the 'norm'. If we all agreed to normalise stims (or accept them) and encourage them, they wouldn't be seen as faux pax. And if we did the same thing with all ND stereotypically labelled behaviours; then ND's would fit into society and we'd all just be called human. Instead of categorised as NT= fitting into society and being 'typical', and ND= not fitting into stereotypical society and being 'atypical'.

Society is definitely what disables people when we quickly judge something as acceptable or unacceptable dependent on its popularity to mainstream culture. This is why we (ND's) prefer the social model of disability, because it is better at explaining that neurotype is on a spectrum, not more ND or more NT – but more able to fit societies rules – to perhaps 'unable' to fit societies rules.

Neuro-normative is also a term used to explain the typical actions/thoughts/being of the majority of the population.

Social or medical model of disability

The medical (or pathologizing paradigm) model of disability is a deficits model. A way of speaking, writing about, and treating disabled people. This model lists people by their flaws based on societal norms and biases, and labels us as conditions or diseases to be treated or cured. Instead of using those labels to help and accommodate us, they are often used to discriminate against, deny supports or presume incompetence.

PFL is used in this medical model, it causes internalised and external oppression, disables people, infantilises them and is highly offensive, and as Nick Walker writes in "Neuroqueer Heresies" it is: Autistiphobic and is often used by bigots. ABA is the therapy tool within the medical model to make ND's conform.

The social model or **Neurodiversity Paradigm**, started in the 2000's. It is about accepting neurodifference as just another way humans vary. It approaches disability by looking at the way society accepts or disables the person. Eg: society disables people by not accommodating us. If all buildings were built with wheelchairs in mind, then a wheelchair user would not be as disabled, if everyone was taught sign language and or typing etc (and verbal language was not the only preferred way to communicate), then the deaf and apraxic communities would not feel as disabled. The neurodiversity paradigm also uses IFL in order to support disabled people and empower them.

Allistic

A way of describing someone that is non-autistic. There is a Parody Article written by Terra Vance (22 September 2018) "Allism Spectrum Disorder": Psych Central (www.psychcentral.com/blog/aspie/2018/09/allism-spectrum-disorders-a-parody)

A good article written by an Allistic, is by: Louise Sutton (27 June 2019) "Are you Worried that your child might be Allistic?" (http://ablogaboutraisingmyautisticson.com/are-you-worried-that-your-child-might-be-allistic/). It goes into the question around the issue that; if your child shows signs of being Allistic... would you take them for an "**Allistic** Spectrum Disorder Assessment"??? Are they "disordered?"

Another one by Terra Vance describes an allistic woman's reactions in an all-autistic presentation. The allistic woman was raised by an autistic family. "When a Non-Autistic

Child Is Raised by Autistic Parents, Their Experiences Are Similar to Autistics Raised by Non-Autistics" (2022) www.neuroclastic.com/having-autistic-parents-when-you-are-neurotypical/?amp#top.

PFL   Person First Language.

This is a way of using language to describe people (eg: has autism, with autism etc). This language has predominately been used by Doctors and scientists to talk "about us". Please read the article by Noelle Sinclair (11 October 2021) The Autistic Perspective: "Language Matters: The PFL v's IFL debate" (www.theautisticperspective.com/post/language-matters-the-pfl-vs-ifl-debate). This article will prove to you; that how you talk about autism and your child is extremely important, and the right language can empower your child, while the wrong language can cause negative self-image, poor mental health and long term, lifelong stigmatism around autism and self-acceptance.

The idea that someone **has** autism, implies that one day they will not **have** autism, this is never going to happen, autism is for life because it's a person's brain/neuron structure.

If you use the excuse of "'my child refers to themselves as **having** autism"; please be aware that this is most often because that is the **only** language that has ever been used around the child. Children are taught language by adults, if they are never taught another way of speaking, or are not taught the meaning of words and their negative connotations, then they will never know that there is another option. Please don't use this excuse unless your child has actually been taught both forms of PFL and IFL, and why one is harmful to their own psyche and that of autistics worldwide. Once they **fully** understand and grasp the ramifications of PFL, **and** have made a fully **informed** decision – and they still choose to use PFL – then it is their choice, not yours, and you should be supporting their rights as an individual. They can speak about themselves using PFL if they choose. But if you meet other autistics or interact on any public pages; you should revert to IFL out of respect for our culture and our preference for IFL, otherwise you are highly likely to offend a great majority of people. If you are not autistic, you do not have a say.

Eg: if you know someone's name is John, but you call them Nancy, or Drew, even when you have expressly been told (like I am telling you in this book) that their name is John – you are being a bigot, you are discriminating against that person, bullying that person, and you are upholding that you are better or superior to John, you are being Johnphobic. Call us autistic, that's what we want, that's what we are, it's even been proven in surveys and through our advocates for decades, respect us, listen to us, follow our lead.

PFL and language is part of learning. We will all make mistakes, give yourself grace and time to learn and adapt. It took me quite a while to undo the ableist language I'd been taught through my teaching degree, and from medical professionals while my children were being assessed and through consequent therapies. But once you do adapt, I promise, it's liberating and so much more positive.

IFL   Identity First Language.

This is also a way of using language to describe people (eg: autistic person etc). This language has predominately been used by autistic people to be self-affirming and positive about autism. This is the preferred way of communicating about and with the autistic community, and what I have used for this book.

See the AUCADEMY for more information on the use of IFL (25 November 2021) "Resources supporting preference, but importantly wellbeing properties, of identity-first language: we are Autistic" www.aucademy.co.uk/2021/11/25/resources-supporting-preference-but-importantly-wellbeing-properties-of-identity-first-language-we-are-autistic/

ASD /ASC/HFA   Autism Spectrum Disorder (ASD), Autism Spectrum Conditions (ASC).

Both of these terms are considered to be PFL and are deemed as offensive to the autistic community. The UK has mostly adopted ASC recently instead of the DSM-V's medical model/ diagnosis language of ASD; but it is just another added term that the community does not like or accept. High Functioning Autism (HFA) also comes under this PFL bracket; please don't use it, it's just another way to segregate our community using outdated terminology and functioning language.

ABA/PBS   Applied Behaviour Analysis or Positive Behaviour Support.

Please see the comprehensive section about this type of therapy for more information

OT   Occupational Therapy/therapist;

can help with 'doing', learning skills and finding tools to help your child self-regulate or co-regulate. They can help with skills building and finding tools and resources that can help your child achieve their goals or needs.

Please see the following article for more information on identifying a neuroaffirming OT (this article is also for OT's to make their practice more in line with Autistic preferences): Julia Sterman et al (17 June 2022) Sage Journals: Occupational Therapy Journal of Research: "Autistic Adult Perspectives on Occupational Therapy for Autistic Children and Youth" Volume 43, Issue 2 www.journals.sagepub.com/doi/10.1177/15394492221103850

SP   Speech Pathology/pathologist:
can help with developing speech sounds, talking, and eating etc. I have a lot of respect for speech pathologists, there aren't enough of them around and they can help in so many different areas that you wouldn't originally think about. But some are not neuroaffirming, and they can value mouth words over all other communication methods (which is wrong), check out the Neurodiversity Therapists Collective for more information, mentioned throughout this book.

PT   Physical Therapy/therapist;
can help with movement, exercise, personal space, continence and diet, and things like 'toe walking' etc. A paediatric physiotherapist is what you are probably looking for. A sports physio can help with some things, but a paediatric one will be more specialised to help with things like relaxing, regulating and releasing tight muscles from things like toe walking.

AAC   Speech Generating and Augmentative and Alternative Communication (AAC),

this can refer to different types of devices as well as other means of communicating. This is a human right – everyone has the right to communicate in the way they prefer; whether it is through sign language, a tablet, writing an email, YouTube videos, pictures, or a speech generator, mouth words or other methods. Please see the section on AAC for more information on AAC's and help with your non-speaking, partially-speaking, or Situationally non-speaking child.

RPM   Rapid Prompting Method.

This is one education method of teaching non-speaking people to communicate (there are others – see the AAC section). The article by Terra Vance, 17 August 2021 for the Website NeuroClastic "An Interview with Soma Mukhopadhyay, Pioneer of Rapid Prompting Method (RPM)" (www.neuroclastic. com/an-interview-with-soma-mukhopadhyay-pioneer-of-rapid-prompting-method-rpm/); is a good one, that is more unbiased, and tells a more rounded story of this particular method of communicating.

AA   Autistic Adult, or Actually Autistic (depending on what site/support group you look at).

AA is only used to talk about yourself (if you are autistic)– not about your child. If you are talking about your child – they are an autistic child / person.

TW   Trigger Warning.

Please use this on posts in Facebook groups where you are asking questions that could upset/trigger people. There is a huge list of things that trigger people, some include (but definitely not limited to): Food aversions, pictures of food, pictures of kids in hospital, ABA, Reward systems, not letting someone stim or use an AAC device, puzzle pieces and "lighting it up blue", 'picky eating', chores and being forced to do certain things, bullying, person first language (PFL), the group Autism Speaks, vaccines and needles, throwing up, Functioning Labels (eg: high/low functioning/high IQ, Asperger's or aspie etc), forcing eye contact, Autism Society (founded by same person who invented ABA), National Autistic Society (UK) etc.

The list can go on and on – just try to be respectful; the people you will be asking for help about your child – were once children themselves and have cPTSD from all sorts of different things. And these people are fantastic to ask help and advice from (because of their lived experience), but if they are not prewarned about what you are about to write about, it can truly upset them and cause more trauma. Respect is key.

PTSD and cPTSD   **Post Traumatic Stress Disorder or Complex Post Traumatic Stress Disorder.**

The difference between these two is that PTSD is usually from one event, where cPTSD is a build-up of multiple events or repeated trauma. Most autistic people will have CPTSD from therapies and living in a NT world that doesn't accept them.

PANS/ PANDAS   **Paediatric Acute-Onset Neuropsychiatric Syndrome or Pediatric Autoimmune Neuropsychiatric Disorders Associated with Streptococcal Infections.**

PANS and PANDAS are often confused with autism. But PANS/ PANDAS requires a medical diagnosis. If your child has sudden onset symptoms similar to OCD (it can also happen slowly, that's why there's testing available for PANS/PANDAS), aggression, consistent meltdowns, or picky eating, or your child suddenly 'gets better'; it could be a sign they have/or had PANS or PANDAS – and is not autistic. But you can be autistic and also have PANDAS/PANS – any child can have it, but it needs a medical diagnosis.

If your doctor has asked for "The Cunningham Panel of Tests" (available in the US through Moleculera Labs); they are probably trying to ascertain if the child's symptoms are auto immune in nature, or if the child just thinks differently (Eg: ADHD or autistic).

If you would like more information on this topic, please see the following links:

"Charlies Law" to help families get the help they need: Check out information on Tom Cullerton

PANDAS Physicians Network: www.pandasppn.org/what-are-pans-pandas/
www.adhd.com.au/pandaspans/pandas-and-pans-misunderstood-conditions
New England PANS/PANDAS Association: www.nepans.org
Dr Susan Swedo: Historical Perspective of PANS and General Overview – YouTube Videos: www.youtube.com/watch?v=4SBowHxnL_8 (Dr Swedo has quite a few videos you can check out).
To Find a Lyme Disease specialist in America: www.lymedisease.org/find-lyme-literate-doctors/
www.moleculeralabs.com/pans-diagnosis

Meltdowns

These are **not** tantrums, hissy fits, manipulation, bullying, or obstruction, a bad temper, a rage episode, outburst, explosion, bad mood, huffy, sulk, crazy, insane, aggravation/frustration, the persons inability to control their temper, attempt at hurting others – or any other ableist discriminatory remark. Meltdowns are a reaction to things like; trauma, pain, or their environment, being abused, sensory overload, not being respected or treated badly etc etc. There are many reasons they can occur. We try to control them or subdue them but eventually they are like an overfilled cup – they eventually spill over as our ability to contain them stops or is inhibited or gaslit into a response.

All people do well when they can, their behaviour is a sign that they are not doing 'well'. That they are **not** coping, and they need help. They do **not** need more people adding to the issue and making it worse by calling them; overemotional, aggressive, manipulative, violent, and/or bad tempered. They need you to work backwards and find out what triggered them in the first place – and then stop whatever it is that is triggering them. Once the trigger is removed, the behaviour goes away – because when we aren't triggered, there's no reason for us to have a meltdown. Autism does **not** cause anger and aggression – our environment causes these things.

Meltdowns are also not 'burnout' – burnout happens over time and is truly horrific – burnout can be a build-up of many meltdowns and shutdowns. Burnout affects everyone differently. Perhaps ask some autistics why it is different, and how it affects them; to get a better idea about this important topic.

When I suffered a major burnout (which has lasted about 10 years), I had both a meltdown and shutdown at the same time – I was then completely useless to anyone, let alone myself. I couldn't do anything! And even someone looking at me, sent me into a meltdown. And now, I'm gradually crawling my way out. But every time something occurs (even if it's relatively small) it sends me into another meltdown, because that's what burnout does to the autistic individual. A burnout is when the person has hit their ultimate limit and they can no longer contain anything. It can relate to **Unmasking**. At least in my case it did. I did not know at the time, that I had started my unmasking journey, but I look back on it and realise that my 'breakdown' was actually an autistic burnout caused by masking my true self for 30 odd years.

Meltdowns are when there is too much going on, and the person reacts outwardly. This can be a show of bodily movements or

102

actions, or verbally. The person has minimal to no control over it once they are in full meltdown (depending on the person and the situation). I've had a couple in my life, they take over, I have no control, I even felt like I was in someone else's body looking out. And afterwards, I'm exhausted, embarrassed, and I'm unable to do anything at all. It's horrible! Sometimes if I'm in the beginning of a meltdown, I can pause it.... This can look to outsiders as if I was just 'having' a tantrum – it is NOT! What happens, is I manage to control it enough to get through for a few minutes or sometimes even hours – but when I feel safe again, I will hit play (or something else will happen to trigger it)– and then I cannot stop it. Not all people can control their Meltdowns, but I know some who can. Usually, people who have learnt to mask for years are very good at it. Do not assume that because your child seemed to stop – that they have full control or that it was a tantrum instead of a meltdown. If you poke a bear – expect a reaction. Same with a person who is holding in a meltdown – it is a tenuous hold at best and anything at all could burst the dam.

A tantrum described as; purposely doing a bad behaviour to get something, people think you have control – as soon as you 'get' the thing, you stop the behaviour. But a child who has a tantrum is likely not coping either and trying to show you through the only method available to you (through their actions and behaviour) that something is not right. The person is likely not trying to 'get' anything, they are usually overwhelmed by something/number of somethings, and are trying to control themselves outwardly and inwardly, but lose control. The person is sometimes unable to hear, see, calm, or think. Sometimes you can't even remember a meltdown, or parts of it afterwards.

My Meltdowns have always involved other people doing or saying something that truly pisses me off, being stuck in commuter traffic, or in a highly populated space also overwhelms me, and a couple times when I've been so hungry that my whole body reacted – this is a sensory and interoception issue with me. Others meltdown due to an inability to do something for or by themselves, or out of frustration with something in their immediate surroundings, or from sensory overload. There are many reasons for a meltdown.

See the Tools section on how to avoid a meltdown before it becomes overwhelming. Once you're in 'meltdown mode' – it is hard to stop (and unhealthy to stop it); just make the area safe for everyone.

It is important to fully understand why the meltdown occurred. This is because you need to figure out ways to avoid it ever happening again. If you do not address the "why" – it will keep occurring and become worse. Behaviour is communication – and they are trying to tell you that they are in severe pain, and that is why they are reacting so severely. Please see the section on Alternative ways to help your child, and the information on Violence and aggression.

Shut down

A shutdown can be like an internal Meltdown. You can become mute (non-speaking), or look like you have a blank face, while internally more is going on. Most people will need rest and to be left alone. But make sure it isn't a seizure first – some seizures can look like a shutdown. Both my kids and I have experienced shutdowns on multiple occasions. In my experience it was because I was so overwhelmed and oppressed in a certain situation that I couldn't see a way out. My brain, my mouth, my feelings all went to sleep.

I'm having more of them as I age. I think it's my new coping mechanism to trauma and unmasking. I used to 'explode' (in their words -meltdown in mine) and I was told off for it and told I didn't fit in, or I was fired. Now I shutdown instead. It's just as toxic to me, but it is a self-preservation and survival skill. I will tell my best friend about something that happened, that I was mad about. And their response is always "Why didn't you say something?". It was because I was physically incapable of responding with anything. I was either too hurt, too angry or too flabbergasted to open my mouth. This causes situational non-speaking... but it goes further – my brain then shuts down, I can't hear what is said afterwards, I can't remember what happened, and I have no idea what I did or should do. It's really quite awful to not be able to control anything about yourself, even your ability to remember a moment in time.

Regression

Regression can exist, but not really when you are talking about autistics. We find this term highly insulting. When a doctor or therapist says 'your child has regressed', what they are actually seeing, is the 'typical' development of an autistic or ND individual. Autistics develop differently to NT's, that's why it's called a developmental 'disorder' by the DSM 5.

When autistics grow and develop, we become aware; like any newborn baby growing into themselves. When this occurs, we become more ourselves. What you're seeing is not a regression, but our natural responses to our environment and things that can harm us. It can seem out of the blue, or sudden. This is why some uneducated people believe that medicines or vaccines cause autism; because we don't start to show our autistic stereotypical 'traits' until something in our world harms or hinders us. Uneducated people wrongly attribute the change in behaviour or skills to things that occurred around the same timeframe.

Some of us may start out our childhoods doing what is assumed as typically developing, but then we may suddenly stop doing a skill or behaviour, this is not a regression, this is us – discovering that something went wrong (around us or to us), that we must respond to in our own natural way. That may be by limiting our speech, so we don't become overwhelmed, or have room to take in more information. It might be that we stop giving eye contact, which may or may not be due to us becoming aware that it gives us pain, feels uncomfortable or don't like attention directed at us.

Often times, a sudden regression is attributable or a result of a meltdown, shutdown or burnout. When our brains, emotions and physical being is under attack; we go into shutdown or meltdown, and when we move passed these two – we enter burnout. This can also look like regression. We are now unable to do things that we could do previously. We are not regressing; we are burnt out! We have reached the limit of our abilities to cope- so we literally are **unable**. It's not that we've unlearnt things, or forgotten, or been 'struck down' with something – that's offensive. You need to see us as the same as we were, but needing help, support, and rest – in order to recharge and get back to 'our normal'.

If more autistic children were seen as needing to rest, instead of being put into more therapy (to re-learn the things that we supposedly lost) we would show you the proof in this.

A child that 'seemed to be typical', and then 'suddenly had autistic traits' is often really hiding their true struggles in order to fit in and be loved by those around them (masking their autism). The same is said in reverse when adults think the child is no longer showing traits and 'lost their autism' – they have not, because you cannot lose neurological wiring in this way – they are masking their traits.

Children are smart, they pick up on everything. They know when other children are loved, hugged, and accepted for behaving a certain way, and doing certain things – so they mimic their peers, to gain love and approval. But there is always a limit to a child's ability to do anything. They can hold it in for only so long. The dam eventually breaks, and that's what you're seeing. Not regression, not being 'struck down'. You are seeing a child that's dam has broken. And once those walls fall, it's incredibly hard (if not impossible) to get the water back behind those walls. Don't expect them to get the water back inside or try to make them; it will just cause more leaks. It is not a sign of autism – it is a sign of trauma and not coping.

Another explanation of regression:

The caterpillar into a butterfly. When a caterpillar is metamorphosing into a butterfly, we do not say "oh that's awful! That caterpillar is regressing, oh no, it's regressed; it lost all those legs, it lost too much weight, it's no longer a caterpillar, something went hideously wrong, that's not natural, that's wrong – we must fix the butterfly to become like a caterpillar again". No! We celebrate the butterfly; we look at the new creature it has become. It has not lost skills and abilities; it has gained others. It may not look like a caterpillar or do the things that other caterpillars can do. But it can do all these other things – and those things aren't wrong or bad, they are just different. There is no need for a butterfly to ever become like a caterpillar ever again, or to act like one; and the same goes for your autistic child.

For more information on this, check out the article by Baden Gaeke Franz (from ASAN Winnipeg, 5 June 2017) "Help! My child is regressing!- On Autistic Burnout and How to Manage It" www.adaptmanitoba.ca/autistic-burnout/

Note: sometimes a regression is a sign of something else; like an illness or PANDAS etc. You need a medical profession to diagnose this.

Radical Acceptance

This is when you change your life and the way you do things to make accommodations for another person. Eg: we don't have mealtimes or screen time limits – because to do so would mean that I'm not accepting them for who they are. I'm imposing social normities on the person that don't suit them. I radically accept everything I need to do, to accommodate them – even if it isn't what I've been taught to do my entire life. I change everything I am doing to accommodate the other person. This is not spoiling them – or not having any discipline or rules. You can set mutually acceptable boundaries, while still radically accepting and adapting to the individual. It's not about pandering to the person or letting them 'get away' with things, it's about coming up with 'out of the box thinking' to help the individual learn something, live their life, or cope etc. This can be especially helpful for people who are experiencing burnout.

Echoing

I do this, and I get in trouble for it. This is when you hear an accent, and you start mirroring it. You do not usually realise you are doing it, but some people think you are making fun of them – but I'm definitely not making fun of anyone, I seriously have no idea I'm doing it. A signal or polite "you're echoing again" is what I want from friends when I accidentally slip into this very common autistic speech trait. Australians have been identified as having a very adjustable palate that allows them to slip into different accents easily. If you are from Australia, please be aware of this tendency – as we don't want to be known as a country of people making fun of accents. I like to let people know that I can't help it or stop it from starting. Imitation is the highest form of flattery, so hopefully whoever is being mimicked is flattered, not insulted.

Masking

Masking is when an individual hides their true self; their feelings, thoughts, habits, stims, eating preferences, toilet rituals etc. They can hide their need for: movement/ silence/ accommodations/ fidgets and different ways of learning. Masking can also happen when a child is bored or overstimulated and when they don't understand a teachers/adults/therapist's way of teaching, or the instructions or content. Not just autistics mask – all people are capable of masking, and do mask, and it is something to be extremely careful with. Please see the section on Masking for more information and help.

Transitions

You will probably hear a lot of teachers and therapists talking about transitions, and how it's; 'hard for your child to transition". Or that you may need timers and schedules in order to help your child to transition more easily. See the section on Timers.

But the reason why transitions are hard is often never talked about. I'm not even sure if the people who tell you this, know why it's so hard for autistics and ADHD'ers to transition. Please see the section on Transitions for more information.

Transitions are movements from one task to another, but for some autistic people, it can be very hard to do without careful planning and accommodations.

AUDHD

This is the acronym most used by people who are both autistic and ADHD.

Spicy Autistic

This term actually has two different back stories – depending on the person. One back story is that it started in order to make light (or fun) of people who say their child has mild autism (which is not a thing, we are all just autistic with different support needs, and have different things occurring co-currently). But in response to the word mild – people started saying they are spicy – as the opposite of mild. The second back story is for those in the community that identify as autistic and ADHD, but don't like the literal meaning of the ADHD acronym. So, they are autistic with a little spice added (the spice being the ADHD); hence Spicy Autistic. This second one makes more sense to me, as my AUDHD'er is definitely spicy and so am I.

Puzzle pieces

Do **not** use this as a symbol for autism. Autistic people are very triggered by this symbol and find it offensive. You can research why people don't like it, but one reason is because it is like saying you are a missing piece or have a missing piece – that you are broken and need 'fixing'. It was originally brought about by the National Autistic Society in the UK and the Autism Society of America, because they believed autism was a "puzzling" 'condition' and paired it with the image of a crying child; because autism is a 'tragedy' and we 'suffer' from it. The American group was also partly founded by the same man who invented ABA and one form of gay conversion therapy.

It is also used by the group Autism Speaks, (they use a blue puzzle piece); the autistic community considers this group to be a hate group that wants to cure us and use eugenics to make sure the next generation of ND's never exist.

Please read the article by Cassandra Crosman (20 March 2019), In The Loop About Neurodiversity – Wordpress: "The Ableist History of The Puzzle Piece Symbol for Autism" https://intheloopaboutneurodiversity.wordpress.com/2019/03/20/the-ableist-history-of-the-puzzle-piece-symbol-for-autism/?fbclid=

Light it Up Blue
This is also offensive to autistic people. It's original meaning was to raise awareness for autistic people – but only the male ones (hence the 'blue'), as they didn't believe it "affected" females, or

anyone else (including the LGBTQIA2S+ community). It started with the group Autism Speaks. This group has been known to support people who think about/talk about killing their autistic children (YouTube video "Mother talks about killing her autistic daughter and herself") and the article: www.autism-advocacy. fandom.com/wiki/attempted_Murder_of_Issy_Stapleton. Autism Speaks also worked to get the US government to take away AAC devices from non-speaking autistics, so that nonspeaking people would no longer be able to communicate. Anyone wearing blue on World Autism Day (April 2) is seen to be supporting Autism Speaks – **not** autism or autism awareness or autistic people. There are also a number of articles and proof that the money they raise for autism hardly ever actually reaches autistic people or their families.

There is a whole website dedicated to this, check out: www. boycottautismspeaks.org There are also Facebook pages like: www.facebook.com/people/Autism-speaks-doesnt-speak-for-me

Also read the article by Emily Willingham (13 November 2013) Forbes: "Why Autism Speaks Does Not Speak For Me" www. forbes.com/sites/emilywillingham/2013/11/13/why-autism-speaks-doesnt-speak-for-me

National Autistic Society has also been deemed as problematic by the autistic community, check out their use of PBS and do an online search of their bullying and law suits for abuse or neglect of autistics. One such article is by Steven Morris (8 March 2019) The Guardian "Autism Charity escapes prosecution over care home bullying" www.theguardian.com/society/2019/mar/07/national-autistic-society-escapes-prosecution-over-care-home-bullying

This is your decision; if you want to support them, that is your decision. Just be aware that you are offending the autistic community as you do so. I personally would not wear a known hate symbol; so, I do not wear light it up blue shirts or puzzle pieces, or support Autism Speaks, as they are considered to be hate symbols by the autistic community. These symbols for autism awareness also steal the show every year – it makes everyone talk about the controversy around wearing this or that symbol – instead of talking about what really matters. If we all agreed to wear gold or rainbow colours and infinity signs; then we'd be able to move the conversation onto really concerning topics. Some people even suggest to "light it up RED INSTEAD" – but I still think this is causing some confusion as to whether it's just a political statement against Autism Speaks, or acceptance for autistics.

It has been suggested (within autistic groups) that people who continue to use these symbols and ignore the autistic community's views; are 'fair weather' friends. Some have said that you cannot be an advocate or ally of autistics if you continue to do the opposite of what the majority of autistic people are asking of you. That you are in fact opposing autistics. Some have also said that the puzzle piece is mostly only used by warrior parents that monetise their children's diagnoses or use it as a symbol of martyrdom, but I think it's more down to educating people as to the correct symbol. People do not know what they do not know; you cannot blame a parent for using a hate symbol if they are not aware that it is one.

There has been discussions around the idea that if you continue to put your head in the sand and echo the voices that suppress minority groups – you are becoming one of the suppressors yourself. And if you are giving money to groups like Autism Speaks, you are supporting the eventual eugenics and possible genocide of autistics. I'm not sure about this myself. But I'd rather give money directly to autistic people than to a group that has been proven to not help the very people they purport to support.

Some people have argued that the autistic community as a majority are also suppressing other autistic voices (because some autistics may like puzzle pieces or the colour blue). If your child 'likes the puzzle piece" that is their right – but do they know the history of the symbol and why it is considered offensive and how it is holding the community back from making positive change and inclusion?

What the autistic community is trying to do- is be heard, and to raise the voices of those in the community that cannot be heard. No minority group can ever effect real change without becoming a movement, a larger group of people that represent the majority view. Listen to them, ask them questions, you will see that there truly is a majority of autistics that have the same view – and it's a positive step in a good direction. The biggest group I know is Autism Inclusivity with over 150,000 members and growing; and they do **not** support Puzzle piece, Blue ribbons or other paraphernalia, or Autism Speaks.

But autistics need your help – they need you, your friends, your family to help lift their voices high (when I say 'voices' I also mean the communications of non-speaking autistics who are also a part of the movement, and some are very prevalent in this movement). Please never assume that I'm talking about only white autistics, or male autistics or 'high functioning' autistics. The autistic movement and community has people from all over the world, from different walks of life and with different abilities and disabilities.

This is up to you. Do you want to educate yourself? Do you want to help raise those voices; and the future adult voice of your child, or do you want to ignore it? Your child will likely join the autistic movement when they are old enough to choose for themselves. Would you want them to be able to be heard, or would you prefer that people talk over them, and perpetuate harmful signs, groups and words that keep the stigmatisms around your child and autism in general.

Gold/Rainbow Infinity

Autistic people prefer a symbol of a gold-coloured infinity sign. Or simply wearing gold/yellow t-shirts. It more closely represents the infinite possibilities that comes with being autistic. And the infinite ways in which our nervous systems and brains are wired- no two neurodivergents are wired the same way, that's why it's so amazing and interesting.

Gold is used because the symbol for Gold on the periodic table is AU. It has no political agenda and has not been started or used by any controversial groups to start their own press or used as a logo for any nefarious groups. If we all agreed to use this instead of fighting over politics – we'd have more time for actual understanding, acceptance and change.

A rainbow-coloured infinity sign represents neurodiversity or neurodivergence. It also links nicely into the huge LGBTQIA2S+ community (who also use rainbow colours); and are huge part of the neurodivergent community.

There was a good YouTube video put out in 2022 for Awareness Day. It can be used in schools to help kids understand differences. Autism acceptance 2022 The Neuro Bears - YouTube – (www.youtube.com/watch?v=_490q6LaHIY) It's cute and quite simple to understand; it's a drawing/cartoon for kids. If I was still teaching the younger years, this is what I'd use on Autism Awareness Day, I'd probably also print out some black and white pictures of the bears for the kids to colour in themselves.

Autism Awareness

Every year autistic people fear this time (April; Autism Awareness Month). It is a time of fighting and arguments and people talking over the top of autistics. We do not need you to talk for us, we have mouths and computers and any number of ways of communicating, and we're good at it. Leave it to the autistic community. And do not argue when they tell you something.

Just accept it. Because that is what this day/month should be about — ACCEPTANCE not awareness. We all know autism exists, but what is needed — is for the autistic community to be accepted and to be the first port of call as experts on autism, and for information/training and education on autism. You wouldn't ask a lion to explain about being a fish — so don't ask a NT to explain to you about autism.

There are also some people that sell offensive products for autism awareness and profiting from it (puzzle pieces, blue jewellery etc). Most autistics would prefer you buy your products directly from other autistic people and support the community, awareness, acceptance and support. Both "Ausome Training" and "Autism Inclusivity" Facebook groups/blogs have lists of autistic owned businesses that are preferred autistic sellers. And there is an Autistic Marketplace group on Facebook that is full of autistic artisans and creators that would love your patronage.

If autistic and neurodivergent people are going to be accepted, change needs to occur throughout the world, not just one island, village or country. And that is what the autistic community is trying to achieve by telling you to stop using puzzle pieces, ribbons (ribbons usually represent disease — autism is not a disease) and the colour blue to represent autism. They are trying to achieve a cohesive and united front against abusive people/groups, ABA, and negative use of language/labels and titles, non-autistic led charities that pretend to be advocating for autistics, stop the misinformation and prejudice, remove the stigmatism around autism and stop the negative cycle.

Yes even 'new ABA' is not accepted by the autistic community: see ABA book 3 for more information.

Some autistic groups are trying to have the World Autism Day changed to the 8th of August – as this would represent 2 infinity signs (two number 8's)– for neurodiversity and autism. I would love to see this happen.

Please also see "Autism Level Up!" Website for more information on the "Levels" of **awareness**. https://autismlevelup.com/the-essential-guide-to-the-autism-level-up-levels/ (Fede and Laurent 2020). They have a brilliant table explaining "Awareness, Acceptance, Appreciation, Empowerment and Advocacy" that is in an easy-to-read downloadable pdf. (This is also available in many other languages on the website – as this is something that needs to be taken seriously – worldwide). I stuck it on my wall because I love it so much. I didn't realise I was stuck in the

"Awareness Zone", even though I'd realised I am autistic, and my kids are too. ... Once I expanded my knowledge and willingness to listen to, and truly acknowledge, and do what other autistic people were telling me - I'm glad to say; that I finally feel like I'm reaching the "Advocacy Level" – but I'm always willing to learn more, like all people should about any topic.

Check out the following article for information about the puzzle piece: Cassandra Crosman (20 March 2019) In the Loop About Neurodiversity: "The ableist history of the puzzle piece symbol for Autism" www.intheloopaboutneurodiversity.wordpress.com/ 2019/03/20/the-ableist-history-of-the-puzzle-piece-symbol-for-autism/

"Autistic Pride Day" is held on the 18th of June annually. "Pride Month", is the month of June.

ASAN & Advocacy   **Autistic Self Advocacy Network:**
www.autisticadvocacy.org/

This group is the biggest network for advocacy across the US, Canada, Portugal, Australia, and New Zealand. Check out their site for information about what is happening in the community and for resources and how they advocate for autistics.

In America, there is also: Communication First www. communicationfirst.org (great for AAC users)

Autistic Women and Nonbinary Network (AWN): www. awnnetwork.org

Autism Inclusivity Meets (AIM), in both the UK and US: www. autisticinclusivemeets.org

NeuroDiverse Self Advocacy (NDSA): The UK advocacy group: www.ndsa.uk

Or the I CAN network www.icannetwork.online They are also on Facebook, Instagram, YouTube, and LinkedIn. This company conducts a program in schools for neurodivergent students, to gain confidence, self-awareness, to meet other ND people, and it is autistic led – which is the important part. If you want to find out more, check out their website where you can download a brochure to give to your schools' inclusion staff member: www.icannetwork.online/high-schools/ Ask you child first if it's something they'd be interested in – it's not for everyone, as I personally would've found it triggering and overwhelming as a child, but some love it and swear by it).

LGBTQIA2S+   **Lesbian, gay, bisexual, transgender, queer or questioning, intersex, and asexual, non-binary, two spirit and more (+).**

More neurodivergent people identify as LGBTQIA2S+ than any other 'group'. Please ask the person what their preference is with pronouns before you make a big mistake, eg: he/she/they/them etc. Some people use the terms AFAB or AMAB etc (Assigned Female/Male at Birth), but some can find it unnecessary or offensive; always ask – don't assume.

The article by Mere Abrams (updated 25 March 2022) Healthline: "47 Terms that Describe Sexual Attraction, Behavior, and Orientation" www.healthline.com/health/different-types-of-sexuality; may be of interest (as a starting point) to familiarise yourself with the sheer scope of this topic, it's huge and there's simply too much information for me put in this book (see section Minorities within Minorities). It's an incredibly important subject with respect to the ND community; awareness and acceptance.

This topic becomes vital when thinking about how best to help/support your ND child, eg: if your child identifies as any of the above; they may need support/help in some specific areas.

Eg; bathing techniques (see the section on Showering and Bathing), help with bullies, and perhaps violent discrimination, or sexism, where to get extra information, specific support groups, how to positively support their human right to choose/acceptance and what to do when discriminated against, information on surgeries and hormone treatments (if applicable), etc, etc, etc. The section on masking to save your life may also be of interest – masking can be harmful, but in some cases, it can also save your life, especially if you are a minority within a minority (intersectional). I hope some of the tips and tools in this book will help – but since I'm not an expert on these things – I refer you to the people and groups I've linked in this book for more information.

There are also many great book/blogs and Facebook writers that cover this topic; see the section at the back of book five for links to these people and forums.

As transphobia has been a big issue lately, and ridiculous offensive laws are being made in some countries; now is a good time to reach out to your fellow ND's and support each other and those around you. Especially to help stand up against bigots and discrimination.

Asperger's

This term is no longer part of the DSM-5 (diagnostic tool). It has been recognised as a slur against autistic people. The name originated in Germany with a doctor (Asperger) that had Nazi links, that believed some autistics were 'better' than others (nazi supremacy thinking).

This information about Asperger's work is now under more scrutiny, as there are some reports that Asperger may have stolen his work from other leading psychologists in the field, (before and during the war).

Please read the research by Herwig Czech (19 April 2018) Molecular Autism: "Hans Asperger, National Socialism, and 'race hygiene' in Nazi-era Vienna" www.molecularautism.biomedcentral.com/articles/10.1186/s13229-018-0208-6 There is actual proof, from Asperger's own hand, that he sent autistic kids to die at the "Am Spiegelgrund Clinic" during the Second World War – because they were "a burden to their mother".

Also read the book by Edith Sheffer (2018) "Asperger's Children: The origins of autism in nazi Vienna". This is a fantastic book, and I recommend everyone wanting to know the origins of the autism diagnosis, and how involved Asperger was with the Nazi regime to read this book.

Please stop using the term Asperger. It is harmful to autistics, and it is a horrible way to segregate the community, but most importantly - it sullies the memories of the children that were killed because of this doctor.

Some people now use "Autistic with high IQ", or '2E' (twice exceptional), or level 1; which are all offensive. This is because labelling some autistics as 'smarter' or 'better' or 'more useful' than others divides/segregates and devalues the rest of the community and assumes that some autistics are superior to others. It creates supremacy – just like Hitler intended. And should be needless to say – it's wrong!

There is no difference – we are autistic, all of us – none are better or less than! Functioning labels and different names for different groups of autistics is wrong and harmful. Putting any group of autistic above or below another is wrong. Eg; white above Black or Indigenous, Asian etc, or speaking above non-speaking, or straight above LGBTQ+, seeing above blind, hearing above deaf, or physically abled above physically disabled - it is all wrong! We **are** all autistic, no less, no more – just are!

High/Low Functioning

These terms shouldn't be used either. This old method of diagnosing autism and creating "categories" so that people can 'pigeonhole' us or separate us into useful groups is repulsive. Many also believe that the High Functioning tool is used to choose the children that can be "helped" and taught to be "normal". And the Low Functioning is used to label children that are to be segregated to 'specialist schools' and forgotten about, ignored or belittled – it's truly hideous.

Functioning labels are also used to deny support (to "high functioning") or to presume incompetence (to "low functioning"). This label only considered how the person was 'functioning' on the day of the assessment; and not a holistic look at the individual and their ongoing needs and required supports. The original intent of these labels was to ascertain funding /insurance /help etc. In all countries, it has now been moved to a number 'Level' system (Using the internationally recognised DSM-5 or ICD).

The levels are also unhelpful and offensive to autistics because (they are the same as the original low or high offensive grading of humans) they are seen like this:

Level 1 – you might not get any help/support or funding (basically the same as 'high functioning' was seen).

Level 2 - usually means you will get support and funding, but your child has the ability to be more 'normal' one day, or perhaps they might 'regress' and become useless to society. It's so offensive and wrong.

Level 3 - is lots of support and funding (like the old 'low functioning' label), but the person is often seen as a 'lesser' being, and not presumed as capable or able – which is disgusting. None of these labels or systems are good for professionals, or for the people being labelled with them.

Just because you are 'Level 1' does not mean you don't need supports in place. I, myself could be labelled level 2 for anxiety, level 1 for social skills, level 3 for meltdowns. Please see the section on Severity of Autism for more information and a better understanding of labels.

There is a very useful diagram that better describes the "functioning" of autistic people, it is in a diagram format of bar chart compared to a pie graph. It perfectly shows that you cannot use a label like High or Low to describe autistic people; we are not linear. Please check out @Autism_Sketches on Twitter.

Specialist Schools

Special schools for the disabled (in Australia) usually have a cut off IQ rank of 70. This means that any child ranked above 70 cannot attend these schools. This means most autistic kids can't attend special schools in Australia. It also doesn't help that IQ tests are aimed at white heterosexual neurotypical males from western society; if you are not in this demographic, then it is likely that you will not score as well as your white NT male western counterparts. Also, some non-speaking autistics are relegated to specialist schools without doing IQ tests – as people wrongly assume that non-speaking means non-understanding. If your child is non-speaking, please do not automatically assume that they need a 'special school'. The 'special school' closest to me is more of a glorified day care – they do not teach reading or writing or communication, or really any educational subjects except for daily living skills. This is wrong. All children have the right to education – equal education! – and should be presumed as capable!

Special schools in Australia are currently under a cloud of doom. If you read the article by Nicole Precel (2 May 2022) in The Sydney Morning Herald: "Push for special schools to be phased out under inclusive education plan" www.smh.com.au/education/push-for-special-schools-to-be-phased-out-under-inclusive-education-plan-20220428-p5agxd.html?utm_medium=Social&utm_source=Facebook#Echobox=1651460233. You will see that under the UN Convention; countries around the world are trying to make segregation of disabled students against the law. This means that all students will eventually be attending mainstream schools. Although I agree that segregation is bad, I also think that the current mainstream schooling system cannot/does not support ND kids, or children with disabilities; and a lot of work needs to be done if special schools are to be abolished.

If you are looking at a specialist school for your child, keep this information in mind for the future. Also, if your child starts out in a specialist school, it does not mean they will always be able to stay in that school. IQ tests for ND kids are often done every 2 years, and many will test higher as the years progress, and they can meet more of the tests "white NT male" and "speaking" criteria / type stereotypes – as they are often taught how to act and think like a neurotypical person, which will bring the very biased score up. This means they will be kicked out of their specialist school if they test higher than 70; even if the result is 71 or 72.

There are some autism specific schools in some metropolitan cities around Australia – but some still have IQ cut-offs. I recommend asking when applying what their criteria are. Also ask if they use any ABA /PBS techniques/rewards or consequences etc – see book 3 on ABA techniques.

For more information on IQ tests, see the section on Spiky Profile, or read these articles by Terra Vance from NeuroClastic: (12 April 2020) "On Autism and Intelligence: Language and Advocacy" www.neuroclastic.com/on-autism-and-intelligence-language-and-advocacy/ OR (12 April 2020) "On Autism and Intelligence: Measuring and Understanding IQ" www.neuroclastic.com/on-autism-and-intelligence-measuring-understanding-iq/

Assistive Technology
Also shortened to AT in Australia. This is any tool or resource that is usually technological in some way that may help your

child navigate the world. Eg: it could be a Phonak listening device, an iPad with speech or AAC apps, or an AAC device, a lift to help you in and out of bed, or even an automatic soap dispenser. These items are so damned important, they can be the difference between struggling and living a great life.

In some countries you can ask for an Assistive Tech Assessment, to assess what type of tool would best be suited to the individual needs of the disabled person, and how they can use them in different ways to do different things. In Australia these are often called AT forms (by NDIA) that your therapists (OT, Physio, SLP, psych or paediatrician) fill in; to prove the necessity of the products/tools, or the effectiveness of them, and they can also recommend different therapy or sessions to help the user learn how to use them.

DSM-5

Diagnostic and Statistical Manual of Mental Disorders (the number 5 is for the latest edition of the manual in circulation and current use, from 2013). Used by medical professionals to diagnose your child with a particular "disorder". It is based on the deficit model – medical model of disability.

ICD

Diagnostic Manual (Predominantly used in Europe) from the World Health Organization (WHO) – International Classification of Diseases (ICD – they are currently up to their 11th revision of this document). Under this there is the International Classification of Functioning, Disability and Health (ICF) and the "WHODAS" = World Health Organization Disability Assessment Schedule; that is used to diagnose people as autistic. It also uses the deficit model of disability.

Ableism

Discrimination of people with disabilities, or discrimination in favour of able-bodied people. Example of ableist language: "you don't look disabled" or "what's wrong with you?", "you can't be disabled, you are too pretty", "you look normal", "you must be high functioning", "you can't be autistic because you're not severe enough like my child" etc. See the section on Ableism for more information. Please familiarise yourself with ableist language, so you can avoid it, if possible (we all make mistakes from time to time, we are human, but we need to learn from these mistakes)

You can also have an ableist business culture; where you do not accommodate, hire, or adapt your premises for disabled people. Eg: no wheelchair access, insisting on face-to-face interviews / mouth words or eye contact, not allowing people to work from home (when it could be an option, or they have worked from home previously), not using clear direct communication and punishing people for their communication style.

Othering

This is a term that is used to describe a situation/prejudice or segregating of a group or individual away from others. Eg: when some kids are put in a separate group from the rest of the class, because they need extra support or 'special' education etc – that group is being 'othered'. They are being separated and segregated from the rest of the class. This can cause the rest of the class to see them as 'less than', or for the segregated group itself to lose confidence and feel they are different and not worthy, or perhaps even broken. My child was "othered" by his teacher; the teacher moved the rest of the class away from sitting next to him (no one was seated in the spot next to him). He told me at age 5 that he thought everyone hated him. It was bullying and othering – by the teacher.

I've even read a story about a parent who removed their child from a school because the teacher asked the whole class to put their hand up if they thought the autistic child in the room was annoying. This is bullying and othering, and truly abusive. I would've loved it if the child had responded with "put your hand up if you think the teacher is ugly" – but two wrongs don't make a right.

Othering can be very obvious, or it can be more subtle. Obvious: like the example of the teachers above. Or subtle: children that have an aide consistently with them are othered. The children who do not have an aide or adult constantly beside them, start to realise that the one child is different, and 'other' to the rest of the group. It separates and divides them.

Difference

There needs to be a discussion about difference. While **Othering** can and is often used to segregate and bully, the word difference is often bandied about in the same way. People will tell us that we are not different – that we are human and just like all humans. Let me say; we are not the same. People tell us that we shouldn't use the word different because it puts the idea in people's minds that we **are** different and perhaps wrong or defective. It is also sometimes used by some people to make ND people feel more included or accepted, by trying to tell us we belong – but it sets the tone that we are accepted- **only** under the condition that we

are like everyone else, and only if we pretend to be like everyone else. But we are not!

In some ways they are right about **difference** being used to **other** a person, and make them feel rejected, or like an outsider. But, It is also liberating to use the word difference to show that we actually **are** different, and that's why we need accommodations, adaptions and support. We diverge, we are unique, we often don't fit in. When people say things like "we love you because you're no different to us"; they are actually trying to negate our differences, and they are not actually seeing us, or accepting us and our divergences. They are only willing to accept us if they can see similarities between themselves and us. If we diverge too much, then the fear that we **are** truly too different, and causes them to reject and other us.

Using 'you are not different' is yet again another form of infantilising and pandering, but not acceptance, and another way to deny supports. If you do not accept that we are different, you cannot also accept that we need support or additional tools and resources to help us cope in a world that is not built for us.

Eg: if you tell a deaf person that they are exactly the same as a hearing person; that they are in fact **not** different, you also can't see that they need adjustments and support and they will not be given accommodations. Because if they are the same, they wouldn't need supports.

Denying differences is denying human variance, it's not seeing the person for who they are, and what their individual needs are; it is in fact rejecting us for our differences. It would be like telling a person of colour that you do not see the colour of skin; thereby negating their struggles and discriminations against them and their lived experiences. It stops people from changing and becoming allies or advocates of that segregated group. If you can't see the differences of people around you, you also can't see their struggles or help them overcome them.

I use the word difference or different in this book to show the need for people to help and support us, **not** to other anyone or any group. Difference is not a dirty word, how people use it is where they problem lies and needs to change.

Stimming

Please note that ALL humans stim, it is not limited to or owned by autistics. It is NOT something to stop unless it becomes harmful. And even then – it should be redirected to another stim, not stopped.

Stimming is sometimes called stimulating behaviours. What it is, is using sensory and or motor experiences to connect to ourselves and the world around us. It is often a repetitive movement, a vocal noise, or something entirely different, see the examples below:

Sound Stimming: making noises, talking, singing, biting your lip, sticking tongue out when thinking, holding your breath, repetitive words (see the section on Echolalia)

Mental Thought Stimming: running something through your brain on repeat, even a song, sound (listening to the same song over and over). Being stuck in a loop of a thought or seeing an event or incident play over and over in your mind can also be a stim. It can become a problem, if the loop is a negative one and you can't get out of it; this causes depression. Doing something else that engages the mind fully (like reading or watching something very stimulating or something that takes a lot of brain power to master or understand). This is why limiting reading, a hobby, or screen time is very dangerous for the ND person – we need these things to fully engage our brains in order to get out of the depression mind loop.

Touch stimming: patting a cat, drumming, scratching, knitting etc

Visual Stimming: I used to watch the same 2 movies on repeat during school holidays as a kid, but it can also be looking at things from different angles repetitively – watching the wheels on toy cars move back and forth. Watching lava lamps or fish swim, or lights on a ceiling (from a projector) move and flow.

Smelling Stimming: sniffing, snuffling, smelling, flaring nostrils.

Basically - Stimming is anything you do repetitively in order to calm, control, think, emote, process, take in and recall information, and of course stimulate.

Sometimes stimming can become harmful. Like picking skin until it bleeds (Excoriation: see the section on this for ideas), or eating to excess, or overuse of alcohol or drugs, or overuse of a muscle until it hurts. One of my kids went through a stage of eating until he threw up, we think it was a taste and texture stim. We also needed to investigate interoception to make sure he could feel when he became full. It can be common for ADHD'ers to not feel, sense or know when they are full.

You need to find out what is behind the stim, eg; what is causing them to want to stim until they hurt themselves, and how the stim is helping them to calm – or overcome the thing that is upsetting them. Once you find out what is going on; you can redirect or stop the thing that is causing the child to stim in an inappropriate way. And help them find a new stim that won't cause harm.

Never stop a stim for the sake of stopping a stim. This is more harmful than the stim itself. You need to remove the thing that is upsetting them, find the cause of the harmful stim, eg: this could be too much stress, arbitrary rules or punishments, bullying or pain etc. Or you can try to find something else to stim with (eg: a fidget: See the section on Useful Tools for more ideas) – but this needs to be their decision. You can't choose a stim for someone else, you can help find possible alternatives, but it's up to them.

STIMS are healthy and important for everyone – they help us self-regulate our emotions and thoughts, they allow us to calm and should **never** be stopped. Redirected **only if** it has become harmful!

Harmful Stims: For Excessive eating; try chewing gum (only if they are older than 7, AND able to handle gum; as it is a choking hazard), food with less calories (needs to be their decision:

check out the section on ARFID for more info), cutting the food into smaller pieces, a spit bucket or flavoured drinks instead (for some people they only like to taste foods and use tasting as a stim). If they are eating because they are bored; redirect and find something to interest them and get rid of the boredom. If it is because they are an emotional eater – get rid of what is causing the trauma, eg: if bright lights are upsetting them – turn them off. If it is chewing or mouth stimulation sensations, they like; try a chew toy/Chewellery or electric toothbrush etc. It needs to be their choice.

For people who throw up: try the above methods, and explaining that throwing up can burn the oesophagus, rot the teeth and cause other serious health issues. And make sure there is not something else that is causing it. What may look like a stim may actually be medical or bulimia, constipation, or a number of other issues, such as; Prader-Willi Syndrome, reflux, overly large tonsils, or other gastrointestinal issues etc.

If it is some other sort of harmful stim – look at what is causing it, and remove the cause – do not remove the stim: this is what ABA does – and removing peoples comfort and coping strategies is abusive. It takes away their ability to self-regulate and can cause meltdowns, cPTSD, and suicidal thoughts. It can also cause more harmful stims to be adopted – like teeth grinding or cutting (self mutilation). Many autistics who have been stopped from doing a stim (like hand flapping) have adopted invisible stims; because you cannot see them do this stim, they feel safe in doing it, because you will not be able to stop it if you can't see it. I will say it again to drum it home – NEVER STOP a STIM.

A stim can also be using a tablet or iPad etc; to relax and calm and 'get out of your head' – and to think about something else. By limiting screen time or removing these stimming tools – you are stopping the stim! Which will cause meltdowns, more harmful behaviours and what you may see as a 'tantrum'. It is **not** a tantrum, and it is not an addiction to screens. If they do have a meltdown because their screen has been removed or limited; they are likely communicating to you that you have removed their only 'safe space' or regulation tool – and they were not regulated (yet) at the time it was taken away. See the section on screen time for more information.

My kids also use tablets to help them to do certain tasks – they cannot eat without them turned on – because the sound of YouTube and the TV on in the background muffles the sound of people chewing (Misophonia) and distracts from looking at food they do not like to look at but like to eat. If they do not have this distraction – they are unable to eat (see ARFID or Misophonia for more information).

There is a great cartoon about stimming on the NeuroClastic Website called "Stimming is fun", by Meg Raby, Elise Palmer and help from Trevor Byrd – it's under the Infographics PDF section: www.neuroclastic.com/infographics/#elementor-toc__heading-anchor-51 it's about an autistic crow called Otto Crow that loves to stim and it tells the audience why. Meg Raby has also written a book using this character called: "My Brother Otto".

Spoons

Many ND people will talk about not having enough "Spoons" to deal with something. This term was first coined and written about by Christine Miserandino in her article "The Spoon Theory", 2003. https://lymphoma-action.org.uk/sites/default/files/media/documents/2020-05/Spoon%20theory%20by%20Christine%20Miserandino.pdf. Trigger warning- it may make you cry (I cried).

Many disabled and ND people have adopted this explanation (of the authors Lupus Story); to describe their own lives and how they cope/adapt and get through every single day. Please read the 3-page article by Christine, it's brilliant.

Basically, the spoons are a visualisation tool of the amount of energy you have and the energy you expend daily, and you only have a limited number of spoons per day – once you're out, you're out.

This theory ties in nicely to Executive Functioning (see the section on this for ideas and more information). We all can suffer from not having the executive functioning to get certain things done, but it is worse for ND people, often due to our already depleted nervous systems working overtime to deal with the world that was not built for us.

Fixations or Special Interests

When NTs have a 'special interest' or a 'fixation', it is not called by these names, it is instead called a hobby, a passion, a leisure pursuit or just 'interest'. This is why changing the name to 'special interest' or 'obsession' is ableist. It is the invention of a word, specifically to pathologize, ostracise or insult a disabled person or persons. They are words used to tell a disabled person that when they have a hobby it's wrong, or they are doing it incorrectly, but if they were 'classed' as NT – it would be called something nicer and less offensive.

ND people can 'fixate' on things, subjects, collections, items/ objects, information, discussions etc – but it is just our **hobby**, just like anyone else can have. We can interact with, or use, our interests, or hobbies differently to a neurotypical people – but it's still just a hobby, and hobbies are good for all people. Encourage it! Once we find a love for something, it can become all encompassing, but it can create so much joy and comfort. We learn through our own different ways, and if we want to immerse ourselves in a topic – let us, and then learn from us – we will soon surprise you with our depth of concentration, varied knowledge, and our passions.

Once a child tells you all their knowledge, they will likely stop talking about it. But if you interfere, stop them from talking about it, talk over them, or ignore them – they will keep going. Rudeness can go both ways. NT people telling us to stop talking about our interests is rude, it would be the same if, for example, we told NT people to stop talking able idle gossip – it's rude. We are different, but it doesn't make it wrong. We all need to get along, and sometimes the way ND people communicate, is through their 'info dumping' of their interests. I may sometimes see NT communication as indirect and 'fluff', if I told them instead to info dump or to stop talking – this is me being rude to NT's. I accept NTs for their way of living and communicating, it needs to go both ways.

If your ND child is 'info dumping' - it is a sign they are proud of themselves and their knowledge, and you should be very glad that they chose **you** to talk to about it – it means they like you and value your input, and perhaps want to impress you with all their new knowledge. Sometimes it can help us to solidify our knowledge by repeating it and talking about it. Think about when you were at school, teachers would make you learn about something, and then do a speech about it – it's a learning process of: read, think, repeat, absorb.

If the child is repeating one particular thing over and over again, this could be a sign of something else, eg; distress, or stimming (which can be a good thing), or perhaps a sign of trauma that they are trying to understand and cope with. You will need to delve deeper to find the meaning behind the behaviour.

Never use our hobbies to 'get us to do something', or 'as a treat' or a 'compliance tool' - it could kill our interest in it **and** we will often lose our faith/trust in you (this is what ABA does to get autistic kids to do their bidding; it's abusive to manipulate people and use their beloved things against them). You can use the child's interests to create further learning experiences and it can be helpful when home-schooling. By helping the child expand their knowledge of their beloved interest further into other fields (see the section on Schooling for more information)- but never manipulate.

Interests and hobbies only become a problem if they interfere with daily life – this is entering OCD territory and requires more specialised support. Not behavioural therapy, as this will only teach the person to hide themselves and their beloved interests; it instead requires gentle psychiatry and identifying helpful strategies – not rewarding or punishing the behaviour away.

Some people refer to our unloading of information about our hobbies as: "Info Dumping". The person writes or speaks about a particular topic constantly, until they get all the information out. I'm sorry if some of this book seems like I'm info dumping, I'll try hard not to overload you, but remember; I'm autistic too – and yes, I info dump, it's my way of communicating.

NT's have asked why we info dump, and there are varied responses like; it feels good, it's like a big warm hug, we love to delve deeper, we don't like superficial chit chat etc. This is our way of communicating/ sharing and being 'social', it can be a stim, or emotional regulation tool as well. We can feel energized by it, it's predictable and we know we won't insult someone, or get into a social incident; because talking about a subject in terms of facts and figures does not take a lot of nuances or reading into what is said. It feels safe and we feel like we can finally be appreciated for our depth of knowledge, instead of criticised for not fitting in, or understanding what people are talking about.

For me: I must get the information out, it feels like a song on repeat in my head (on an endless loop), and once I unload the information, I feel free and calm again, and it helps to increase my working memory capacity. Eg: Once my brain is clear, I have more room in there for other things.

If your kid is information dumping and it is affecting their relationships with people, or they say they want to stop but don't know how. First, I would recommend educating people about our hobbies and our communication style. If the child themselves, needs to clear their head (like I need to), I'd try and get them to write it all down, create videos about it, or find a group for them to join and talk about it with other likeminded people. This is why things like Comic Con and conventions were invented in the first place. For likeminded people who love a certain topic to do a deep dive. It can also help your child to find real friends and a lifelong connection to people that understand and appreciate them the way they are.

Work, or a career, or a job, (for an adult or teenager), can become like a hobby or interest, to the point that we overwork ourselves to burnout. It's often why many of us only stay in jobs for a short amount of time, we work ourselves to the bone. The need for a hobby outside of work is paramount, and a boss that keeps an eye on the number of hours we do and does not take advantage of us is also imperative. If work is your interest, be kind to yourself, try not to be taken advantage of (I know it's hard) it's happened to me multiple times, and I regret that I did not see my self-destructive pattern sooner.

Monotropism

Monotropism can explain our need for hobbies and our 'hyperfocus'. This is a term and theory that was developed in 2005 by Dinah Murray, Mike Lesser and Wenn Lawson. It is important because autistic people came up with this theory, and it does accurately describe some autistic people's experience. It is a theory about how our brains work. Basically: the polytropic (the stereotypical Allistic) brain looks at things 'a little bit', they skim the surface and move on. The monotropic brain (autistic and some ADHD etc) can focus deeply on a thing/topic/interest etc to its full capacity. We look at things in an in-depth way until we have discovered every in and out, and every nuance (sometimes to the exclusion of all else). And sometimes explains why we are not interested in other things at all.

Check out the website: www.monotropism.org for more information, or Damian Milton explaining "Flow States" on YouTube; Damian has quite a few useful videos, it might be good to browse as my explanation is very basic and does not do it justice.

NOTE: Not all autistics are completely monotropic, and not all allistics are polytropic. This theory explains how some autistics are able to hyperfocus and how it affects their ability to transition, deal with sensory input and even communicate; but like with everything – not everyone is the same, and this theory is more applicable to some than others.

Hoarding

If your child is displaying hoarding symptoms, don't jump to conclusions. Talk to them and ask them why they are holding onto something. If you want to do a clear out; I'd suggest you do a re-arrange instead (that's what we do in our home). Especially for the first time. Ask them to group things into different boxes; one full of things they use all the time, one for: use sometimes, and the last for: haven't used in a year or two. Then put them away – do **not** throw them out (never throw anything out without your child's permission, what looks like rubbish to you, may be a cherished memory to them). Sometimes we take photos of our items and put them into a book, or album, or onto a slide show or into a movie; this can help us to come to terms with getting rid of items we no longer need.

Obviously if they say they are fine with donating the item, or throwing it out, then follow their lead, but sometimes we can feel pressured to get rid of things, and regret the decision later; which can cause meltdowns and instil distrust between the two parties.

Once you have kept the; 'box with things in it that haven't been used'; for a while, get it out again, and go through it again with the child. Ask them to go through the process again, to ascertain anything that can be donated or thrown away. Repeat the process once a year if necessary. Make sure the child has plenty of spoons to do this in the first place. It can be traumatic and emotionally draining to be asked to throw away things that we have put emotional memories and experience into. Yes – we can occasionally assign an object a memory, or be emotionally attached to things that may seem odd to others; like an empty chip packet. We might be keeping it because it was the very first time we tried that type of food and it may remind us that it's sometimes alright to try new things. It may seem ridiculous to some people, but sometimes we need it, it doesn't have to make sense to you, only to us. If we throw it out, we feel like the memory and experience will also be lost.

By using this method, in this way; you are creating a gradual and kind process of getting rid of things, without upsetting your child or breaking their trust. You will be building good habits and a way of controlling the amount of things in your home. You will also be helping your child to develop good coping strategies, without hurting your relationship with them.

Taking photos of the things that you throw away can also help some people to identify bad spending or buying habits. Also check out 'object permanence', to find out why some of us buy multiples of things.

Because some autistic people have a special ability to remember things very well – they will know when something is missing. If you do throw something away – it can be catastrophic to them. They will no longer trust you or anyone else, and the hoarding will become a lot worse. This happened to me as a kid, I have trouble getting rid of things, and I have trouble trusting people. I couldn't even share a room or house with anyone when I went to university, and I have trouble living with others. There were other issues involved, but it's a big fear of mine that something will be binned/donated or stolen. The things you do, without your child's permission or knowledge; have huge psychological consequences later in life.

Companion Card

Companion Cards in Australia are hard to get (I'm not talking about the QLD card here) – unless you are a 'level 3' diagnosed autistic – or have another disability that requires a carer at all times (for life; this is sad, because it implies that autism and being ND are temporary, or that autistic level 1 or 2, don't need a carer or support person in certain situations – which is completely wrong – see section on Functioning Labels).

Every state in Australia has their own card – which is a total pain in the bum if crossing boarders/travelling or going on holiday; see: www.companioncard.vic.gov.au for Victoria or www.companioncard.nsw.gov.au for NSW etc etc. or The national site: https://www.dss.gov.au/our-responsibilities/disability-and-carers/program-services/for-people-with-disability/national-companion-card

These cards can get you cheaper tickets and/or free entry (for the carer) into certain events/places etc, if you are accompanying a disabled person – the card belongs to the disabled person, not the carer specifically. It's worth looking at the criteria for application to see if your child is eligible: www.companioncard.nsw.gov.au/apply/eligibility-criteria. These cards are not income tested.

Carer Card

A Carer card (in Victoria, Australia) is totally different from a companion card and does not get you as many things, but it is easier to get, see www.carercard.vic.gov.au

This card will give you cheaper travel with things like www.MyKi.com (public transport) or cheaper tickets at places like the Melbourne Zoo. These cards are not income tested.

Search your state government website for more information on what is available in your area, NSW has the group Carers NSW which may be able to help www.carersnsw.org.au

With either a companion or carer card, it would be worth your while checking out www.pwd.org.au/services/qantas-card/ for discounts on Qantas flights when travelling with your child. If you are travelling – also look into airports to see if they have a "Hidden Disability Program"; these programs can be useful for your sensory avoider and for special lanyards that identify your kids to airport staff and crew, some have social stories and other tools to help you navigate planes and airports. There are mixed reviews from families who have taken advantage of this program. Some say it did nothing, some say they were discriminated against, and some say it was wonderful and helped immensely. I've also heard stories of airport staff not being trained or even told about the program – so it sometimes becomes redundant and useless.

Hidden Disabilities website might be able to help in your country (available across north America, Europe, Middle East and Australia/New Zealand). A sunflower ID card and lanyard that identifies the person as identifying with a 'hidden disability' (please be careful about displaying a disability publicly, some unscrupulous people can take advantage of this information – these lanyards and identifiers are usually only used in special circumstances): www.hiddendisabilitiesstore.com

Health Care Card (Australia Only).

Your child will be eligible to apply for their own Health Care Card – through www.Centrelink.gov.au once they are diagnosed. You can also receive a healthcare card if you have already applied for either Carers Allowance or Carers Payment, or other disability service or payment etc (contact Centrelink for more information). You can apply for a Healthcare Card without a payment (as long as you meet the requirements), they are very worthwhile. They make it possible to get cheaper transport tickets, and cheaper entry into certain venues, cheaper energy/electricity bills in the winter, Bulk Billing for GP's and other medical services, and cheaper prescriptions etc.

Carers Allowance (Australia only)

You can apply through Centrelink for a fortnightly Carers Allowance (if you meet the criteria), it isn't much – but it helps with money for petrol to get to all those therapy sessions (well that's what I use mine for). The government also has a 'bonus' payment sometime in July or August that is for each child you have applied for. (This payment may stop, or be changed depending on government policy, but was in place when writing this book). For the bonus payment; you need to be on the payment before July in order to receive it). You should receive one bonus payment per disabled child that you have under your allowance. But you only receive one Allowance fortnightly. I hope that made sense, see www.centrelink.gov.au for more.

Carers Payment (Australia Only).

This payment is harder to get. If you are already on Single Parenting, Youth Allowance, or another pension – it is the same thing (a fortnightly payment), but for Carers. It is **not** an additional payment; you would need to come off single parenting and change over to carers payment – you won't receive both. You will need to prove you are a full-time carer. For parents, I suggest applying if you cannot work due to your child's disability; it is well worth it. The application is like all other Centrelink applications; you need to supply a lot of information and meet the requirements; but definitely worthwhile (it is means/ or income tested). They may change the rules, but at the time of writing this – this was the rule.

You will need to send in all documentation of diagnoses and reports from specialists, as well as a 'carer statement' that estimates the amount of time you spend "caring" for your child – that is **not** age appropriate. Eg: if a parent of an NT baby spends 5 hours a day changing nappies. …. and you still spend 5 hours a day changing the nappy of a 10-year-old – then this is what a 'Carer' does – not a general parent – as

159

it is assumed a parent of a non-disabled child would stop changing nappies after the age of 5. It is the time you spend helping your child that you wouldn't do if the child didn't have a disability etc.

These Carers Statements will depress you – you need to write it from a "worst day' scenario eg: on your worst day – you will spend eg: 5 hours changing nappies, 3 hours dealing with meltdowns, 4 hours a week in therapies and taking them 'to and from' appointments, 2 hours dressing and feeding kids, etc etc etc. (Carers Statements can also be used for NDIS reviews).

The statement may also need an estimate on how much extra you spend on your child (not including other funding like NDIS). Eg: if you spend money on your child that a parent would not spend on their non-disabled kid – then this needs to be added. (Not funds that NDIS pay for; you are telling them the gap you make up between NDIS and Medicare). Eg: your kid has an eating disorder – NDIS say they will not cover it, so you have to pay for a Gastroenterologist, food supplements and nutrients and hospitalisations etc. This information helps Centrelink ascertain the additional energy and money etc that you and your family expend because of your child's disability. By stating this information, you are providing proof that the carer payment is reasonable and necessary, because you can't work because of the time that is needed to spend with your child.

NDIS/NDIA (Australia Only).

National Disability Insurance Scheme / National Disability Insurance Agency.

See the section on NDIA for more information. NDIA is not Medicare – they do not cover funds for things covered by Medicare, or by private health insurance, they also do not cover anything for schools or education. It is a government scheme to bridge the gap between private health, income payments (like the above mentioned carers payment or youth allowance) and Medicare; to help families and individuals with disabilities, to live above the poverty line, and live their best lives. I'm immensely thankful for it, especially after researching for this book and finding out that Australia is one of the only countries in the world that offer this type of extremely important and vital service.

Carers Gateway (Australia only)

www.carergateway.gov.au this part of the government is for the carer – not the disabled person. Which means that you as the parent can call the hotline 1800 442 737, to ask about respite care, financial aid and other things like free counselling and support. This is a great place to talk to a counsellor and vent.

The Carers Gateway can be a life saver. When I finally heard about them, I was at the end of my tether and desperately needed help … it's OK to **not** be OK. And asking for help is what you should do. This organisation can help with organising help for you. Unfortunately, they are understaffed for support workers – but hopefully that will change in time. They can also sometimes help with a small monetary assistance during hard times, but again, you need to meet their requirements.

Finding a Therapist

It is not easy to find a good Therapist of any type, (eg: Speech, OT, aqua therapist, etc), especially if you are looking for someone that likes your children, and your children truly likes in return, ones that do not use ABA techniques, rewards or consequences, or has a lot of experience with autistic or ND kids or adults. Because there is a huge shortage of properly and suitable qualified therapists, we often are left without support, or given the wrong support. It is a large skills gap, and Australia is not the only country suffering for this.

There are a lot of graduates that do not have much experience yet – but you have to learn somewhere – and if you get a university graduate therapist, one of the positives; is that you can train them up – if you are confident with what your child needs and responds positively to. You are the one paying for the service, so you get a say in what you are paying for.

In America there is a website that has a directory for Therapists who are also ND themselves (www.ndtherapists.com) or the Therapist Neurodiversity Collective (www.therapistndc.org/our-directory/). These websites can help, as these ND Therapists are going to understand your child better, from having the lived experience.

Facebook Group New Zealand: "Neurodiversity affirmative therapists NZ"

www.meaningfulspeech.com is an SLP site in America, which also has parent training on gestalt language processing online. Or Divergantz may be able to help in Australia: www.divergantz.com.au There is a Facebook Group called "Australian Neurodiversity Affirming Health Professionals" for healthcare professionals to learn from actual ND professionals.

And another group called "Neurodivergent Affirming Service Providers Australia".

One of the reasons that therapies like ABA became popular is because it makes businesses a lot of money, but also because the 'therapists' only have to undertake an extremely short course, they even advertise these courses as being only 40 hours in duration to complete the certificate; which is less than they recommend hours for the child who undertakes the therapy. The ABA therapist does not need a degree or qualification, and they don't need to know anything about any sort of disability at all. This is also one of the biggest problems with ABA; as 'therapists' are not trained properly, and often have no understanding of autism. They are often only taught how to reward your child until they give up or comply. I do **not** recommend ABA or PBS in any way.

To find a good therapist, you will have to ask to be put onto a lot of different waiting lists (usually 6 months to 2 years wait in Australia depending on location and quality of therapist). Once you make it to the top of the list, make sure you trial them – you do not have to accept any offer. Many therapists bank on the fact that they have a captive audience. By this, I mean that if you are in a very regional area, there is usually only one or two therapists (and sometimes none), and you have no choice but to go with them. This is a crock! Of course, you have a choice. If you read the rest of this book, especially the section on ABA – you will see that often no therapy is better than the wrong therapy, or wrong therapist.

Online therapy sessions are hard – I will not lie, and it will not suit every child. It did not suit my kids.

Choose a therapist that will measure the success of each session by how much fun your child has – not by whether or not they achieved the set goal for the day or week. This is important because the child is still a child. Therapy is usually something adults do because they have chosen to do it – it needs to be the same for the kid. If they are not having fun, they will soon resent it and not do it. But also, if the therapist is putting all the emphasis on learning a skill instead of letting the child lead and have fun, they are probably do more harm than good. Read the section on ABA techniques for more information on this.

We do not make NT kids do therapy to fit into society, or teach NT kids to be able to interact with ND kids. ND definitely don't need to learn to interact or 'fit in' with NT either, we have our own way of communicating and interacting, find a therapist that works with the child's style and preferences – not against it, and not in a way that invalidates the child's way of communicating, or try's to change their methods, or show's preference for NT skills over autistic skills.

Try to pick a therapist that is **not** going to teach your kid NT skills, but rather work on skills that your child already has, or your child specifically asks for help with. It can be helpful in certain circumstances to learn certain skills, to cope with mental health problems, to build core strength or other muscle tone or flexibility, to learn to use mouth words **or** use an AAC device (depending on the child's preference), or to channel our emotions into more productive areas. But it needs to be the child's choice, not just what the parent and therapist want them to learn.

There is **a lot** that therapists **can** do for your child, but I'd be wary of any therapist (or any well-meaning person) that is not willing to listen to autistic people and **act** on their advice.

NOTE: If you can, I advise writing up a document that tells new therapists everything great about your child. Every new therapist will ask you for a very detailed list of their background information, including family history, pregnancy, birth and growth. It's handy to not have to go over every detail a million times (believe me it becomes exhausting, and a printed document can save time you don't have). This background info is important for building a clear picture of what might be going on, but they also only let the therapist see the medical model of disability. Show them the positive things about your child so they can build a good relationship and find common interests and ways to work positively and cooperatively together. If the therapist only wants to know the struggles – they are probably not going to be a great positive influence.

Support Workers

It's even harder to find a good support worker in Australia. One that you trust, your kid likes, and one that sticks around; many good ones move on to better jobs with better pay and benefits. Support workers in Australia are not highly paid.

Support workers are sometimes a necessity for families with disabled children. They help you access the community where you would never be able to otherwise. Eg: if you work full time or have multiple other children to care for; the support worker can take your disabled child to their appointments or help them participate in an activity that they are unable to do alone.

They can also help with your child learning certain skills and developing confidence in public.

Unfortunately, there are not enough Support Workers in Australia and a support worker is even harder to get approved through NDIS, especially for kids under school age (6 and below), unless there is a significant disability.

"Hire Up" and "Mable" are often recommended by parents as the first port of call to find a support worker. They are agencies that hire Support Workers and send them out to you. It also helps that they deal with all the payments, insurance and things involved in hiring someone as well. Once you get an idea of how Support Workers work, and how the system works; you may feel confident to hire your own support worker. Especially if you require one full time.

It is cheaper to pay a Support Worker directly; as you are not paying for agency fees, but the convenience of an Agency sometimes out rules money. After you've used an agency for a while, you'll also have a better understanding of how much support workers are paid and how to best utilise their help.

In Australia there are two main support worker organisations (there are more than two, but these are the biggest):

HireUp: www.hireup.com.au
Mable: www.mable.com.au

In other countries, I'd recommend asking fellow parents for recommendations for support worker agencies or individuals.

What is Autism?

If you are looking for a definition of autism (or an explanation of it); there are definitions in Medical Journals, but they are not great. They are usually written by Allistics, and they are written using the medical model of disability. Nick Walker ("Neuroqueer Heresies" page: 85) describes autism as "a genetically based human neurological variant" …. "autistic brains are characterized by particularly high levels of synaptic connectivity and responsiveness", "Autism is a developmental phenomenon, meaning that it begins in utero and has a pervasive influence on development, on multiple levels, throughout the lifespan. Autism produces distinctive, atypical ways of thinking, moving, interacting, and sensory and cognitive processing". This is probably the best definition I've seen so far, please check out the NeuroQueer website (mentioned earlier); Nick is a great writer.

Medical journals may also be confusing or difficult to truly comprehend, so I'd recommend reading the article by C. L. Lynch (4 May 2019) "'Autism is a Spectrum' Doesn't Mean What

You Think" From the NeuroClastic Webpage (www.neuroclastic. com/its-a-spectrum-doesnt-mean-what-you-think/).

Or, if you want a good idea of autism through the years and where we're headed, I'd point you towards the book by Steve Silberman (2015) "Neurotribes: The Legacy of Autism And How To Think Smarter About People Who Think Differently".

Or, as explained earlier: check out "Aspergers Children" by Edith Sheffer.

If these brilliant explanations aren't enough, and you are still confused or unsure, or you need something more, I will try to explain about our brain, wiring, emotions and experiences, and how they work differently to the typical person, below.

Spiky Profile

IQ tests for neurodivergent individuals often result in a "Spiky Profile".

When taking an IQ test, you are tested on four main areas: Verbal Comprehension (understanding spoken language), Perceptual Reasoning (using visuals and senses to interact with the things around you), Working Memory, and Processing Speed (how quick you learn, interpret and process information).

For the majority of the population (NT's), all four areas will usually be fairly similar in score. Eg: an NT person might receive 100 for Verbal, 90 for Memory, 105 for perceptual and perhaps 95 for processing speed. Which would give an average IQ score of 97.5. You can easily find the average IQ because all the results are within the same standard deviation. And this can be a more accurate representation of IQ. (if you ignore that IQ tests were made and biased for White, CIS males, from middle class, heterosexual backgrounds. More about that later).

For most autistic people and some ND; their score will be more scattered. Eg: they might get 100 for verbal, a 75 for memory, 90 for perceptual, and 150 for processing. This means you can't accurately calculate a mean score as the scores are scattered across multiple deviations. In other words, to give them an average is actually lowering their true IQ score and it would not be a true representation of their intelligence. This can also show why we often need supports in some areas, and not in others. And why many people will get frustrated with the fact that we can't understand what you are saying, or perhaps able to tie our shoes, but we may be able to get a PhD, or play piano like a savant, or play soccer like Lionel Messi. Everyone of us is different and will have a very different spiky profile; that will show needs in one area and perhaps better proficiency in others.

This is why autism is a neuro-divergence and can affect development, and it is **not** an intellectual disability. Yes, some people can have an intellectual disability as well as being autistic, just as NT's can also have intellectual disabilities; ID's are not restricted to one neurotype. This is definitely why you can**not** separate us from our autism. It is the wiring in our brains, it is how we think, learn, experience and feel, sense and act – it is who we are! Not a **thing** we **have**. This is also why autistics are so hugely insulted when you try to therapy it out of us, give us medication, try to change us or reward it out, or even poison us with bleach to get rid of it. Yes, there is an actual day of filicide remembrance (on March 1st every year) because parents have murdered their disabled children. For more information on filicide, Please see ASAN: "Find your local Day of Mourning vigil site" (9 December 2022) www.autisticadvocacy. org/2022/12/2023-vigil-sites/?emci=7a32213d-94a8-ed11- 994d-00224832eb73&emdi=39368eb2-bca8-ed11-994d- 00224832eb73&ceid=26999051

Autism is a different brain wiring, and that's why so many of us are so proud to be autistic and don't want a cure or a fix! Because we love that we think differently, it gives some of us opportunities we wouldn't have had if we had typical brain structures. Yes, our co-occurring disabilities can suck, and cause some massive problems for us – and are often what we see as disabling. But brain wiring differences are amazing complex things that help make the world a better and more diverse place to live and love.

An interesting article that proves that intelligence in autistics has been underestimated by IQ tests, is by: Michelle Dawson et al (August 2007) "The level and nature of Autistic Intelligence" National Library of Medicine: www.pubmed.ncbi.nlm.nih.gov/ 17680932/

Differences in Neurotype Communication

One way of explaining the difference between communication styles of the autistic and the NT; is that it's a way of thinking, feeling, developing and expressing. We tend to experience the whole world differently, and that can be extremely disabling for some of us.

The 'thinking' part of being autistic is like using a different language. Some people think in Spanish, French, Cantonese etc, and if you are reading this – then you can probably read English. But you may find it difficult to understand someone who only speaks French. You may have a basic understanding of French (taken a class in high school), but you will never understand the person properly, unless there is a bridge, or a mutual respect of each other's languages and communication styles. A bridge that helps both sides learn to understand what the other person is trying to communicate. It is not good enough to ask the French speaker to learn English, and the

English speaker does not learn French. There will continue to be a breakdown. Because a native language is just that – it is native, it is your inherent, instinctive way for communicating; you will revert to it in your mind when you are trying to translate something you want to say to the person who speaks the other language.

This is what autistic people do all day long, when interacting with NT's; we are continually thinking in our predominant autistic way of thinking, and then translating our thoughts and feelings into a NT socially acceptable format – so that the NT's around us can understand us and hopefully not be insulted or offended by what we say or do, how we act, react and even our facial expressions have made us targets for bigotry and hatred.

We also have to interpret what NT's are saying and doing, feeling and expressing; and try to translate it back into autistic. It's exhausting. And I truly feel for those autistics that are also living in a country that speaks a different language from their native language. When I visited Asia and Europe I was in a constant total state of heightened meltdown, over having to translate into NT and then into the language of the country, and then back again. It was unbelievably exhausting.

Having different communication methods and styles from the NT population is often one of the biggest problems with maintaining a mask, and keeping ourselves from entering meltdown, shutdown, or burnout. And it is not fair that the onus of understanding is put on the disabled person. We already have so many disabling things to deal with, without adding communication to them. There is often a break down because we don't speak the same language. Please read more later about the Double Empathy Theory for more information.

In order to understand your autistic child, and for them to understand you; you may need to learn to speak or understand autism (for lack of a better term). If you are having trouble communicating with your autistic loved one, it may be because they feel like you are currently speaking a foreign language to them. In order to bridge the gap between your child's language and your own, you will need to educate yourself, ask autistic adults to educate you (eg: speak their language). Even if you are autistic yourself, you may want to understand more about other autistics – because if you meet one autistic person – you've met **one** autistic person.

I had trouble understanding my kids at first, because I hadn't realised there was a communication breakdown. I realised that I was translating everything I said into NT communication before I spoke to them or interacted with them; because that's what I'd done my whole life; so others could understand me. But it was causing a breakdown between myself and my children. Once I reverted to my natural instincts and my 'normal' way of communicating; we stopped having issues. They now understand me, and I understand them. We all think, feel, sense, behave, learn differently; that's what makes humankind so wonderful – we are all different. But if a whole family is all ND – the communication usually flows easily and freely. And the same for an all-NT family group. But if you mix the two neurotypes, or if the ND's are masking and using NT communication and styles to communicate with other ND's; it can be almost impossible to understand them (well I find it impossible).

Just because I'm autistic doesn't mean I'll understand everything about the autistic person standing next to me, because I have learnt to be more NT over the years and have lost a fair amount of my authenticity. I'm learning to unmask and to be more authentic, but in the meantime, I'm learning from autistic adults about how I can help myself to become more natural and happier, and by association; this also helps my children to do the same thing. It also helps with my energy levels, ability, and communication with others. I always used to meltdown when others couldn't understand me or called me argumentative or rude. Now I know what the problem is, I can bridge that gap and help both parties to understand, be heard and helped.

To learn another language, to the point that two people can cross communicate using two different languages (without misunderstandings); both parties need to be willing to learn, and willing to admit that miscommunication is not the responsibility of one individual and should never be the responsibility of the disabled person alone.

This book can't tell you what your child is thinking or feeling, but I hope it can help you to cross the language barrier, build a bridge to understanding your child, deciphering their language - and moving on to helping your child.

Autism can be simple to understand if you are willing to change your view of it and accept that it is just a different way of thinking, developing, and experiencing. We are disabled, but we deserve respect, and want understanding.

Identifying Autism

You can't see autism! Many people will try and identify autistic 'traits' in kids. They will say; meltdowns, anxiety, fear of social situations, depression etc are autistic traits – they are **not** – this is actually often trauma or perhaps pain that a child is showing or has developed over time, it is **not** autism. Read the section on ASD assessments, or the DSM-V if you want more information on how professionals 'identify' autism.

I had my child's school Aide tell me that "not having friends and living with anxiety is **a fact** of his existence". I've never wanted to punch someone more (but of course I wouldn't). These are not facts of someone's life or existence, these are consequences of living in a world that doesn't understand or accept him. And he will eventually have friends, I have friends, so why wouldn't he? If he learns to avoid people like this Aide; he will hopefully not live with anxiety and/or trauma either. This has been studied by Botha, M., & Frost, D. M. (2020). "Extending the Minority Stress Model to Understand Mental Health Problems Experienced by the Autistic Population", Society and Mental Health, 10(1), 20–34: www.journals.sagepub.com/doi/full/10.1177/2156869318804297

If your child is showing signs of anxiety or depression, seek help and try removing the triggers that are causing the trauma. Remember their trauma is not **them**, it is not 'their autism', it is a result of something in their environment, in their lives (which is external to them), that is causing them emotional pain and negative mental health issues.

Other so-called Traits can also be problematic as they are not reliably visible or identified in every autistic person. Some autistics **can**, and **will** look you in the eye, some are extremely sociable, some are extroverts, some are brilliant, some have learning disabilities, some can't use mouth words, some are hyperlexic, some use lots of stims, and some will only use one or none.

My point is, is that you cannot 'identify' an autistic person by looking at them, it is an invisible disability. Children are sometimes easier to diagnose because they haven't learnt to hide their inherent nature, and because children react instinctively. They will say and do what comes naturally. They will also often react to trauma by using behaviour as communication; this is where you will 'see' behaviours that have been mislabelled as 'inappropriate' or 'problematic'. No behaviour is inappropriate because it is often their only form of communicating with adults. What is **inappropriate** is trying to stop the behaviour or punish the behaviour; without learning what they are trying to communicate.

Sometimes it's easier to diagnose children because we base the diagnosis on what they can't do, and their developmental delays compared to neurotypicals of the same age. If we compared them to other neurodivergents, there would be no 'noticeable' difference. And if we waited for them to catch up to their peers (eg: they became adults), their delays are no longer noticeable. This is why many adults will tell autistic adults that they can't be autistic, because they do not show visible signs of delay, or because we no longer use behaviour as our only method of communicating. Of course, we don't; we're adults, and we've had years to overcome our individual challenges. And most of us achieved this without therapy, because a huge percentage of autistic adults were undiagnosed until adulthood; just like me and many in my family.

Do not judge us by our covers, or our masks. Our struggles are real, our autism is real. Just because you can't see our disabilities, does not make them any less real or as valid as the next persons.

BAP – Broader Autism Phenotype

This is when a person exhibits many autism "traits" – but not enough to be diagnosed as autistic, so they are given an **un**official diagnosis of BAP (as BAP is not actually considered a diagnosis). This originated with two psychiatrists; Susan Folstein and Michael Rutter in 1977. They were researching autism in relation to twins. They would often identify autism (and diagnose autism) in identical twins – as the subjects in the studies would act and think very similarly. But they would often describe one non-identical twin as BAP; because they did not show stereotypical traits of autism, and one twin would show more of the stereotypical traits than the other twin.

The problem with BAP:

In Fraternal twins, the researchers would identify the twin that showed more obvious signs of autism as autistic, and then say the other twin was either NT or BAP, or another neurotype as they didn't have enough evidence to diagnose as autistic. In pigeon twins, they often identified the boy, and not the girl as autistic; as it was originally thought that autism only 'affected' boys – and because they didn't know how autism presented in people who identified as anything other than cis gendered male. The researchers would then identify that the fraternal or female twin (that wasn't diagnosed as autistic) may show some signs of autism, but not all of them – so they came up with the term BAP, to identify people who seem that they may one day be able to diagnose them as autistic, or show some traits, or if they don't know what exactly is going on.

The study of BAP went onto studying the parents of autistic kids. When these researchers were studying the children, they also noticed that the parents showed a lot of autistic traits, but not enough to diagnose them under the DSM– so they labelled them as BAP. The major problem with this, is their criteria for diagnosing autism. The DSM is not infallible and there is a lot to learn about how to diagnose adults and people who do not identify as heterosexual middle-class Caucasian cis males.

Parents have had a lifetime of pretending to be NT or been trained how to fit in with the NT world, which would make them mask their autistic traits. I'm not saying all parents of autistic children are autistic themselves; but there is a consistent and ever-growing percentage of parents that are identifying as autistic late in life and are unable to be diagnosed because therapists do not know how to identify autism in adults, and especially in females, BIPOC or BAME communities, or the LGBTIQ+ community.

This lack of information about how to diagnose people who do not fit into the stereotype of middle-class heterosexual Caucasian cis males; leads researchers to look at autism as something that is either increasing (as each new generation is born), or defining a new subcategory like BAP.

In the article by Lydia Denworth (15 May 2019) Spectrum News: "What the 'Broad Spectrum' can teach us about Autism" www.spectrumnews.org/features/deep-dive/broad-spectrum-can-teach-us-autism/ : the writer talks about researchers that are investigating the difference between autism and BAP. I believe they've missed the mark entirely and heading towards eugenics (which is wrong). They were inferring that autism is becoming more prevalent in children because parents carry the gene but are not autistic themselves – utter BS! And is unbelievably insulting and leads to supremist thinking, cure rhetoric's and people believing in epidemics and other clap trap.

These researchers were looking at it from the viewpoint of the parents not having autism at all – because they either do not understand masking, or the diagnosis of adult autistics, or because they are looking at it as something that needs to be fixed and eradicated (eugenics). They are not looking at it as a neuro difference, but as a gene mutation. If they did research of late diagnosed autistics (which there is very little about, approx. 2-5% of all autism research is on adults) they'd figure out there's a lot more to learn.

If you ask late diagnosed autistics, or self-identified autistics directly (like I have) about their diagnosis journey – you would figure out that they were often misdiagnosed as either depressed, bi-polar, BAP, SPD, etc etc etc. When they finally figured out their true autistic brain, (often because their child was diagnosed first, or because another family member or friend was diagnosed first); it was a relief to these people, life changing and made so much sense. Adding additional labels like BAP, subcategories and levels and 'severity' to autism creates more and more confusion about the diagnosis and treats us as lab rats to be studied and eradicated. If these researchers asked actually autistic people what they would prefer to be studied under the 'Autism' topic, we'd probably have better outcomes and research we want and need.

Severity of Autism

This is **not** a 'thing'. There is no 'level' or 'severity' of autism. They are just autistic. Your child's coping ability changes, they develop in their own time, their support needs change, their co-occurring disabilities can impact them in different ways throughout the years, and they can enter into and out of burnout. But the way they think and experience the world should not be defined by severity, it's insulting. How we deal with external pressures and influences, and how we are accommodated and supported will make us 'appear' to be more or less 'severe'. But our neurology, brains and nervous systems do not change – and that is all that autism is; a different neuro wiring.

If you look at the research by Benjamin Zablotsky et al (20 March 2015) National Library of Medicine: "Factors associated with parental ratings of condition severity for children with Autism Spectrum Disorder" www.ncbi.nlm.nih.gov/pmc/articles/PMC4652641/ You will see that severity is seen as subjective to the individual family, or individual parent. "Children whose parents reported poor mental health, high stress levels, and greater burdens requiring higher levels of personal sacrifice were more likely to be described as having moderate to severe ASD". This tells the story, that it is the parents' perception of the 'level of burden the child is to them', which indicates a severity level. Children whose parents didn't see them as such burdens; indicated their children to be 'mild, or moderate'. This body of research comes down to people's perceptions of us and implies that severity of autism is actually people seeing us as burdens. Eg: if you don't see your child as a burden, you do not use the word severe.

This is why I hate the term **severe**; it implies that the parent of the 'severe autistic'; sees them as disabling to their life – a burden – a severe affliction upon them. Surely no parent wants to see their child in this light. And surely no parent would want to use this label as a way to compete with other parents, eg: "my child is more 'severe' than yours" – what a hideous degradation of a child.

The article also found a correlation between the year the child was diagnosed, and the severity inferred, eg: if the child was diagnosed after 2008, they were more often to be considered 'to be mild'. Which can point to this method of labelling (as severe); to be a term of its era; that most people have moved away from (since 2008). Or perhaps that parents were learning how to help and accommodate their children; (so they saw less 'severe traits'). And/or perhaps it indicates that doctors after 2008 were beginning to understand how to diagnose autism in children and were not using words like severe to label the child. Parents will often use the terminology that medical professionals use; if the doctor calls the child severe; then the parent often takes their lead.

One way of thinking about this differently is by using "severe" and "profoundly" to describe other people – if it's offensive – then it's discriminatory. Example: I would **never** call someone Severely Lesbian, or Profoundly Paraplegic, or Severely Short. Do you see how offensive it is to call someone profoundly autistic, or severely autistic?

What makes people think that there are levels and severity; is the way insurance companies apply levels to assign funding. Levels are assigned to people, to gain different levels of funding and supports, and to deny agency or to deny supports and funding – see the section on High/Low Functioning and NDIA/NDIS. Your child will be given a diagnosis of 'ASD' – the level is irrelevant, unless you need to ask for supports through insurance. The word severe was often used by parents or doctors, so they didn't have to explain exactly what needs the child required. It was a quick way of saying; the child needs a lot of support. But I'd rather just say that, instead of insulting the child and making their diagnosis into a competition, or by using outdated levels and functioning words to deny or give support. We all deserve support, we should not be graded like beef cattle in order to receive what we need.

Read the blog by Yenn Purkis (18 May 2022) "'You don't speak for my child'. Actually No, I don't". (www.yennpurkis.home.

blog/2022/05/18/you-dont-speak-for-my-child-actually-no-i-dont/). It may help you to understand functioning labels better, help with understanding that 'severity' of autism doesn't exist, and that a non-'verbal' child is **never** 'doomed' to silence and **can** learn to read, write, learn, or communicate, and become a useful member of society (whatever that really means). The doom and gloom mentality of labels like: Low functioning/ severe/level 3 etc needs to **stop**. Please presume competence. We need to stop referring to our children in terms of levels or functioning ability compared to others. I do not point to random people in the street, and say "they must be a level 3 human!"... or to a person who is laughing and talking with friends: "they must be a high functioning human".

Once you know your child is autistic, then you may need to know what else is going on. The child may also be given a co-diagnosis, (a secondary diagnosis); this is often what people see when they label the child as severe. They will see behaviours that are resulting from trauma, medical conditions, or other disabilities that are hindering movement, speech, coping mechanisms or something else. These things are what often disables the child and increases their support needs. Please do not use negative language. If you talk about us using negative language, we can either think that you don't love or like us, or we will eventually adopt your language, and start seeing ourselves as damaged, broken, profound, severe, or extreme etc. We will measure ourselves and compare ourselves to those around us. This can lead to depression and suicidal thoughts.

Note: When most non-speaking children grow up, they will 'tell' you (in their own form of communication) that they understood everything you said and did, as they grew up. Do you want them to remember you talking about them in positive ways? Or negative ways; using severely? profoundly? Or using positive language that will lift the attitudes and thoughts of family members and those around your autistic child, and the individual positive thoughts about themselves.

The reason 'Level 1' autistics don't receive supports:
The main reason that "high functioning", "Level 1", "2E" (twice exceptional), "high IQ" or "Asperger's" people don't receive any supports is because of these functioning labels. (I use quotation marks because I do not like any of these terms).

Functioning labels segregate our community into (literally)

- High functioning: ones who can function to a high NT standard – and therefore; need no supports. Thereby denying our disabilities even exist.

• And non/low functioning: who apparently require an overabundance of support and are often not (considered able, or) presumed competent.

The change to using Levels 1, 2 and 3 instead of "high/low functioning"; did not change this concept or outcome. Levels and functioning labels only look at the person at one moment in time, usually the day they are diagnosed. This is extremely problematic. Because all autistics vary so dramatically, not just to each other, but throughout their own individual lifetimes. We change day to day, and year to year, and our functioning and ability to cope changes constantly. To give someone a level, is to say that they will never change. We do not label babies as babies forever, or children as children forever. But professionals are forced to label a person (because of insurance requirements in some countries) with an arbitrary number that dictates how people view them and support them, without acknowledging the fact that the only constant in this world, is that things change.

One of the reasons that labels and levels haven't changed, is because our family, friends, therapists, teachers (and ourselves) still use these labels to describe autistic people. There are even autistic people within our community that still want to create more segregation and class distinction amongst ourselves. They say it is in the guise of finding friends who are also 'high functioning'. But what they are doing is perpetuating the concept that there are classes within the community and that some are better than others. This continually tells the world (that doll out the supports and help), that some of us either don't want the help; or more likely incorrectly infers that we do not need the help. Those people are often seen as wanting to separate themselves from the rest of the autistic community. Creating classes only hurts the rest of us who are trying to gain necessary supports, and get the world to accept us as we are; as a group and culture of our very own.

Medical professionals often base their decision of our 'level' based on how well we communicate, or if we are too social, or able to make friends. These highly valued NT skills, tells them that we don't need support because we can get a job, talk, and make eye contact. If we were just thought of as being autistic (and not categorised into levels), we would be more likely to be seen as individuals and human.

Disability needs access should be assessed on an individual basis, because everyone is different. We are not a number or a level, we are people, individual people with different needs. There is no definition for a level. All level 3 autistics do not have apraxia of speech, and not all level 1 autistics can make eye contact and hold down a job. Our individual needs are different from the person next to us. A 'level 3' child, will need different supports from another 'level 3' child, because they have different co-occurring disabilities and needs. The level is superfluous and redundant. Insurance companies and NDIA (in Australia) base their decisions of support funding based on an individual by individual bases. The number level is irrelevant and actually causes more issues, not less. It is only used to deny supports and offensively categorise us.

It is a very sad fact that people who want to see themselves as more elite, or high functioning than the rest of the community, are actually hurting themselves. The more we use these terms and separate into subcategories, the more the world will continue to deny support to those elitest groups. As we see from the Uncanny Valley Theory; these 'elite' groups are the ones that need a lot of help but are sadly overlooked. I cannot say it enough, as long as people use functioning labels it will perpetuate the stereotypes of how people will view us, and how we are treated and receive support.

If you are a parent; you may have been relieved when your child's paediatrician diagnosed your child as high functioning, or level 1 – but I can tell you, I was damn glad my kids were not given that label, as they were able to get the support they needed. And as they grow; I never want their 'label' to change because they will be denied so much if it's based on levels instead of needs. As I was not identified as autistic as a child there was no support for me. But a level would not have helped, it would've hindered me. It needs to change to a no label /or no functioning criteria – as we all need support: we are disabled! It's not a dirty word (unless it's used as a slur), it's only dirty if people use it to deny us things, which is often what is happening now (and has been for generations). The denial that some autistics don't deserve help because we can 'fit in', we can 'work', we can 'talk', please help us stop the discrimination against all autistics and allow all of us the support we need, without the 'level' and indignity of comparisons.

Examples of Levels and PFL:

by Author: C.L. Lynch from 'NeuroClastic' explains it like cupcakes: "Imagine if ASD was described like types of cupcakes. You have some with icing, some with sprinkles, some chocolate, some vanilla but they're all cupcakes. 'But how cupcake is it?' 'What?' 'Like is it a little bit cupcake or severely cupcake?' 'It...............it doesn't work like that'". See more of C.L. Lynch's work at: www.neuroclastic.com/author/cllynch/page/2/ The website is great for a whole range of articles and information about autism, neurodiversity, and research, it's well worth looking at.

How you talk about your child and 'their autism', will affect the way they see themselves, feel about their diagnosis, and make them either feel broken, disconnected, or proud and happy with who they are. "On the spectrum" is a euphemism and "with autism" or "has autism" can also create a disconnect between understanding what the person is talking about. Eg: "On" sounds like you are talking about a linear thing, a line, an invisible cloud or something else that's more concrete that you can stand on (eg; "on the spectrum"). I don't want to be seen as something that people stand on. "With autism" makes the person think you are carrying something extra around, or you live with something, like: "Have you seen my autism?" – "Yes, it's over there by the phone".

An important thing to realise about PFL; is that euphemisms and using alternative words for autism /or autistic; further stigmatises the use of the two words. Avoiding saying them is autistiphobic (like Nick Walker suggests) because it is the avoidance of a word to the detriment and continued shunning of who we are. It shows a disrespect of our chosen terminology, and it makes saying it 'a dirty word', anathema and something to be avoided – which in turn makes **us**, something to be avoided and shunned.

A diagram is often used to describe the 'wheel' of the spectrum. Autism Spectrum Disorder is **not** a line (not linear), because we are not more or less autistic. Using the term 'spectrum' (as linear) shows that the person using this term still thinks of us in terms of 'more' or 'less' autistic. Eg:

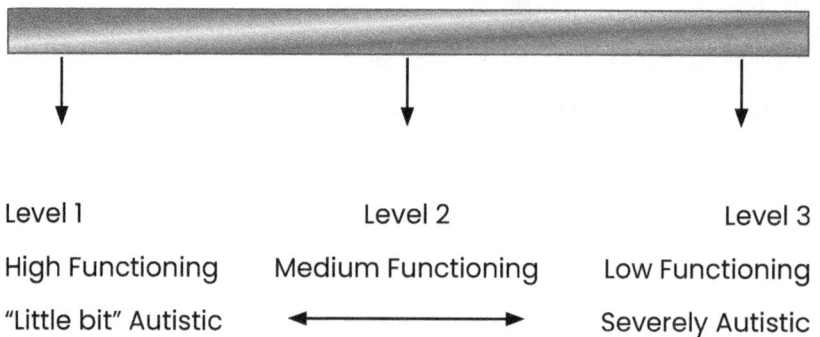

Level 1	Level 2	Level 3
High Functioning	Medium Functioning	Low Functioning
"Little bit" Autistic	←————————→	Severely Autistic

Autism 'Spectrum' is more like a wheel, eg:

Spectrum

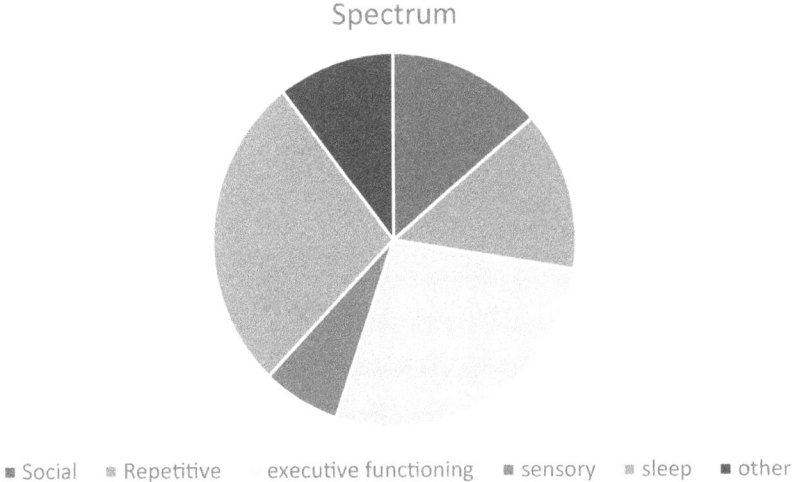

■ Social   ■ Repetitive   executive functioning   ■ sensory   ■ sleep   ■ other

Everyone's wheel will look different from the person sitting next to them – but it will also change for the individual from moment to moment. More colours will enter the wheel and more will leave over time. This is why there is no 'level', 'high/low', or 'severity', and why it's not linear – it's a "spectrum".

I've filled this wheel in using my own thoughts about how I feel right now, eg: I don't get any sleep, and my executive functioning is out the window. But tomorrow I might get enough sleep, and it will affect every other piece in the wheel. This is how you can help your child. You can think about the things your child likes and dislikes, and how it affects them.

I know if I have to stand in a queue for very long – I meltdown, or if someone purposely aggravates me – I meltdown. But if I get about 5 hours of alone time, or TV time, use fidgets, get a good night's sleep, and avoid incidents that I know upset me; I can function really well across most pie pieces.

You need to find ways to accommodate your child and to teach them about their own wheels. I'm not the first person to come up with this concept, this site that calls it a "Spiky Profile" (but this is confusing as IQ tests are also commonly referred to as spiky profile: see section on Spiky Profile): www.employmentautism. org.uk/blog/the-autism-spectrum-as-a-spiky-profile

This can help your autistic family member to manage (or self-regulate) and teach them how to use different tools in different situations. You can use a pie chart or table etc. Add in all the things that do affect them and how it affects them in different ways, and how to overcome them, avoid them or lessen them (perhaps a chart like below):

	Influencers	Result	Fix/Solution
Internal	Needing to use the toilet, but can't feel it	Hurts/can't concentrate	Take regular breaks, use reminders and/or timers, try interoception skills building
	Thirsty/hungry, or can't tell when these occur	Shakes/can't concentrate	Take regular breaks for food & drink, use timer on iPad or smart watch
	Too Hot or too Cold, or can't tell when these occur	Pain/Meltdown	Change fabrics that you wear, new clothes, thermometer use, turn on heater or cooler, allow child to choose clothing and temperature of bath water

	Influencers	Result	Fix/Solution
External	Bullies	Pain/anxiety/ trauma/meltdown	More complicated, discuss options in greater detail & plan what to do
	School work	Bored/stimming/ anger	Ask for harder or easier/simplified work. Or for more clear instructions. take a break/move around/ speak to teacher
	Loud sounds	Pain/fear/meltdown	Headphones/earplugs, move away from the sound, hoodies that muffle some sound
	Bright Lights	Pain/fear/meltdown	Sunglasses, hat with a peak, light dimmers, move seats

By doing this, you will be able to identify things to avoid, things that can help before a Meltdown begins, and have tools and strategies in place for every option. Make it as detailed or as simplified as your unique child needs. Some situations will still occur that you didn't plan for or know would cause an issue for your child. But having a list of solutions will have you better prepared. A list like this can also help a school or day-care centre better plan for your child's needs.

Myths about Autism

There are so many myths, stigmas, misinformation, horrible stereotypes, and offensive things that seem to be considered as 'common knowledge' about autism. Most of the autistic community are trying to dispel them, correct them, or give the world the right information, and educate, but they are being overshadowed by an overabundance of allistics talking for us and over us. We need your help to spread the word and to help us to be heard over the ruckus. Most of the misinformation is from hate groups or from people who are trying to help, but don't realise they are making it worse.

The good intentions are usually from the media and from stereotyped tv and movie personalities, like; 'Rainman' (Dustin Hoffman's character in the movie), 'Dr Sheldon Cooper' (Jim's

Parson's character in 'The Big Bang Theory' tv series, which I love, but many autistics dislike), or Dr Temperance Brennan (Emily Deschanel's character in the tv series 'Bones'), or even Sherlock Holmes. These characters build on the stereotypes of; brilliant but rude, or stuck in their ways and uncompromising, and very hard to love or get along with. It's often insulting and hurtful to watch these sorts of characters played out for people to laugh at. That's why many of the creators, writers or directors will say the characters have OCD instead, or say "we don't label them", because if they did, they might offend people. Audiences make up their minds about characters without the direct 'label' anyway. Most people think Sheldon Cooper is autistic, and yet the official people who made the series, say he isn't. If people are laughing with us, it's better. But most of the time, it feels like people are laughing at us. I loved The Big Bang Theory, and Sheldon, but some scenes made me physically cringe and very uncomfortable. To the autistic community, Sheldon resonates with some of us, and offends others; he is more than just someone with OCD, and that's fine – if you are laughing with us, not at us. Please be aware though, that many of us have realised that many of the other characters in TBBT were heavily coded characters that had many differing autistic or ND traits, eg: like Raj's situational non-speaking. Sometimes characters are heavily ND coded because they make for more interesting and varied people and for varied entertainment.

It seems the media and Hollywood can only present autistics as either eccentric brilliant people, or 'profoundly' disabled. Neither of these stereotypes represent the community as a whole. And I'm sure most would agree; even if one or two of us did fall into (perhaps) fitting into one of those stereotypes; we'd still be insulted by it. That's the problem with stereotypes and trying to make **one** character that represents all people in that community; it can't be done, because you often end up insulting the majority. Because everyone is unique, and everyone has their own life experience. I'm trying to take less offence at things and take them at face value; but that's a skill I don't really have. I'm autistic, so I tend to overthink everything.

ASAN helped to develop the autistic puppet for Sesame Street ('Julia'), to try and lessen the offence felt by the community when people represent us without our consultation. They did a pretty good job of trying to come up with a character that is still fairly universal, and less confronting or insulting than most. But the partnership ended with Sesame Street siding with a group (that the community consider to be a hate group) and Sesame

Street refused to break ties with them, even after ASAN pointed out the problems with the group. This means that there is no longer autistic representation for this character, and I find that incredibly sad, and ableist.

See the article here: Sara Luterman (16 August 2019) Slate: "Trouble on Sesame Street" www.slate.com/human-interest/ 2019/08/sesame-street-autism-speaks-controversy-julia. html?utm_medium=social&utm_campaign=traffic&utm_ source=article&utm_content=web_share . Note: Autism Speaks has lost their connection with the Build A Bear company due to their 'cure for autism' mentality. Well done to Build a Bear for listening to the Autistic community.

Many autistic advocates and writers have been asked to consult on characters, which is great news and sounds like it's heading in the right direction. Some of these autistic consultants have been attacked by the community for the outcome/ or final product of the character. They are not responsible for the final product, as the director has the final say. But also remember that one consultant alone, will only be able to talk about their own life experience. The character that results will be a representation of that 'one' autistic person. Since we are all very different, and have such varied lives and experiences –

is it any wonder that many of us will not identify with that 'one' character? Of course, we wouldn't, because you don't identify with every single character that's ever been written.

Many other misconceptions about autism can come from within our own community. Some autistic people are known by our own community to be problematic and cause more harm than good. These people can be anyone, not all ND people are good people, just like not all NT people are good people.

Please be careful about who you follow or admire, by doing so, you can perpetuate harmful myths and stereotypes.

Myths arise and develop most quickly through media forums. **Some examples of terrible myths are seen below:**

1. **Autism can be seen.**

2. **Autism can be cured. Or we want to be cured – we do not!** We want help with co-occurring disabilities and support for things we struggle with.

3. **Everyone is a little bit "on the spectrum".** This is invalidating to autistic people, their lives and their experience. I love the

Yenn Purkis blog (22 May 2022) "Things Ableists Say" (www.yennpurkis.home.blog/2022/05/22/things-ableists-say-2/) that states: "if (we were all a little bit on the spectrum) then there would be no autism spectrum because it would just be called being human". It's also like being "a little bit pregnant".

4. **Some autistics are more autistic than others.**

5. **Vaccinations cause Autism.** The doctor that alluded to this was disproved by the medical field, he lost his license and it apparently ruined his career.

6. **Autistic children cannot learn.**

7. **Autistic people don't feel empathy or understand feelings.** We can show and experience our feelings and understanding in different ways than Allistics. Sometimes we show empathy by telling stories. Eg: A person may talk about something horrible that happened to them, and they are probably expecting the other person to say something like "I'm so sorry, that's awful". But to some autistics, that is not showing empathy – it is more flippant and can seem insincere. Some people would like us to hug them, but some of us are incapable of that as hugs are painful to some of us.

I prefer to tell my own story, that is similar to theirs – to show them that I know exactly how they feel, that I really **do** understand and it's also like paraphrasing their story back to them (like you do when you are practicing 'active listening). To me, this shows true empathy and compassion, and makes the person feel less alone. But, I have been told that it sounds like I'm trying to compete with the person about who has the worst story. This is never our intent; we are empathising not competing. But we are doing it using our own method of empathy, it is **not** wrong, it is not an example of **not** feeling empathy, it is just a different way of expressing it.

8. **Autistic people don't understand sarcasm –** Nope! I've been told I'm one of the most sarcastic people in the world. And I know other sarcastic autistics too.

9. **Autistic people have no sense of humour.** Autistics are some of the funniest people, in fact there are quite a few comedians who are autistic – like Dan Ackroyd, or Hannah Gadsby.

10. **Autistic people can't make friends.**

11. **Autistic kids don't know how to play.** They play in their own way, with their own preferred toys. Just because it's

different, doesn't mean it isn't playing. Let your kids play the way they enjoy it, and don't feel bad or sad for them – if you watch carefully – they are happy doing what they have chosen to do.

12. **Autistics can't love –** I don't know where this came from. We love – very deeply. Sometimes, too much, some of us can have trouble showing you (in your preferred method), but if you are willing to learn our way of communication, you will see how very much we love our family, friends, life, learning etc. Check out "Different Not Less" by Chloe Hayden, page: 227. She has a fantastic dot point list of red and green flags for relationships with disabled people. I can't do it better than her words, so I refer you to her book. The 'flags' can be used for any type of relationship, eg: parent/child, romantic, siblings, friends, work colleagues etc. They are a good list of ways to help the autistic and allistic person navigate, person to person interactions throughout your lifetime.

13. **All autistics are savants.** Just like NT people – not everyone is fantastic at something – we can't all be Da Vinci or Beethoven. Autism is just a neurotype difference – it doesn't necessarily correlate with intelligence. In other words, you can have any level of intellect and still be autistic.

14. **Autism is becoming an epidemic.** For starters, an epidemic is insulting and implies there's something wrong with having a neuro-difference. But also; numbers of diagnosed people are rising. And that is in part, due to it finally being widely recognised, and slightly easier for people to get a diagnosis (it is still hugely out of most people's means to afford, or ability to obtain due to gatekeeping). Many parents also find out that they are autistic after their own children are diagnosed – which is increasing the numbers exponentially.

15. **Autism only affects boys.**

16. **Autistic people are intellectually disabled.**

17. **Autistic people can't talk.** Some of us can't because of co-occurring disabilities like Apraxia of speech. See the section on apraxia, dyspraxia and AAC for more information.

18. **Autistic people are violent.** Violence, aggression, or anger is communication, and most often a trauma response. Reduce the trauma, reduce the aggression. Autism does not cause violence or aggression – this is a trauma response of fight/flight/freeze etc.

19. **Autism is caused by mercury poisoning, or by gut microbiome imbalances and can be fixed/ and or cured; by cutting out red dyes, heavy metals and taking multivitamins or by murdering your child through using bleach -**This is seriously one of the worst and damaging myths in the whole world. Check out ASAN and their information about filicide. Please stop people if you ever hear or read anything like this, these completely untrue things are causing irreparable harm and even deaths in our community. Please see the section under ARFID (in book 2) called "cutting out red dye, carbs and other foods" for more information.

20. **Early Intervention will stop your child from being diagnosed 'with autism'** – No! If your child is autistic, they will be autistic their whole lives. Early 'Intervention' can teach them to mask their inherent wants, needs, stims, behaviours etc, which is bad. Good therapy can help them to learn new skills or build on existing skills. But they will be autistic forever- no matter what you do.

21. **ABA is the only therapy for autism.** The opposite is true – ABA is called abusive by the autistic community (whether it's the 'new' ABA or the 'old' ABA). Please read the section

on ABA in book 3 and read articles from autistics that have been through this type of therapy; listen to autistic voices. Especially read the research by the American military that has proven that 9% of autistic children are deemed to be worse off after receiving ABA therapy.

22. **Teaching desensitising skills to autistics can help them –** Sorry, mostly this technique causes the person to internalise their discomfort. Eg: they still hate the thing that they are being 'desensitised' to – but now they don't make other people uncomfortable by showing their discomfort. Sexual predators also use this technique to pray on kids and 'groom' them. See more in book 3 in the topic headed desensitising.

23. **All autistics are rude.**

24. **Autistics are immature –** No! Maturity is subjective, but also - society makes the rules around maturity. They deem people as immature if they cannot abide or fit into social expectations that are arbitrary. Maturity is often based on what is popular in the moment. Eg: Marvel comics used to be considered geeky or immature for an adult to like; but now that Marvel Studios, with people like Chris Hemsworth,

or Robert Downey Jr making certain roles famous and popular; the empire of Stan Lee has become the epitome and gold standard of some blockbuster movies, they are now deemed appropriate for adults to watch and enjoy.

Other myths or stereotypes revolve around the traits of autism. These myths and stereotypes often prevent people from self-identifying or seeking out an autism diagnosis. Things like; autistics never make eye contact, you must have a stim to be autistic, autistics are never social, we all love trains and maths, autistics must have a routine and a 'special interest', or there's a female presentation of autism, which there simply isn't!

Some of us do not identify with any of these things, at all. The myth that there is a female presentation of autism is very wrong, and so is the 'boy' presentation. Neither are right or even close to helping professionals 'identify' female autistics, because neuro-wiring has an infinite number of ways it can come together, so no one is really going to fit perfectly into a set of stereotyped traits.

Some 'girls' can be great at masking and be very social, and very easily can see social rules and follow them. But it never means that we would **all** fit these stereotypes or myths. And what about the LGBTQ+ community? If you have a set of requirements for a boy or for a girl, where does the LGBTQ+ fit in? Pigeonholing us into a set of traits makes diagnosis and access to supports a hell of a lot harder for everyone. It's gatekeeping. To see us as a very narrow set of traits, is to not see us at all. It perpetuates the stereotype of; brainy, or intellectually disabled, or as non-speaking "level 3", or as the Elon Musk's of the world. None are right, and all can be offensive and not helpful.

These myths or stereotypes will continue to drag down autistics and prevent us from having real advocacy and support. They prevent us from being accepted and truly respected, known and helped. They prevent us from getting a diagnosis, but they also prevent us from getting jobs, finding love and sometimes from finding fulfilment and happiness.

Another myth is that we grow out of autism or can't be autistic if we don't show our struggles on the surface. By hiding our struggles, we help no one, especially not ourselves. But if we show them, we become "fixable". We can't win! We never stop being autistic and asking for help. If we do ask for help – it will never take anything away from anyone else. Being autistic and showing our struggles can help to make people more aware and willing to help and understand more about autism in the future.

I wish this could go without saying, but it's a huge argument at the moment, and we find ourselves fighting the very people who are purporting to be helping us. The fight is about and for supports for all autistics, but some people believe only a few are deserving of them. it's ableist and wrong.

Some people think that autistic adults, that ask for support and funding, are taking something away from autistic children – or those that are horribly labelled 'severe'. We don't. For starters, there isn't much (if any) support or funding available for adults in the first place (especially in some countries). I'm not sure what exactly these people think we are getting or even asking for. When we do ask for support; we are usually asking for understanding or for an accommodation in our workplaces. Or we may ask society or universities to teach (or ask our workplaces, friends, and family) to learn about autistic communication and social skills – so that allistics can interact with us better. This would help or benefit **any** child when they grow up.

So, what are we 'taking away'? Absolutely nothing! Autism is lifelong. Your child may always have struggles in certain areas, they may need ongoing support and accommodations throughout their whole life. If you advocate for adults, or for 'high functioning' autistics to receive **nothing** – you end up hurting the autistic child who will eventually grow into an autistic adult.

They will be denied supports later in life; **if** they advocate for 'only support for my child or only level 2 and 3. …. and definitely **not** for adults'. There are misinformed and ignorant people in the world, that are trying to have the descriptor of 'profound'; added back into the DSM-6. This would only hurt the autistic community. These people are trying to make it possible for eugenics to be used on this new category of autistics. Adding 'profound' will see a return to Nazism. It is segregating the community and seeing one group of autistics as incompetent or **not** 'useful'. No person – **ever,** should be categorised in this way. Never forget that **every** child has the potential to grow and develop in their own way, in their own time. By giving them a label of 'profound' the DSM -6 would be ensuring that they will never be given the respect they deserve, or the benefit of thinking that they can learn or grow. It pigeonholes them into not being seen as human. It's truly a terrible and inhumane thing to do to anyone. No-one has any idea what the future holds. Just because one ignorant doctor or therapist told you that your child would never do X, Y or Z does not make it a fact. There are groups filled with parents that talk about their child learning AAC (after a doctor told them to give up and labelled the child 'severe' and incapable of communicating) and sometimes those children go on to graduate from high school or even university level learning. Nothing is set in stone, but giving them detrimental functioning labels does put a stone weight around their necks that will hold them back.

I'm not trying to give you inspiration porn, or to upset you. I'm trying to tell you that once you categorise someone; doctors, therapists and even the children's own parents sometimes give up. **No one** should **ever** give up on a child. That's why these levels, functioning descriptions, and labels, need to be burnt and thrown away. All they do is hurt the child and create more myths and stereotypes for that child to overcome and destigmatise themselves from.

Imagine if you were slapped with a label as a child, one you find; offensive, diminutive, infantilising, ableist, inhuman, controlling and belittling? One that robs you of the right to the same education as other children! One that sees you as not deserving of respect or fair treatment! One that sees you as intellectually disabled, even though you may not be able to use mouth words, but perhaps you are not intellectually disabled at all! Or perhaps you do have an intellectual disability, but with the right help you could achieve your best. But the label robs you of the right to those educational tools! How do you build yourself up? How do you make people see anything but the label? How do you get the help and support you need if you have been labelled as 'never be able to read, write and communicate'? When you know inside that you could, if only someone could see beyond that label?

Once you are labelled, often people never see anything but that label. We need to be seen positively. As a person that is capable, competent, and able to grow and learn. The label (or identifier) of 'autistic' does not measure us against each other or see some as better or worse. It identifies us as a minority in society that need supports, accommodations and understanding, in order to live our best lives. But only if people stop trying to segregate us and say that some are more deserving of support than others, or use negative language about autism to give the word a 'damaging' label. How we view and use a label matters.

Some of us will need more specific supports than others, but I can almost guarantee you; that all of us will need some sort of support throughout our whole lives to live in an ableist, neurotypically controlled world.

Please help us break down these myths and stereotypes, to help us be truly seen, helped, and supported. All of us! All the time!

Not some of us, and **not** when some random person suddenly deems us as 'struggling enough' on a particular day to qualify for it. This gatekeeps supports and makes it harder for us to cope and get help when we suddenly do need it.

Some benefits of Autism

Many people go on and on about the traits and myths of autism, but hardly anyone ever mentions the benefits. There has even been research that has proven being autistic can be of benefit long term and medically, in some specific areas.

Yes, some people are good at certain things (as seen in the stereotypes), those stereotypes had to come from somewhere, they were based on something. But not all of us are great at maths or science etc. I'm talking more about the benefits of hyperplasticity. Some researchers have found that the cognitive or physical delays that we can sometimes experience in childhood is from not shedding unneeded, or unnecessary synapses or grey matter. The autistic brain apparently shows more grey matter then their typical peers. This is thought to help in some areas later in life, like being able to learn things later in life, because the brain has kept so much grey matter. Throughout anyone's life, you shed synapses and grey matter. Some research even points towards delaying Alzheimer's for longer. Hyperplasticity is also thought to help slow the aging process.

Lindsay Oberman, Alvaro Pascaul-Leone (17 June 2014) National Library of Medicine "Hyperplasticity in autism spectrum disorder confers protection from Alzheimer's disease" www.ncbi.nlm.nih.gov/pmc/articles/PMC4392915/

Most of the research into autism is investigating things that NTs perceive as negatives. It would be nice if there was more research, like the one above, that investigated the benefits and positives.

Other benefits include things like our ability to hyperfocus or our sensitivities help us experience some things more deeply and expansively. We can be incredibly inciteful, knowledgeable, deep thinkers, and have an awareness of things around us that allistics do not often notice. Also, look at the top people in their fields, a huge number of them are ND, they are exceptional because of their neurodivergences not despite them.

It's important to look at the autistic individuals' strengths, we all have them, don't put yourself down if you are ND, I'm sure you'll find something great about yourself. But often, we are taught to only see the negative things in being ND. This causes depression and negative self-image. Build up a list of your autistic loved one's fantastic traits. Ones like; attention to details, finding the literal in things, being able to sense more than others, their wonderful depth of knowledge in their hobbies or interests, or any other thing they might do. Every autistic trait can have a positive connotation, try, and see it from that point of view.

Autism and Medication

There is **no** medication for autism. Full stop! And it should be the end of the conversation and a mic drop, but I will try to explain.

As I've stated many many times, autism is just a different neuro wiring – you cannot medicate to change 'wiring'. People have been trying to medicate us for decades. It often doesn't help, and (often) all it does is mask our issues and sometimes it makes us dependent on drugs.

Some medications will help us to cope with our co-occurring disabilities. But there is **no** actual medication for autism.

My children's paediatrician understands this very well, I'm lucky I have a good one, I know I'm privileged in this regard. Please if you have a GP or paed (or even a support group) that constantly recommends trialling new drugs – leave them, go searching, and find one that understand autism properly, because I can guarantee- that a doctor or other adult that recommends drugs over accommodations, does **not** understand autism at all!

When my child passed out (from extreme anxiety and stress) on his paediatrician's office desk, she prescribed an anti-anxiety med. But before she handed it to me; she stressed the utmost importance of **not** giving it to him until we had exhausted **all** accommodations and adaptions first. This is because giving a drug to someone that is still being thrown into the hornets nest, or the lions den; will not benefit from drugs. The drugs won't change the persons circumstances or make people be understanding or accepting. It won't teach the child how to deal with bullies, or how to self-advocate. All it would've done for him was to superficially make him appear more in control (to appear more NT), and it might've made the people around him feel more comfortable. It would've helped him in the short term, but detriment him long term.

We may be struggling or showing classic signs of depression, anxiety, aggression, or violence; which are also signs of depression and of unmet needs. But until you dig down to

225

the route cause of the behaviours, you will not solve anything for them. They will possibly never learn to identify the issues for themselves and how to be self-reliant or how to help themselves. They will possibly never learn how to deal with their emotions and use tools that may help them to avoid situations and people that trigger them. By giving them drugs, instead of teaching skills and helping them understand themselves better; it is most likely teaching them helplessness, reliance, and dependence, but also possibly drug dependency.

Please don't get defensive on this one. I'm not trying to make you feel bad for trying everything you possibly can to help your child. If you are resorting to drugs, then you are obviously struggling and desperate to help. And sometimes drugs **are the only option left** (as my paediatrician nicely pointed out to me). But unless you have exhausted all other options first; that child will likely become dependent on those means for a very long time. No child should have to be dependent on drugs, when what they most often need is a school that accommodates them, teachers that act on bullying, and a society that accepts them for who they are.

If you are thinking about trialling meds for their co-occurring disabilities, please seek a second medical opinion, but also

226

try and look at the opinion of ND people. Some autistic adults have said that they were drugged as children, for anxiety or behaviour. These people have often said that it didn't help, or that they are now dependent on drugs. **But** some have said it helped them get through a very rough time, or to deal with a certain issue – but it's not for everyone. It's a slippery slope. And when I'm talking about drugs and meds here, I'm not talking about ADHD meds or diabetes meds etc; some meds are vital to some individuals, and necessary for survival. I'm more talking about anti-depressants and behaviour modification or other things that only make the individual mask and hide their pain.

Please also see the section on ARFID, eating disorders and cutting out food.

Note about medications: Some medications for anxiety, ADHD, depression, and others can lead to autistic burnout. Because some of these drugs can hide or push our experiences below the surface, we are less aware of our feelings and natural responses. We sometimes push ourselves too far, without realising it when we are medicated, because the medication has numbed us to the extent of not recognising stress, triggers, and burnout. Sometimes these meds cause a bigger problem than they help.

I'd know because this is what happened to me. I was feeling better, so I felt I could do more. It's a false feeling of 'better'. Be aware that the meds may make you feel better, but it's not the time to go out and do more, sometimes the opposite is the best move. It's sometimes better to do nothing until you are feeling better, so your body/mind can heal properly. Medications like these are usually only meant to be a temporary solution. You take them to heal, allow yourself to heal, and then slowly reduce the meds until you don't need them.

Some people expect meds to be a fix all. Where the patient will be better, so they'll return to a 'normal' life, without fixing the underlying issues like removing triggers, changing your lifestyle to better adapt to your needs, or to stop unwanted 'behaviours'. Usually the 'behaviours' will still be there, just numbed and not as visible – because the reason for the behaviours (the feelings behind them) has not been dealt with or helped – just numbed.

Making Friends
Why it's so hard – Double Empathy Problem – and relationships between NT and autistics

Dr Damien Milton coined the Double Empathy theory many years ago. It is simply; when two differently minded people, (or groups of people) meet – they will have trouble empathising, understanding and communicating with each other. This happens between NT and autistic as we interpret things differently, and therefore understand things in a different way.

I believe that in some instances, when communication breaks down between an allistic person and an autistic person, the blame is put on the disabled person. Often because there is often a misconception that all autistics have comprehension issues. We don't, in most cases, it is the breakdown between two specifically different communication styles and methods.

It has been proven that autistics can communicate easily with other autistics without there being this Double Empathy problem. But when we try to communicate across neurotypes a breakdown begins.

There is a total miscommunication and inability to comprehend from **both** sides, both people are competent and able to communicate clearly – just not to each other, in a way that is fully comprehended by both parties.

Instead of blaming the autistic person for their type or form of communication and seeing them as faulty (and then tell them they need to learn your form of communication or language); try and see it from the other side.

The autistic person also may think that the NT person is 'faulty' and has an inability to communicate effectively. Two wrongs don't make a right. Instead of trying to fix just the one person (which is what ABA and many other 'therapies' do to autistic people)– we should be working with both sides to find a middle ground and a new way of communicating. We should educate both sides how to communicate and get along – "it takes two to tango" – but the only side that is taught to tango is the autistic one.

Take a look at the people in your life; how many are willing to go to therapy, or talk to autistic adults and learn about your autistic child, and are they willing to make a change within themselves in order to bridge the gap. What was your personal statistic? One in ten? Two in ten? Apply that statistic to the rest of the world. How many people worldwide do you think would be willing to learn to communicate with us? To learn from us, to listen to us? I'm going to bet not many, because I'm a pessimist. This is the issue, until we have worldwide change, autistics will be the ones that are told to change our method of communication, to continually change ourselves, because that is the easiest way. Things that are easy are not great, the things that are worth doing, are the things that require effort. Autistics will continue to struggle unless we are met halfway. It's sad and depressing, but it's true, this is why change is needed and acceptance is vital.

Teaching one person to communicate in a way that is abhorrent to them, makes no sense, it is not their natural communication method and will always cause discomfort and miscommunications.

The following article may also help you to understand why there is a communication break down between NT and autistic people: Noah Sasson, Daniel Faso, Jack Nugent, Sarah Lovell, Daniel Kennedy, Ruth Grossman (1 February 2017) National Library of Medicine: "Neurotypical Peers are Less Willing to Interact with Those with Autism based on Thin Slice Judgments" www.ncbi.nlm.nih.gov/pmc/articles/PMC5286449/

Autistic Researchers are also looking into this important issue between neurotypes, but their results have not been published yet – keep your eye out: Sue Fletcher-Watson, Catherine Crompton, Claire Evans-Williams, Cos Michael (2022 – 2024) The University of Edinburgh: "Diversity in Social Intelligence" www.dart.ed.ac.uk/research/nd-iq/

Or, if you are autistic and interested in research, I highly recommend the group: "Autistic Researchers Researching Autism (ARRA)".

For great advice about inter NT/ND friendships, check out the article by Abby Sesterka and Erin Bullus, Psyche: "How to be a good friend to an Autistic person" www.psyche.co/guides/how-to-be-a-good-friend-to-an-autistic-person

Questions and responses

When talking to autistic people, make sure your questions are clear, direct and contain a direct explanation of what you are asking. It also might be a good idea to not use too many words, don't talk too fast, and give us time to process. Not all autistics will need this, (as we all have different needs) but the Double Empathy theory has proven that we sometimes mistake Allistics communication and meaning due to most allistic communication preferences being for chit-chat, small talk, superficiality and avoiding conflict or saying anything directly (I realise this is because allistics do not want to offend anyone), but by speaking in metaphors, riddles and not coming to the point; the autistic person can become confused or outright not understand at all. By making yourself very clear and concise – you will avoid making a miscommunication.

Rachel Cullen has hypothesised about the Autistic Language- (check them out on Aucademy or YouTube), which builds on Damian Milton's work on Double Empathy. They ask (like many of us do) to look at how you ask questions. When you ask a specific question, without context and variables, you are limiting our ability to answer. Eg: if you ask "What's your favourite movie?" I specifically can't answer that question and will become mute. I have many more questions before I can answer it, eg: "today or yesterday?" "Winter or summer?" "Comedy or Action?" "Which actor?" "Which country of origin? I have favourite English movies, and favourite Australian movies etc" "Which era?" I love 'classic' movies, but then I also have to break them down into westerns, musicals or dramas. And "who am I watching it with?" I can't even watch some of my favourite movies with certain people, because they don't appreciate them, or talk through them, or walk out of the room, or want to press pause constantly.

Autistic Community

This is the group of people who are autistic – not the NT parents of autistics, or people who live with autistics, but **actual** autistics themselves. We are a community, and we have our own culture, language and behaviours. We are here to advocate for ourselves, and our kin; including your autistic children.

We want to help, because by helping your children we help the community as a whole.

The **autism** community are the people surrounding us, helping us, or living with us; the allistic people who often try to raise the voices of autistic people. It is the request of the autistic community, that the autism community stop and listen, not talk for us, or over us; but to lift us up and support us.

I want both communities to be on the same page. And I want to stop the fighting. Read the book by Meghan Ashburn and Jules Edwards "I will die on this hill", for a better example of how we can all move forward together in a positive and neuroaffirming way.

I cannot see the world becoming a better place for autistic people and the autistic community as a whole; unless both communities work together to listen to the minority; the autistic people.

Autistic Led Facebook Groups: (not a complete list, but it will get you started)
Autism Inclusivity: www.facebook.com/groups/autisminclusivity/
Autistics Worldwide: www.facebook.com/groups/autistics worldwide/

Ask Autistic Adults – Resource for Parents of Autistics: www.askautisticadults.org

Asking Autistics About Helping Autistics: www.facebook.com/helpingautisticspage

Unschooling Every Family: Embracing Neurodivergent and Disabled Learners: www.facebook.com/groups/UnschoolingSpecialNeeds/

And Next Comes L - Hyperlexia + Autism Support: www.business.facebook.com/pg/andnextcomesL/posts/?ref=page_internal

Kelly and Claudia: Moms on the Spectrum: www.m.facebook.com/Kelly-and-Claudia-Moms-on-the-Spectrum-107263375017145?__nodl&ref=external%3Awww.google.com.au&_rdr

Autistic Union: www.facebook.com/AutisticUnion/

Autistic UK: www.facebook.com/AutisticUK/

TAC: The Autistic Cooperative: www.facebook.com/TheAutisticCooperative/

The difference between Autism Community and Autistic Community

If you are allistic – but support someone who is autistic (maybe you are a parent, therapist, extended family etc) then you are part of the **autism** community.

If you are autistic yourself – you are a part of the **autistic** community. If your child is autistic – they are in this group.

This is why it is important that you listen to the autistic community – as that is the group that your child is part of.

Some people have described the difference between the two differing mentalities as well. Check out "Parenting Through the Fog" a Facebook blog by Vanessa R. Blevins – or see more of their wonderful work at: www.parentingthroughthefog.com Vanessa has a table that breaks down the differences between the two groups perfectly.

► Please read the book by Jules Edwards and Meghan Ashburn (19 January 2023): "I will die on this hill". This book is the first of its kind trying to bridge the gap between the autism and autistic communities. And it is written by one NT author and one Autistic author; so you get both perspectives.

Difference between NT led parenting groups and autistic led parenting groups

Below: I'm specifically talking about support groups for parents of autistics – I'm not talking about any other type of group.

The majority of NT led parenting ND kids groups are about supporting the parent, and the majority of ND led parenting ND kids groups are about supporting the child. I think both models have their benefits and their drawbacks. I'd like for there to be just one group, but unfortunately many groups have tried this, and the outcomes are quite often horrific and usually to the detriment of the autistic adult.

Let me explain. When I started my journey, I first joined 'autism parenting groups', because I didn't know the difference or that there would be anything other than this available. These are support groups, for parents of autistics. But what I didn't know, was how much ableism and offence can be spewed out in these groups, I mean no offence, but it's true. If you don't agree; perhaps you need to unpack some internalised ableism. These groups use PFL, they allow functioning labels, and they allow parents to vent about their autistic children. The problem with this, is if you are an autistic adult: **every single one** of these posts, comments and rants will affect you deeply. It is like they are purposely trying to hurt you. They say things that make you realise; "these are the things they hate about their child, **and** are the exact things that I do! They hate me! They hate autistics". It hurts!

It may be a comment about them always being inside instead of going outside "like other kids" or being 'difficult' or not being able to do certain things, or about meltdowns, or their lack of executive functioning, or having 'school can't', or about their eating habits, or anything else at all. These are all part of being autistic, and having co-occurring disabilities and can't be separated from the child.

To quote Lyric Rivera (The Neurodivergent Rebel): "It is impossible to love the Autistic Person but 'hate the Autism' because it's impossible to separate an Autistic Person from their Autism. If you hate 'the Autism' then you also hate the Autistic Person".

I've seen this a lot in these groups. They'll say: "they hate the 'tism", or "the 'tism won today" and many other horrible things. This is unbelievably insulting, and I call it hate speech. Some will say things like, "the problem isn't ARFID, (or executive functioning etc) – it's the autism". It's the same thing. We have co-occurring disabilities that affect our ability to cope and do things, because we are autistic. And you still can't separate the autism from the person, as we are born this way and wired this way. What you are saying, if you say the autism is the problem – is "the **person** is the problem". And if you are saying this about your child: you are saying "your child is the problem". How do you think that would make your child feel if they read it? How do you think that makes adult autistics feel when they read it? They used to be kids, and many now have autistic kids of their own, and they join these groups for support. But these words are words of hate, they are condemning a whole community and our way of thinking, feeling and being. It's ableist, rude, insulting, and downright offensive and needs to stop.

I understand parents need to vent and let off steam, I've been there – many times, sometimes constantly in a state of overwhelm. But spewing ableist and derogatory hate speech in a support group for parents of autistics will only hurt and offend. You may get sympathy from the NT parents in the group, but you will irreversibly hurt those people who are like your child. That's the biggest reason I have left most of these groups, I was sick of being insulted and sick of hearing them insult their children (who are like me). I could've helped so many parents with my knowledge and experience of being autistic and a parent, but I couldn't stand being abused multiple times a day, every day.

I tried to educate parents about how offensive our community finds the things that they are saying, and how hurtful they were being. But instead of stopping, or simply apologising for hurting me and many others (and then moving on), they double downed and told me "There's nothing to be offended about". Let me stop this right here. **No-one** has the right to tell me or anyone else, what, or how, or when we should be insulted, offended, or feel abused or suppressed! That is the definition of gaslighting someone. Telling them their experience or thinking is not real, not true, not valid, and not worth anyone's time. This is what happens to autistics on a daily and sometimes hourly basis (especially in these types of groups). It happens throughout our entire lifetimes.

If someone insults another person, 'NT society rules' places an expectation on the insulter to apologise, and for the insulted to accept the apology and hopefully move on. Often it's the autistic that is the only one expected to obey or complete these rules. What happened to me every time in these groups, was: I was insulted, I informed people of the insult and (if I had the spoons) I'd tell them why it's insulting – but they would **never** apologise or move on. They usually always doubled down on the insult, or other parents would dog pile on me and do it for them. This is what happens in general society to autistics all the time. The autistic person asks for help or tries to explain their side of things, but instead of apologising, accepting, and helping autistics; the people in the majority neurotype suppress us even further and make it intolerable until we retreat, leave, or explode.

This is often what happens at schools. The parent goes into bat for their autistic child. They have meetings, they try to get accommodations and they try to point out to the faculty what is being done incorrectly or show that what is happening is harming or hindering their child from attending school, or from feeling safe and able to learn in toxic environments. Instead of the faculty apologising to the child and doing what it asked. The opposite often happens. The faculty double down, refuse to change, refuse to listen, offer excuses, tell the parent they see none of the issues at school, tell the parent the child needs to change – not the school. They even deny IEPs to some people or offer more abuse (in the form of ABA or behaviouralist intervention), they do tokenistic listening and then go back to doing what was harming the child in the first place, or they ignore the IEP altogether. Parents are told to stop bothering the teachers, or to take it to the district or education department in their state, or to local MP's etc.

Parents are ignored, talked over, gaslit, abused, threatened with things like having their children taken away, threatened with social services and fines, threatened with court action and all sorts of hideous things. The parents end up feeling alone, useless, powerless, insulted, abused, hated, downtrodden, disrespected, and suppressed.

If this sounds familiar, and you hate it – good! Because you should hate it! Its discriminatory and horrible, time consuming, ableist and toxic, for both parent and child. But it's also how autistics and other NDs are treated our whole lives. But especially in these groups where we have **exactly** the same things said and done to us – by other parents. Now do you see why these groups that allow insults, venting, functioning labels, PFL and bitching about autistic children can be harmful to autistic adults?

If you feel offended by what I've written here, you need to re-read it and sit with it for a while, and realise they are exactly the same. The way you feel when you try to advocate for your child – and you constantly get pushback, ignored, and talked over, is how autistics feel every single day. And that's why Autistic Led support groups have rules in place to protect autistics. Some good groups include rules, like:

- No PFL or functioning labels

- NTs not to respond to questions until autistics have had a chance to speak, **or** not allowing NTs to talk at all

- No bigotry or anti-(anything) talk (eg: antisemitic, anti-gay etc)

- No talk about curing or fixing autism, or medication, dietary advice

- Nothing pro ABA or behaviouralism

- No puzzle pieces or light it up blue

- No dirty deleting (because it takes away the emotional energy of a disabled person that badly needed it, and they were kind enough to try and help by commenting – but deleting removed their help that others could've learnt from, and it is also a form of gaslighting the disabled person).

- No pictures of children, and none depicting a meltdown

- No sharing screenshots outside of the group – as many people share very personal and sometimes heartbreaking and or embarrassing stories that are not safe or permitted to share.

If you find any of these rule's offensive, sit with it for a while. Re-read everything above and realise that these rules are there for the protection of people who are just like your child. Do you want your child to grow up and feel respected and heard and valued, or do you want them to continue to be treated like you are often treated when you advocate for them? Also try and imagine what happened or occurred within those groups, for those rules to even become necessary or mandatory in the first place. Check your privilege and realise that autistics don't have the same privilege as others. We don't get the chance to be heard -usually at all! These groups are often the only place that our voices are seen, heard, or listened to in the slightest. If NTs talk for us or over us, how can we be heard through the din.

If you don't (specifically) like the rule about NTs listening instead of speaking; also realise that autistics are often born from ND people, it's genetic. Autistic people can be autistic parents. And as autistic parents; we go through the exact same experiences in supporting our kids that NT parents go through. What do you think you could learn from NT parents (about autistics) that you can't learn from autistic adults that were once autistic children themselves, and are now also autistic parents of autistic children? We have information for you, that could be of significant life changing help. Because we are the only ones who have the lived experience from both sides – from being autistic and growing up autistic, **and** of being a parent to an autistic.

We all want a better life for autistic children – but also a better life for autistic adults, because one day **your autistic child will be an autistic adult**. I think some people forget this important part. That the children we advocate for today – are the autistic adults of tomorrow. And fighting against, or not listening to autistic adults about their thoughts and feelings, is the same as fighting against, or not listening to your future child.

Remember: if you are part of a parenting group for autistic children, many of the parents will also be autistic, please don't offend or insult them. And if you don't have any autistic parents in the group – it's a good sign that it's a toxic environment for autistics; and therefore, not going to be good for neuroaffirming advice about your child. Sometimes these groups might be good for the sympathy or support that NT parents may need, but I wouldn't know because I found them horribly traumatic. Be careful which groups you join, and what you say or do within the group; not all groups are safe.

Example of group differences:

I came across the same question in two very different parenting groups – by two different posters in 2 different countries. The question was: "what do I do about my daughter that is self-harming?"

In the NT led parenting group (which is led by NT parents of autistic children), the answers were all the same: "Take your child to the emergency department at the hospital". No other advice was given other than to get onto a waitlist to see a psychologist or psychiatrist, or "I'm so sorry, it's so common for our kids", or "I sympathise, we're in the same boat". The original poster said, was left with nowhere to go and no way to help their child, they said: "We tried that, the hospital sent us away, and said we have to see a psych and use a mental health plan from a GP". And that was that. There was a lot of NT empathy, "I'm so sorry" etc. But empathy only builds solidarity, and sometimes pity; but it doesn't fix or help anything.

In the autistic led parenting group, (which is led by autistics who are also parents of autistic children) the answers did include the suggestion of emergency (only if there was an injury or immediate danger), and to see a psychologist when one became available. But the autistics also asked a lot of questions of the OP. They asked the following types of questions; this list is not the full list — it's just to give you an idea of how thorough they were, and how much they truly wanted to help:

Had things changed recently for the child? Eg: moving house, school, someone dying, new teacher, new pet, new neighbour, new light globes, new bedding, new food, new therapist? – the list is literally endless for what might have changed.

What age is the child? Are they likely to be in or entering puberty? Can the child communicate with you about what is wrong? If not, what are you doing about teaching them a communication method that suits them? Eg: AAC, sign language, typing, gestalts from music or TV shows or YouTube etc.

Has the child been doing this for a long time? Or just started? And if so – how long ago exactly?

What kind of school does the child attend? And for how long? What behavioural methods do they use? Do they have an IEP etc? What sort of therapy are they in? And how much/ how long/ what methods are being used etc etc?

Does the child have sensory aversions? And what are they?

Has the child ever been in ABA? For how long? How long ago?

What sort of self-harm? Is it excoriation, hair pulling, pica, cutting, headbanging, punching kicking, picking fights, bruising, throwing yourself around, actual suicide attempts, drug abuse, alcohol abuse, etc etc etc?

Are they seeing a psychologist? What sort of psych? Is the psych neuroaffirming? What techniques are they using? Is the parent present at every session – or does the child go in alone? Has the child seen a GP to rule out medical conditions and pain etc?

Have you used Dr Greene's CPS method? Or read "The Explosive Child"?

What tools does the child have at school or at home to help with regulation? (they would also suggest tools that may help, and did help them as children, and helped their own children)

Are they being bullied or abused?

What are the co-occurring disabilities? And how do they affect her?

Is your child struggling with their identity, or wanting specific help with gender specific care?

What else is happening?

What safety plans do you have in place? If they are suicidal, what measures have you put in place to lock away dangerous things?

Is it a stim, or is it purposeful? What is the purpose behind it?

If it's a stim, what have you tried? Then they'd suggest better alternatives for the stim – instead of stopping the stim (which is also harmful)

Is it only happening at home, or other places? If so, where? Why? And how can you minimise the risk in those places?

Is the child in severe burnout? Does the child need to be totally removed from the environment that is causing this behaviour? (eg: if school is causing it, removing them may be the only option to stop serious harm or death)

This list goes on and on.

Result:

After the OP answered these questions – the autistics in the group then continued to drill down to find the cause of the self-harm, the self-harm talk, and whether it was actually self-harm or if it was sensory seeking, burnout or something else that was going on, or a possibility of many of these occurring simultaneously. And then the group of autistics gave very detailed and very helpful advice and tools that they parent would be able to use or put in place for the child – on their own, without the need for an emergency visit to a hospital.

In this particular case, the OP realised it had been going on for longer than they thought, that psychology appointments were not going to help in the short term- but perhaps would in the long term, if they used the right techniques and methods that the group recommended. And they were able to help their daughter on their own, in the meantime. By using all the tools/products/suggestions and advice given to them in that autistic led parenting group. This particular parent was also great- they paid attention, did not get offended by all the questions, they listened and learnt – because they truly wanted to understand their daughter and understand and learn how to help them.

Both groups were willing to help these parents, but only one parent walked away saying "thank you, I now feel confident in my ability to help her, I've introduced some of the methods and tools suggested to me – and they're working. My daughter also thanks you". (I paraphrased that slightly – to protect the identity of the specific parent and daughter). The parent in the other group never responded with letting the group know that the child was now safe. And I fear that perhaps they were not, and I feel for those parents and the child.

I was one of those parents, I was desperate for help, and everyone was so nice and so sympathetic, and responded with telling stories just like mine to sympathise with me. They were being supportive as parents are prone to do. And I appreciated it more than anything at the time, but what I actually needed was solutions and methods to help, not more sympathy and stories of other people struggling with the same thing. It actually made me incredibly depressed to think that these other parents had been struggling with the same thing- but for longer than I had – and they still hadn't found a solution. They got sympathy and 'support', but they never found reprieve or tangible help.

Like Jules Edwards says on page 108 of the book "I will die on this hill": "Unconditional emotional validation is enabling. It's not support".

Figuring out if you or a loved one might be autistic.

Here's a list of articles and books that may help you: also check out Embrace Autism website to take the free tests online: www.embrace-autism.com

Cynthia Kim (10 August 2013) "I think I might be Autistic: A guide to Autism Spectrum Disorder Diagnosis and Self Discovery for Adults"

Thomas W Iland & Emily Doyle Iland (15 September 2017) "Come to Life! Your Guide to Self-Discovery"

Jenara Nerenberg (16 February 2021) "Divergent Mind: Thriving in a World that Wasn't Designed for You".

Samantha Craft (10 June 2019) "Females and Autism / Asperger's: A Checklist": The Art of Autism www.the-art-of-autism.com/females-and-aspergers-a-checklist/

What to do next

Nearly every single parent who is new to autism asks, "what do I do?" Well, it depends on your level of understanding of autism, whether you are autistic or otherwise ND yourself, and what help you are looking for. I've made the following list to try and simplify things for parents.

In short: In most cases, the answer is to research, learn from autistic people, get onto wait lists (either for assessment or for OT or speech etc – if it's absolutely necessary), perhaps apply for funding (if you need it). Mostly: it's more important to relax, do nothing or very little. Learn to love, to accept and to adjust yourself. Tell your child how wonderful and unique they are; never hide a diagnosis from them. Just love your kid and spend time with them while you learn, while they learn, and while everyone adjusts their thinking and responding techniques. Kids thrive with love and support, and they will develop in their own time. It is the parent that usually needs more training, support, information, help and guidance than the child. The child will be fine, if the parent can choose love over fear or anxiety. Kids follow the lead of their parent. If you are happy and excited, they will be, if you cry and become overwhelmed and depressed; they probably will too.

- Firstly, have you identified if your child needs a diagnosis or not, and whether you can afford one? Or if you can get into see a paediatrician and/or psychologist to ask for an assessment (due to wait times being so long, diagnosis being a privilege, and costs being out of most people's grasp). Have you identified the possible benefits and pitfalls of a diagnosis (eg: wait until you get citizenship before you ask for a diagnosis- as some countries discriminate against autistic people; by denying access to the country, or even deporting them).

- What is the age of your child? ADHD won't be diagnosed in some countries until they turn 4 (autism usually from about 18 months). If you are an adult or identify as intersectionalled (or a minority like female, LGBTQI+ BAME etc), you may need a specialist that knows more about autism or other neurodiversity's. Eg: if you are an adult, you may need a psychiatrist instead of psychologist, because only a psychiatrist (in some countries) can prescribe ADHD medications.

- Have you asked in "Therapist Neurodiversity Collective" (USA, UK) or other groups, to find a neuroaffirming psych or paediatrician to do an assessment. BTW: autism is **not** a medical condition, that's why it's usually diagnosed by a psychologist, psychiatrist (as it's a neurodifference) and not a GP or something else.

- Once you have a diagnosis, you don't really have to do anything at all. It's up to you. Autistic people do not **need** therapy, they need love and understanding. We may need support and help to do certain things, but we do not necessarily need therapy. So, the logical thing to do would be to learn, to research and love your child. This book will help, and all the articles and books I've referenced will definitely be able to point you in the right direction. Doing anything or something out of fear is often worse than doing nothing.

- I would advise celebrating. I celebrated when I received my diagnosis, it's a wonderful thing, I'm privileged to have received one (and my psych was wonderful and only advised that I read autistically authored books). The whole thing made me feel uplifted, validated and like I finally belonged. Your child will too, give them the great news, make it a party, get a cake and a present; make it like a birthday and celebrate annually if you feel like it (if they want to). This can help to remind everyone in the family that it's a wonderful thing, and to think about it positively for years to come.

- All ND people develop at their own pace, so they will eventually develop; but they will do it when they are ready, not under a therapist's schedule, or due to force. It may not be at the same time as other kids their age (it may be ahead of other kids, or perhaps delayed). But who gives a damn, I'd rather have a happy healthy child than one that will burnout at age 3 because they're being pushed to do something they are not ready for, or told not to do something because it's not age appropriate. Yes, I have been told stories where teachers or therapists have told adults that they are stopping or not letting the child do something because "children don't learn to do that till grade 5" or something similar. This is holding them back, not helping.

- If your child has a speech delay, apraxia/dyspraxia, an intellectual disability, low muscle tone, or something else that may benefit from therapy. Then yes, by all means; check out what insurance you have and what it covers (if you are in Australia I'd recommend applying for NDIS, remember it can take a few months, and in the meantime, you can read some of the books and articles I've recommended). Call some different providers and interview them. In order to apply for NDIS over the age of 7 you will need a diagnosis, before 7 you might get access with a childhood delay of some sort (call NDIA for more information).

- Make a list of the things that your child would benefit from, like an AT assessment, equine therapy, aquatic therapy, speech therapy (help with learning an AAC device and app), OT or paediatric physiotherapist to build muscle tone and joint mobility etc.

- Once you have looked around, done your research on which therapists are not good (the ones that use ABA or PBS), and figured out exactly what your child would benefit from each therapy, only choose one or two, perhaps only an hour (maybe 2) a week to start with. Any more is likely to cause issues, and possibly burnout. Remember that they are still kids, playing and being a kid is more important and more 'therapeutic' than actual therapy. Please make sure that therapy doesn't rob them of having a childhood.

- Remember your child deserves to be a child – not a workhorse or a therapy junkie. Kids need time to play – in their own way. They need their parents love and affection, and they need to know they are loved the way they are. Pushing them into more than a couple hours a week sends the message that you only love them conditionally – that they need to develop at the same rate as other children, or you won't accept them, or play with them, or cherish them for who they are. Be mindful though; that learning a new language (eg: an AAC Device and App or Sign Language) is a full-time job, this is not what I'm talking about when I describe therapy for 2 hours. The child and the people in their life will need to immerse themselves in the new language, in order to become fluent, and be comfortable and happy with their choice of language. And full-time (in class) therapy is not needed to learn AAC; it is more often taught like mouth words are taught- through everyday interactions and playing. Please read the section on AAC and screen time (because some autistic or non-speaking people prefer to use YouTube videos to communicate – don't limit them).

• Make a list of things that your child loves to do and then do it with them. Spend time with them (not manipulating them or getting them to change), but just doing what they love to do, the way they love to do it – whatever it is.

- In the meantime, while your child attends school, (or homeschool's), attends play therapy or develops naturally; you can read and learn (if you have the time). Not all information costs money. Join an autistic led Facebook group, watch YouTube videos, read the articles online that I've mentioned, join the B Team and CPS groups (that are based around Dr Ross Greene's CPS method). Support your child and enjoy time with them.

- Do not stay in toxic support groups that see autism as a condition, or disorder, or something to be cured or changed – they will make you hate your child and your life; they drag everyone down and cause such horrible outlooks on life. I can say that even groups that are run by autistics are sometimes toxic – if they allow PFL (because they have internalised their ableism), and they continue the rhetoric that autism stole my child, or autism won today. Or anything else utterly disgusting like these. Also don't follow people who write this vulgar crap either. Lift yourself and your child high, autism can be awesome, we think about and experience things differently, sometimes it sucks, sometimes it's amazing (it's our co-occurring disabilities that can often hinder us). Go with it, see where it takes you and your child. I can guarantee you will definitely see the world and life in general, in a different way if you see autism as just another human variation; if you join positive groups that talk about autism in a positive way.

- Advocating is damn hard. Take time for yourself, look for a counsellor or therapist that is neuroaffirming that can also help you to deal with emotions and hardships that come up along the way. A non-affirming therapist may continue the negative talk about autism, or blame autism, and/ or make you hate your child. Your child will never be the problem – but I can guarantee that society and their bias for NT behaviours and developments will cause you more heartache than you thought possible. If your child is melting down – they are not the problem, it is the things around them that are the problem and causing issues.

Just imagine how hard it'll be for your child to advocate for themselves throughout their life, if it's hard for you. Yes, you are going to need support and love too. Keep people around you that are supportive and understanding of both you and your children. Toxic people will show their faces soon enough, prepare yourself for a lot of ableism and a lot of things like "that child manipulates you", "give them to me, I'll sort them out" etc. Stay strong, tell them to bugger off and that you know your kid and you've actually learnt from the source; from actually autistic people.

- Also don't forget that neurodivergences run in families, if one of your children has been identified as ND, it's extremely possible that one more or possibly all your children could be ND, and more importantly - you or your partner (or donor; sperm or egg) may be as well. Take the time to adjust your thinking and analyse whether your child's struggles are also struggles you had, or are still having. Are you upset because you aren't coping, or because your child is triggering your sensory preferences and causing you to meltdown as well? (Perhaps you have opposite sensory needs).

Remember it's alright to have imposter syndrome (think you might be ND, but also think you are taking something away from you child by thinking it). Most parents (who eventually find out they are in fact ND)will go through imposter syndrome if their children are diagnosed before they are. It's a right of passage in many ND circles, find a therapist that understands neurodiversity and talk it through. Follow some advocates (mentioned at the end of this book); they might help you to move from imposter syndrome to self-identifying, to maybe diagnosis (if that's what you want). Of course, not all parents are ND, and that's cool too.

- Good luck and congratulations, you now know more about yourself and your child than you knew before. You will have a wonderful journey – if you allow yourself and your child time to adjust and embrace this knew knowledge without bias, negativity or grieving. That road leads to nowhere good. Follow the light – follow your beautiful child to wherever they may lead you.

Diagnosis

The diagnosis process can be different in different countries and even different in different states of Australia. The DSM-5 is used to diagnose autistic kids and adults in Australia, UK and America. In Europe the ICD from the World Health Organisation is used to diagnose autism. Many people will first seek out a Behavioural Paediatrician (this is a paediatrician that has experience with autistic and other ND kids). A multi-disciplinary approach is usually used. This means that you will see a paediatrician, and they will send you to a Psychologist and a Speech Pathologist (or an OT) to have an 'ASD Assessment' performed. Then the paediatrician 'diagnoses' your child based on these assessments.

ASD Assessments

Getting a Diagnosis: These 'ASD' assessments are usually performed by a "multidisciplinary team" (in Australia) for younger children, which means a Speech, a clinical Psychologist and a Paediatrician. But **not** always. Some specialised and experienced Paediatricians will diagnose without the multidisciplinary team. And some very confident and experienced clinical psychologists or psychiatrists will also diagnose without any other professional being involved. You need to check with your insurance carrier, or NDIA (in Australia), or governing body etc - if they will accept a single practitioners report, and which practitioner they prefer (if you want funding or support). Some of the government bodies or insurance companies are extremely picky about who they will accept a diagnosis from. Be careful you aren't wasting your money and time on a report that will be rejected by the company that you need assistance from. In Australia the NDIA usually prefers a paediatrician to do the final diagnosis.

A multidisciplinary team ensures that the diagnosis is a part of a consensus, so nothing is missed or misdiagnosed. It is sometimes hard for professionals to diagnose children; as the children do not have the communication skills to tell you the answers to specific questions. Sometimes the specific professional does not have enough knowledge or experience to make an informed decision, and sometimes the children seem too young to assess (eg: younger than 18 months can become complicated and hard to identify).

Behavioural Paediatrician: This is a special name for a paediatrician that has experience with neurodivergent kids and other specialist areas. A regular Paediatrician will usually not be able to do the assessments or look after your child, for ongoing care (in Australia). You will need a referral from your GP to see a Paediatrician, and there's a waitlist (as always; with everyone you will see).

If you are in the USA; some school districts can perform an assessment – but they will only look at behavioural and educational things – and you may need a medical professional/psychologist or psychiatrist to diagnose if you want to claim anything through insurance (unless your insurance agency has different rules). They will also usually try to push you into ABA if you go through the school system method.

An **adult** can get a diagnosis from a clinical psychologist (who is experienced in doing these assessments) or a psychiatrist. But it is widely recommended in Australia to stick with a clinical psychologist because they are often more thorough with their reports and information, and psychiatrists have often been rumoured to not have a great understanding of autism or perhaps not know how anyone other than the standard heterosexual cis middleclass white male represents. But you may be lucky and find one that has great experience in diagnoses and reporting.

I would note that if you are also looking at an ADHD diagnosis as well as autistic (AuDHD) - for an adult (or person reaching 16 years of old/ or older) – you may want to talk to a psychiatrist, as they are the only ones who can prescribe ADHD meds for adults. Most GP's in Australia stay very clear of prescriptions for ADHD.

Check your favourite autistic Facebook groups for recommendations on therapists in your local area – and for people who identify differently to 'male' (as not all therapists are confident in diagnosing people other than the typical white cis-male from a middle class family), check out Therapist Neurodiversity Collective (www.therapistndc. org) – or in Australia: check out either Divergantz (a group of "Neurodivergent Affirming Professionals") www.divergantz. com.au **or** Yellow Ladybugs Page – they have a list on their website of therapists per state. www.yellowladybugs.com.au

It will become obvious (as you navigate the world and diagnosis of autistics) that the world diagnoses people based on the diagnosis assumption/tool that all autistics must present the exact same as a white cis-male, heterosexual, middle class, speaking person; in order to be easily identified as autistic – see below for more information on why diagnosis is usually denied.

Why a multidisciplinary approach? A Psychologist is used because they will assess your child using the DSM-5. As it is a psychology manual.

Speech Pathology is usually utilised as the secondary professional to back up the psych report; as many autistic kids will also have a speech delay or other speech issue (eg: hyperlexic or something else). But **not all** autistics have a delay of **any kind**. Speech Language Pathologists (SLP) are uniquely trained to diagnose speech and other disabilities that co-exist in autistics. Just because your child does **not** have a speech delay – does not mean that they are not autistic ... this has been a misconception used by many therapists to deny an autism diagnosis. You can be autistic and not have a speech delay.

The SLP's and Psychologists are who the paediatrician will usually send you to (in order to complete two separate assessments), before the paediatrician will make the diagnosis official. Some states in Australia will allow for a standalone assessment from a Paediatrician to be accepted for access to NDIS, and for a diagnosis to be official (check with NDIA for your best options). But in my experience, it is the paediatrician that wants the assessments from other therapists in order to make an official diagnosis, and most won't diagnose without them. It's smart, because they can get a better idea of all the areas that your child may struggle with, and may need support with in the future.

I understand these paediatricians also want to cover their bums, and ensure that your child is diagnosed properly, but it makes diagnosis extremely difficulty for some families as each of these therapists will charge approximately $1000 to $3000 for each assessment. This is denying both the right to diagnosis (for low-income families), but also the right to access support from insurances and places like the NDIA. – And NO – in Australia NDIA will not pay for, or help pay for; diagnostic assessments in order to gain access to supports (at the time of writing this, hopefully they will change their minds in the future). Even if you managed to get NDIS without an official diagnosis (through their Early Intervention Program; below the age of 7 or possibly 9 ; they were discussing changing the age range when I wrote this); their website says they will not pay for a diagnosis – but you will need the diagnosis to remain on the NDIS after the age of 7 (or possibly 9 depending on their rule changes).

I would recommend these extra psych and SLP assessments (if you are privileged enough to be able to get them); as they give you a better understanding of your child and their needs and can help you identify what therapists, tools and therapy might be helpful for your child in the future. The reports can also outline what the child may need in the future, and how to best address any co-occurring disabilities (like a speech delay, learning disability, bipolar, ADHD or depression etc). But it is an expensive exercise and not available to everyone. Check with other parents in your area (through online support groups) if you'd like to find a paediatrician that will diagnose without these extra reports – these paediatricians are extremely hard to find in Australia. You will not want to see multiple Paeds (and pay for appointments) to find out they will only diagnose with these reports. It's best to get a recommendation before you fork out the money.

COST: Each of the separate assessments (from Speech and Psych) will cost between $1000 and $3000 – depending on the individual business and therapist, and it also depends on whether you have a referral from a GP (referrals can help to bring down the cost in some cases, check with your therapist to discuss the cheapest options). Medicare in Australia will help with some of it, but it's not much (but still worth having). It is not claimable through NDIS **yet**. Speak to your LAC or Planner or NDIA call centre for more information. Paeds in Australia can vary greatly in cost and expertise. Paediatricians usually cost anywhere from $100 to $500 per visit (usually a 15-to-30-minute appointment); you will get a little bit back from Medicare; if you have a Medicare Card, and more back if you reach the Medicare levy, but it's incredibly hard to reach that levy in one year – and it resets every year. Be prepared to pay the whole thing up front. You may require either 6 monthly or annual appointments with your paediatrician from then on. Yes, it can be tedious, and expensive – but it's usually best for your child, and if you are going to apply for NDIS – you will need a yearly report from a paediatrician to do your annual NDIS review. Paediatrician appointments are **not** claimable through NDIS either.

You can use private health insurance for speech assessments – but you cannot use both the referral from the GP **and** the Health Insurance at the same time – it's either one or the other – sometimes private health will be a couple dollars difference cheaper (but not much) get the speech pathologists office to check the dollar difference for you – to get the best price option.

Always talk to your therapists to discuss payments and possible discounts or payment options before committing to an assessment or therapy sessions. Most are very understanding and realise that not all people can get access to NDIS, and not everyone is privileged to just have the money spare for such extravagant one-off expenditure. Also talk to your GP for possible options, and discuss with your local support group to find the best and cheapest option.

Other options for assessments:

Go public. This is by seeing an Allied Health provider through your local hospital. The waiting lists for public is approximately anywhere from 6 months to 3 years, depending on the region and back log of patients in your area. Opposed to private, which can be anywhere from 6 months to maybe 1 and a half years. If you call around your local areas (for private providers who can conduct these assessments); ask them if they have a cancellation list for assessments (most providers will have a cancellation list just for assessments). You'll be put on the cancellation list mine came up very luckily within a few months for the first one, and a few weeks for the second time around with my second child, and 6 months for my assessment.

Go to a University: some of the Universities around Australia have cheap assessments available through their provisional psychologists. These psych's are students who are trying to get experience in order to become fully qualified. The assessments are supervised/overseen by a fully registered psychologist and the university gives you a discount because they are not fully qualified. Sometimes these are better options. These provisional people have to be very thorough with their assessments and are often scared of getting anything wrong, if they get it wrong – they may never become fully qualified etc. So, there is a joint interest between you and the provisional – you want a thorough, professional, great job, and comprehensive bang for your buck – and they want to become registered and prove their worth and ability. The Universities are sometimes inundated with requests for assessments, especially with the ever-increasing price of living.

Returning to the Paediatrician: when you have your reports from the Speech Pathologist and Psychologist – you will need another appointment with your paediatrician to ascertain your child's "level" and confirm diagnosis. The speech and psych reports usually only say something along the lines of "Master/Ms/Mx XYZ's assessment was consistent with a Diagnosis of ASD level X" – or other diagnoses. Some other diagnoses can include things like: global development delay, ADHD, PANS etc. These reports are often 20 pages long, with lots of information and details of each stage of the assessment. Read it all, sometimes there is a great tid bit of info that give you insight into what may help your child in the future. Eg: if they have great receptive language, but poor expressive; then they may need an AAC device and apps. If they struggle with working memory; they may need schedules, procedure boards or lots of notes taking in school as they grow.

It is up to the paediatrician to give you a report (usually just a one-page summary) of what your child's official diagnosis is (according to them, based on the info they receive from the other reports). Use this report to gain access to NDIA (or insurance in other countries).

Make sure you like your Paediatrician and trust them – you will be seeing them regularly, and you need one that understands you and your child; and one that is willing to write a report 'off the cuff'. I have had to email my child's paediatrician on multiple occasions, to get a quick one-page update for NDIS or another therapist (and even for the school when they were being discriminatory) and she's been great for that – always quick and pretty thorough, and very understanding about how suddenly you may need a report, or referral or other info from them. I've been extremely lucky in my paediatrician, not all people will be. You will need to book in for your next appointment as soon as the last one ends; it's really hard to get an appointment and to keep a Paed you like – they move on, go on maternity/paternity leave, retire etc. I lost 3 Paeds before finding my current one.

If you're lucky, you can try and coordinate your paediatric appointments for one month before your NDIS review is due – this makes it easier for yourself/NDIA and the Paed to do any reports and updates that are needed for your review. NDIA take the word of a paediatrician in Australia over any other therapist or professional at all! If you can't find any therapists in your area, (which can be the case in regional areas of Australia) – just make sure you have a good Paediatrician who can write the reports and recommendations for you.

NDIA/NDIS: You can apply for Early Intervention if your child is under the age of 7 (if they have significant developmental delays) – before you receive the child's diagnosis. But if your child is over 7 – you will need to wait until you have the diagnosis reports to apply for funding. See the section on NDIA for more information. Note: if you have a Key Worker or Support Coordinator approved for Early Intervention, you may lose them when the child turns 7. When the child transitions off EI, NDIA often cancels the approval for a KW or SC. This is truly unfair and a huge loss to many families. Once you find someone that finally works for you and your family, it is the worst thing that a government can do – to remove them, just because the child is one year older. Afterall, nothing actually changes much from age 6 to 7, but apparently; this is when the government has decided that they no longer to be as supportive – no matter what the needs of the child, or the family are.

In the **UK** there is a group called RTN Mental Health Solutions www.neurodiversity-training.net/combineddiagnosis?ref= https%3A%2F%2Fwww.neurodiversity-training.net%2Fa%2F 2147507961%2F3R6xzMEN That can do assessments (including combined ASD/ADHD assessments for a little less than usual – about 1495 GBP. Which is about AUD$2600 – at the time of writing this. Check with your GP, paediatrician and the NHS for more information and options. I'd also recommend checking out the Facebook page and webpage for "Ausome Training" – They post a lot of information for the UK (as they are in Ireland), and they are neuro-affirming and have lists of businesses and groups that you can contact for specific information – they post helpful things all the time that are not just about training. See the list of advocates at the end of this book, sometimes, some of the UK based ones will post discount codes for this service.

In **America** they have assessments available through the schools and districts or through medical professionals – depending on the state you live in. I've heard good and bad things about school assessments - some will ask you to enrol your child in order to get a diagnosis (which they're not really supposed to do), and then some schools will try to push a diagnosed child into full time ABA therapy (obviously not all – but it's a risk you need to be prepared for). But it seems to be the cheaper option for diagnosis in the States.

I have also been told that you also need good health insurance, if you are going to use any therapy after diagnosis. The therapy that is pushed by insurance companies is ABA – so check out your options and ask for advice from other autistic people and from people who have 'been there, done that'. There is OT/Speech and other professional therapists in the States that can do an excellent job of helping your child. Also read book 3 (in this book set) about ABA – and read the research in book 3 proving that ABA does **not** work.

I'd also suggest joining the "Autism Inclusivity" or another autistic led Facebook page to ask for help and recommendations in your area. These groups have a many members and are international, so you'll get a more comprehensive response.

Reasons why a diagnosis is denied.

These reasons are all wrong, and you can immediately identify that the professional does not know anything about autism if they use any of these listed. If they justify their reasoning because the person does not show **any** signs of autism at all – then that's fine. Or if the child is simply too young for them to make a confident informed decision; usually they can make a pretty reliable decision from 18 months onwards – depending on the child – some are undiagnosed until 3 or 4, or in their 40's like me. But if they just pick out one or two of these stereotypes below – they don't know what they are talking about, and you should probably find a different professional to diagnose yourself or your child. I have actually heard real life examples of people being told that they cannot be autistic because of the following reasons. ...

• The first reason is usually because the person is female or identifies as something other than heterosexual cis male.

• The person makes good eye contact.

• They are too social.

• They do not have a speech delay.

- They don't line up toys.

- They are a person of colour or ethnic minority (POC, BIPOC or BAME etc).

- They have a different cultural background – the professional sees it as a cultural difference instead of autism.

- They do not speak English so they can't be assessed. This is discriminatory to both non-speaking people and to people whose first language is not English.

- They have ADHD so they can't also be autistic (read the section on ADHD for more info)

- They do not go to school (this reason is often given because the specialist wants a second opinion or form filled in by a teacher that sees your child regularly. Some therapists may think you are biased or don't know what to look for. And some therapists are judgemental to home schoolers and just want you to take your child to a mainstream school. It is **not** a valid reason for denying doing an assessment or not undertaking a diagnosis process).

Warning: If you are moving to a new country, please consider holding off and waiting until you gain citizenship to get a diagnosis. Some people in Australia have been denied citizenship due to being autistic, or their child having an autism diagnosis. It is utter discrimination, and I hope it changes, but this is the ableist world we live in.

Also: In America, be careful about loopholes in any funds you may receive from the government. According to the book by Meghan Ashburn and Jules Edwards "I will die on this hill" (page 161): "Laws and policies are still in place which allow Medicaid to recapture any form of wealth that a disabled person earns throughout their entire life (American Council of Aging 2021)". "When a disabled person dies, whatever (they) were allowed to accumulate during (their) life may be recovered by the state- home, vehicle, cash and equivalents". This is truly horrifying and keeps the disabled person and their family in perpetual poverty. When we talk about governments and policies being a detriment to disabled people and their families; this is a prime example.

Extra Warning for Parents: Some people (in some countries) have had their children removed from their care, because the parent is diagnosed as autistic. This can predominantly happen in family courts, where one parent wants custody and tries to use the other parents' disability against them. I nearly threw up the first time I read about this terrible way of treating people, the second and subsequent times I heard more of these stories, I wanted to undertake a law degree and help these people personally; I'm disgusted with humanity. A diagnosis of autism does not prevent you from being a fantastic parent, and I'll fight anyone who says otherwise.

Misdiagnosis

Misdiagnosis is very common amongst the autistic community. I have had it happen to myself. Many of us are misdiagnosed as bipolar or depressed. Depression is one of the biggest ones. Trauma or PTSD is probably one of the second most common to be mistaken and misdiagnosed instead of autism. That's not to say that you can't have both, or all of these things, because you can. It's that people are often only diagnosed as one of these and autism isn't even suggested or mentioned as a possibility – when it's the underlying diagnosis. This is sometimes because the questions that mental health plans and depression questionnaires GP's use are directed at NT people; so it indicates depression, instead of being an indication of being autistic. The answers that we give, often point towards depression over and over again. But we are not necessarily depressed.

If you do an online search for a: "Quiz to see if you are depressed". Nearly every question is actually asking about the autistic experience. They are questions about depression and trauma, but they are equally valid for autistics living their typical, everyday lives. We answer these questions in the affirmative − which gives us a depression diagnosis, but we often aren't depressed and don't feel depressed. These are questions like "how often do you feel fidgety or like you can't sit still?", or "How often do you feel tired?", "How often do you feel everything is an effort?" or even "How often do you feel that nothing would calm you down?" This seems like it is a direct question about a meltdown experience − but they are actually asking about panic attacks. But it doesn't specify that, these questions are subjective and not literal; this leads to the double empathy problem between the patient and the doctor.

How about the question "How often do you feel you are bullied? Don't fit in?" etc. They are trying to ascertain anxiety and/or fear that leads to depression and/or isolation, or psychological conditions. But this is an actual autistic experience on a daily basis that doesn't really have anything to do with depression, anxiety or panic attacks – it is just a typicality of our lives, a daily occurrence. Taking medication or seeing a therapist for these things often don't help either – because we have been misdiagnosed.

Anxiety meds are for people whose brains are in a heightened state (and sometimes having panic attacks or 'overreacting' to things). These medications help to bring the 'heightened state' back to a regular pace (so to speak), but if you are just observing the world around you and feeling that you aren't fitting in because people treat you as 'weird', 'different' or 'disabled' then meds won't help. Because there is no heightened state to repair, or alter, or change. It is important to get the right diagnosis in order to help. I really hope that they change the questions for the depression diagnosis, as it has been at fault for the misdiagnosis of many many autistics, for many decades, and it has delayed them getting the right information and the right support. Including for myself.

During the Assessment

ASD assessments are always catered to the child's age. If the child is still a toddler or has limited mouth words; the assessment will be mostly play based. Play based; is a set of games, toys and activities that your child plays with, while the therapist writes down notes and evaluates your child. They will occasionally ask the child a question or play with them in order to complete their analysis. There is also a 'school, or day care question form' and a 'parent questionnaire'. The questions are very thorough and ask you the same thing over and over in different ways, so that you can't fake the results or get the wrong diagnosis.

TIP: I would also suggest that you write down all the things that you have noticed about your child and their 'behaviour', and things that you and/or your child are struggling with and give it to the therapist. These lists and reports can help them better understand your family, and your child, it can help the professionals to do a thorough job. It also helps to cement in your mind what is going on, how you feel about it, and what you might like to do after an assessment or diagnosis is received.

Assessment timing

Each assessment will take a few hours and is usually spread over a couple of days (for each therapist), depending on both the therapist and the child; and whether they do a thorough assessment or not. There are a few parts to it, eg: parent form full of questions and teacher's form. The therapist can also change the testing to suit your child. Eg: they can skip over a section perhaps because your child's attention span is not long, do more play-based assessments, or do a section of the assessment at a later date. If you want your child assessed specifically for ADHD (if they are over the age of 4), OCD, PDA, Intellectual Disability or something else – make sure the therapist is aware of your concerns, so they can add helpful information into the report for you/your child's teacher/NDIS and any other therapist you may be seeing.

If you are worried about how your child deals with strangers, don't worry. Most therapists will allow you to be in the room while they conduct the assessment. For my first one, I was extremely nervous and didn't know what to expect, the psychologist was so nice, helpful and reassuring. If you want to be in the room – you can tell them, you are the parent after all, and it is your right. The psychologist we saw wanted to see both my children alone for a few minutes (as she needed to ascertain if they still had the same behaviour without me around, eg: I might be influencing them in some way). I understood this, as one my kids also needed constant reassurance and support from me, which showed the psych that he would probably benefit from help with anxiety in the future. The psych also needed to see any other behaviours that being away from me could invoke, eg: fear of being with strangers, extreme attachment to parental figure etc. These types of experiments help to get a full picture of your child and their preferences/likes/dislikes and behaviours. If your child cannot achieve this – don't worry, this is all the therapist needs to know, and they want to complete the assessment – so they will ask you to return immediately.

Sometimes a child who displays a lack of noticing if the parent is in the room or not, can be a good indicator of other things, like ADHD or hyper focus, memory problems, or something else. These little experiments during an assessment are important for the psych to understand and get a full picture. If you are extremely nervous about your child's assessment, ask the therapist to give you a description or a run down of their procedure beforehand.

Outcomes of Diagnoses

Please **NOTE**: These assessments will also look at 'worst case' scenarios. Eg: they'll want to know what your child is like on their worst day. This can be depressing for the parents; this is not usually conveyed to the child in any way. It helps the psychologist and paediatrician to assign a "level" to your child (eg: 1, 2 or 3). Please read the section in this book on High/Low Functioning under the Terms section and the section on Severity of Autism. This level is only valid for assessment of funds; due to the NDIA and other insurance companies not understanding autism and associating level of autism to level of funding – which is wrong.

A common misconception is that the assigned level tells a parent how 'severe' a child is, or perhaps how 'unable to learn'. It does **not**!!!! A genius child can be assigned with a level 3; due to repetitive behaviours or because of support needs. Please be very careful using these harmful levels to talk about your child.

I would not use them at ALL, and especially not in FB Groups – they have no bearing on the child – and do not help other parents to give you good advice. All advice is the same – no matter what 'level' your child is, because they are still autistic no matter what level. The only thing that may impact the advice is: what the problem or issue may be. If they have a co-occurring disability that needs extra consideration, it can sometimes be relevant to add something about it, perhaps things like: the child also struggles with attention, or you've already tried XYZ, or my child is x years old. Context always helps to receive the right information, but you do not need to overshare (I overshare, it's one of my personality traits).

Warning: There have been instances of some groups being 'trolled' for information. These trolls have been using this sensitive information to make fake insurance claims in some countries and to make fun of disabled people, it's horrific, but true. Please be careful with your child's medical information and of over sharing.

Self-Diagnosis

This term is not quite correct, but it **is valid**. It is not correct because we don't really diagnose ourselves as autistic – because we are not all medical or psychology professionals; so we can't officially self-diagnose. What we do instead is self – **identify**. The only place that self-identifying as autistic is not valid, or not accepted – is with medical professionals, insurance and lawyers. But if a person has decided to **identify** as being autistic – that is their right, they do not need outsiders belittling them or invalidating their life experience. You can self-identify as just about anything in the world, and that is our right as humans and individuals. No-one has the right to tell us how we should identify.

In order to self-identify; the person has to go through a lot of personal reflection and stigmatism. They need to overcome 'imposter syndrome' and become proud and positive about their self-identity. Never tell someone that they are not autistic because they do not have a piece of paper to prove it. This is invalidating them as a person and invalidating their immense emotional turmoil that they have gone through to identify as autistic. They are no more, or no less autistic than the person with the piece of paper.

Please read the article and research by T.A.M McDonald (11 March 2020) Liebert Publishers "Autism Identity and the "Lost Generation": Structural Validation of the Autism Spectrum Identity Scale and Comparison of Diagnosed and Self-Diagnosed Adults on the Autism Spectrum" www.liebertpub.com/doi/full/10.1089/aut.2019.0069. This article will give you a better idea of why people self-identify and why it is valid. And it proves that people who self-identify as autistic are correct in their assumptions.

When I was struggling with imposter syndrome, I had a wonderful autistic tell me that: "An NT person does not struggle with the idea of whether they **might** be autistic or not". It is not a question NT people ask themselves, struggle with, fight, and feel they need to explore. But the undiagnosed autistic goes through, what I can only describe as a personal hell; in order to finally tell people "I'm autistic". Looking back, I feel unbelievably silly that I doubted myself. I knew other family members were autistic, I knew it's genetic and runs in the family, I knew how much I struggled growing up and how I was delayed in many areas (eg: speech, walking, playing, social skills etc). I know my kids are little clones of me – in every way (and they had received their official diagnoses) – but why did I question whether I was or wasn't. It's because society puts a price on it. They bottle it, package it, stamp their approval on it and make you pay through the nose for a perfunctory piece of paper, and if you don't go through all of this - they refuse to validate you, accept you or even believe you.

One of my sons' therapists asked about the family history, and I told her that we were all autistic, bar one. She wrote this down to put in her report. I then regrettably added "We're all Self-Identified" – she crossed out what she'd written, because (apparently) we are not allowed to self-identify. There is some unwritten law that says professionals must invalidate self-identity. I was incredibly hurt, and I vowed never again to tell anyone I was self-identified. I booked in for my assessment and made it official so people couldn't invalidate me again. Some adults still try to invalidate me and my diagnosis by telling me

I'm not autistic enough, or that "I'm not like their child", but that is their internalised ableism to deal with. I no longer feel like an imposter, or that I don't have the right to call myself autistic; because I do have that piece of paper now. But why should anyone have to go through that?! This is a rhetorical question – **no-one** should go through it! Yes, we need the piece of paper to access funding or supports (I understand why diagnosis is there for people), but we should not have to get a piece of paper, in order to be validated, accepted, believed and supported.

Many people have remarked in the past: that the autistic community sees nothing to be offended by; in self-identified people, and we have nothing to fear from them. The Community has more to fear from bigotry, discrimination, myths and stereotypes, ABA and ableism than from a person who thinks they may be autistic - and calls themselves autistic. The autistic community accepts self-identity as valid, so why doesn't the general population. What do you have to fear? How do self-identifiers hurt you or your child? The answer is, they **don't** – and it's none of anyone's business how another person identifies.

Testing, in order to be diagnosed, is hard to undertake. The Functional IQ test that is often undertaken during the testing is extremely trying, tiring and nerve wracking. I had to undergo this test to get my piece of paper – and it was horrible. It takes all your spoons for the day leading up to it (through nerves mostly). It takes all your energy, the test itself does not take that long, but it is full on! And it takes all your strength the following days as well; as you replay the whole thing in your head on repeat, berating yourself, second guessing yourself and realising what the answer was; but you couldn't think of the answer at the time- due to nerves, or a frayed mind or from being overstimulated. I found it over stimulating to be asked question after question, verbally; due to my APD. Some of the questions, or tasks were not verbal, but I was so overwhelmed by the whole process and going back and forth from verbal to a task, to a screen, to a game that I was truly exhausted afterwards. Once you finally finish the test, you have to wait for the results; which takes all your strength and reserves until you find out how you did and what the figures are and what they represent. And then the day after you get your results, you are still exhausted and second thinking everything.

It is something that you truly have to be prepared for and be in a good place to undertake. Putting a teenager or adult through this process is hard, don't ever think that it's a simple interview or a matter of ticking some boxes. The assessment for children is a lot more gentle; it's play based (if you get an ND affirming therapist), it can seem like just another day playing; not like an assessment or test at all. The emotional turmoil of an adult diagnosis is horrendous. I was lucky I had a great Psych that split it up into different days and spread it out, so I had time to get over each section of the assessment. My psych was also so kind and understanding that she made me feel validated and supported. If you get one that invalidates you and says "oh, you can't be autistic because xyz" – You will most likely have trauma from just trying to get a piece of paper. After you have the piece of paper, you need guidance on what to do next, and how to unmask. A diagnosis is a privilege, and not something that everyone can undertake.

The book "Unmasking Autism" by Dr Devon Price (April 22) might help after your diagnosis (especially if you are late diagnosed), but there is no book or therapy (that I know of), that is available just for undertaking the assessment. There needs to be; especially with the number of therapists that invalidate autistic people all over the world, tell us that we are not autistic, or therapists that don't know how to diagnose autistic adults.

If you are looking for a fun and interesting checklist to identify if yourself or someone else is autistic, I'd recommend "Samantha Craft's Autistic Traits Checklist" Spectrum Suite (updated May 2016) http://www.myspectrumsuite.com/samantha-crafts -autistic-traits-checklist/ or do the free assessments on www. embrace-autism.com

In Australia: Also read the article on the Autism Awareness Australia Website "Diagnosing Adults" – about the process and where to get more information (if you are thinking about asking for a diagnosis): www.autismawareness.com.au/diagnosis/ adults/getting-a-diagnosis. They also have info about applying for NDIS as an Adult: www.autismawareness.com.au/funding/ adults/ndis - also check the NDIA website.

Diagnosis is a privilege – one that not everyone can afford, literally and figuratively.

Be kind the next time someone says they are self-identified as autistic – you have **no idea** what their barriers are to getting an official diagnosis, and whether it's an actual possibility for them or not. You have no idea of the personal horror and tribulations they went through to get to a place of self-realisation and acceptance. Just accept them for who they say they are. ... we are who we are; the paper doesn't change that.

Reasons for seeking a diagnosis.

A diagnosis can help your child apply for funding at school, for financial support, or therapy supports.

A diagnosis does **not** label your child. Your child has probably already been labelled by others, with words like; lazy, troublesome, weird, different, and perhaps even aggressive and violent (please read the section on aggression to understand more). They may have already labelled themselves (as many of us do, when we don't understand why we are not coping, and why we don't fit it), with things like; hated, useless, unlovable, friendless, broken etc. Labels are all around us, people label and discriminate against people; diagnoses are just information, not labels. A diagnosis does not label someone; the person will be autistic whether they have a piece of paper or not. Paper changes nothing; it only serves to get official funding and support, and to validate the persons experience when people do not accept self-identity.

A person who has self-identified as something, has already come to terms with their identity and the majority of their struggles, but they may have difficulty naming their struggles, or they may struggle to identify the reason behind their struggles. This is where an official diagnosis can help.

The official diagnosis process and the things that the assessments involve and uncover can help the individual to put a name to an issue, help them identify intricate needs and finer details of their brain structure and neuron wiring. This information is sometimes invaluable.

It helped me to recognise my children's needs and identify supports they might benefit from. For myself; the diagnosis validated me, made me see things differently, made me accept myself and my struggles, and to be more mindful of when and where I need more help. It also allowed me access to discrimination legal services and work accommodations. I shouldn't need a piece of paper to make people treat me kindly and equitably; but as it turns out – I do. It's sad, but that's the world we live in.

Hindrances to diagnoses.

Money, time, and professionals not understanding autism properly, are usually the biggest hindrances to a diagnosis.

Many professionals are not neuro-affirming, and some don't even know what that means.

There is also the fear of labels, fear of judgement and fear of consequences that stop parents and adults from seeking a diagnosis (either for themselves or their children). There is internalised ableism that prevents some people from realising there is nothing wrong with a diagnosis, and nothing wrong with being neuro divergent. These are barriers to receiving a diagnosis, but there are also some very real and very scary pitfalls once you receive it.

These are called the **cons** of diagnosis (here's some of the pitfalls):

- Autistics having their own children removed from their care (just for having a diagnosis); this often happens in custody battles, where one parent will use the other parents neurodifferences to manipulate the court system

- Autistic child being put in abusive therapies. Things like electro shock treatment (which is still occurring in America); these therapies are sometimes even court mandated

- Deportation of autistic people, or not allowed access to certain countries. This happens in Australia, the government deems the person will be a drain on society, so they deport them. It's hideous, but it happens.

- In some countries, people with an autism diagnosis are denied access to health insurance.

- "Do Not Resuscitate" (DNR) orders that were plaguing some countries around the world during the height of the Covid epidemic. Read the following article to find out more about this foul discrimination against disabled people, which occurred because some people apparently value certain lives over others; just because we are considered to be disabled. Gus Alexiou (23 June 2020) Forbes "Doctors issuing Unlawful 'Do Not Resuscitate' Orders For Disabled Covid Patients 'Outrageous'". www.forbes.com/sites/gusalexiou/2020/06/23/unlawful-do-not-resuscitate-orders-for-disabled-covid-patients-outrageous

- In some countries (like America) if you use funding like Medicaid or other government initiatives; any money or assets that you accumulated during your lifetime, can be repossessed by the government after your death. This makes sure that disabled people; and their families remain in poverty.

- Career: some careers still discriminate against autistic people. If you have an official diagnosis; you can be rejected from some careers or jobs.

I'm not trying to put you off seeking a diagnosis. But a fully informed person, is a better prepared person. Diagnosis is a long, expensive, and sometimes arduous journey, and it is not for the faint of heart. You need to truly understand the pro's and con's if you are truly going to understand what future troubles your child may confront, and what advocacy you will need to undergo as the parent, but also what self-advocacy the child will need to learn to survive a long happy healthy life.

Drivers licencing rules.

The biggest discriminatory hindrance I've found (for myself) since getting my own diagnosis is from the drivers licensing authority in Australia. From both AustRoads (Australia wide) and VicRoads (which uses the information from AustRoads to produce their own documentation and policies for Victorian citizens/drivers).

Apparently, Australia and the UK (DVLA) have very similar laws about drivers licensing. So, I prewarn you; that getting an official diagnosis may impact your ability to get a licence or keep your licence; in the way you have grown accustomed, or possibly put extra requirements on you once you have your official diagnosis. I am personally looking into law and policy reform (in Australia) to stop this travesty here, and I personally entered a "submission for policy reform" at the end of September 2023; but it's a laborious process.

Until governing bodies stop discriminating against us, (just because we have a different neurotype), please be very cautious about the policies that exist worldwide that may affect a neurodivergent person from living their life parallel (on par with) or even similarly to that of a neurotypical person, just because we have a piece of paper that states our neurotype.

Just because we might be able to get a diagnosis, it doesn't mean it's always safe or prudent to do so.

Please check your own countries (or individual states) licencing laws for more information, before undertaking an assessment for autism or ADHD. Getting an official diagnosis may affect your livelihood, your freedom, independence, and financial security due to these discriminatory policies and procedures.

Pro's of getting a diagnosis

I have listed the con's above. Here are some of the **pro's**:

Validation, and coming to understand yourself and your brain and neuron configuration better. Understanding and identifying your strengths and opportunities. Being able to make informed decisions and figure out tools and resources that help, and ones that hinder. Access to funding and supports. Access to discrimination law and workplace equal opportunities.

The child is still the same child before and after a diagnosis! But the diagnosis may help you to identify what will and won't assist them throughout their lives. A diagnosis will not adversely affect your child; **if** society would stop discriminating against us. If you simply don't want to know; because you and your family are perfectly happy the way you are - this is another option. But your child may get to a certain age and wonder 'why they are different', 'why they are bullied' – or any number of questions, and a diagnosis can help with the answers to these questions. Remember it is easier to be diagnosed as a child, than as an adult. If you allow your child to grow up without a diagnosis, it can be an unsurmountable issue to get a diagnosis in adulthood; and they could be denied that opportunity if it is left too late.

A diagnosis of ADHD has to be officially undertaken in order to be prescribed medication. Since a huge percentage of autistics are also ADHD, the diagnoses often come together to paint a whole picture and demonstrate the specific needs of the individual. Read the section on ADHD for more information but remember that a majority of ADHD adults wish they had received stimulant medication earlier than they did. They often say this, because their ADHD was not identified until adulthood (so they missed out on earlier meds), or some parents are afraid of, or nervous about giving their children stimulants, or they fear the stigmatism around stimulant medication. Once the right medication is found for ADHD, it can be life changing. Don't be fearful; be informed and prepared, follow your child's lead and get second opinions from doctors if you're nervous.

A diagnosis can be life affirming for older kids and adults, and can be extremely helpful for parents of little ones, to understand what is going on. If you know what you are dealing with – there is more understanding and help available to a diagnosed child. I wish I had known when I was a kid that I was autistic, it would've made my life a lot easier, and things would've made more sense to me. I could've made adaptations for myself in everyday life. Instead, I have been blindsided my whole life, I have struggled and been discriminated against. I could've fought those things if I'd had a diagnosis earlier.

Some people have likened **not** getting a diagnosis; to playing a game with one hand tied behind your back. Or, like playing baseball without a bat – and being constantly asked "why can't you hit the ball?". Knowledge is power.

What to do after Diagnosis

Check out the article by the University of Portsmouth (26 April 2022) Medical Xpress: "Study suggests early self-awareness of Autism leads to better quality of life" (www.medicalxpress.com/news/2022-04-early-self-awareness-autism-quality-life.html). This article may help you to understand that it is important to tell your child about their diagnosis as soon as possible. This article and research was conducted by autistic people, with autistic people; so it is extremely relevant. It goes on to prove that knowing you are autistic causes "better adult outcomes" and that it "can be empowering because it helps people understand themselves and also helps them connect with other people like them".

To find the best way to tell your individual child, you need to understand their language and find a positive way to talk about neurodivergence. Depending on your child's language skills and communication preferences, you may want to try different mediums, eg; pictures, words or typed correspondence, YouTube videos, or other means. I found the Neuro Bears (22 March 2022) on YouTube is an effective cartoon for younger viewers to learn about neurodiversity: www.youtube.com/watch?v=_490q6LaHIY. They also have more videos for kids to understand different parts of autism; like stimming, masking etc: www.pandasonline.org (but these are not free).

Also try the cartoon "Amazing things Happen" (19 July 2017) on YouTube; by Alexander Amelines (www.youtube.com/watch?app=desktop&v=RbwRrVw-CRo&feature=youtu.be)

For teenagers: perhaps look into literature by autistic authors that explain autism from the lived experience. It is often easier to understand something, when the author writes from the heart and can speak to actual incidents, real life experiences and thoughts, and feelings. The book by Yenn Purkis "The Awesome Autistic Go-To Guide: A Practical Handbook for Autistic Teens and Tweens" (www.yennpurkis.com/books/) is a good start.

The book "Different Not Less" (by Chloe Hayden) is written by an autistic that was diagnosed as a teenager and has a lot of good examples of what it is like to be a child or teenager growing up in a neurotypical society.

There is also the kids' book "Some Brains: A book celebrating Neurodiversity" by Nelly Thomas (3 March 2020). And the YouTube video "What it's like living on the Autism Spectrum".

It might also be necessary to get your teenager into a support group for teens. There are a few on Facebook that might be appropriate – just for autistic teens, to make them feel less alone, and more connected, and a great place for support and empathy. They might even find some likeminded people to hang out with. Some of these groups are moderated by adult autistics, try a few out first, if you're nervous, but some do not allow parents or allistics in the group; this is for the safety of the teens. I'm not trying to insult allistics, but some autistics do not feel safe around allistic people, especially if they have been traumatised or abused, which a large percentage of autistics have unfortunately experienced.

To find like minded people for your teen, or other children to hang out with, or make friends, you do not specifically have to find other autistics (although that would be nice). Most people make friends by finding people with similar interests, likes and dislikes. There's actually been research to prove that people bond more over their dislikes of certain things, than over their likes.

If your child is into chess, swimming, geography, trains, maths, tv shows, Roblox, Lego, exercising, barbies, astronomy, golf, skateboards, art, etc; find a group that does a deep dive into the topic, a group that is all about exploring every nuance of the specific topic your child loves. It will help with their hobbies, and to get a better education on the topic, but it will open them up to a whole new community that loves the same things. There's nothing like the joy of exploring your favourite topic with people who are equally excited about it; and want to talk about it.

Next Steps

Figure out what you need for your child and what your child wants. What is necessary and what isn't. What helps, hinders and aids or hurts your child (tools, equipment or therapy). What your child wants to achieve, improve or enhance (eg; their goals). What your child wants to decrease that isn't working (eg: bright lights, too much noise, abusive therapies, routines that are too strict, too many demands or chores that are causing executive functioning issues), and what you yourself need, want, help, or hinder etc. Educate yourself and your child. Don't keep their diagnosis a secret from them. Talk positively about autism and their other diagnoses (if applicable), and constantly look for alternatives and other ways of thinking and doing things. Open up the world for them – don't close it. They can be anything they want to be, do anything they want to do; they just need love and support, accommodations and therapists that are neuro-affirming; that can help them achieve their inner desires.

Be positive, stay away from negativity that views your child as broken, or needing fixing. Your child is perfect the way they were born, they need you to be their anchor, their safe person, their rock, and their beloved parent, which I'm sure you always have been, and will always be. Some parents can lose their way, often due to the way professionals give the diagnoses to them, eg; the professional doesn't congratulate them, they instead use negative language, condolence messages and hand them eugenics pamphlets from places like Autism Speaks (remember that this organisation is deemed as an autism hate group by autistics). How you receive your child's diagnosis makes a huge difference to the way you view your child and how you move forward. This is why it's also important for your child to receive the news from a happy parent who is also using positive, happy and affirming language (IFL not PFL). They will gain a negative, or positive self-image, dependent on your demeanour, your language, and your emotions.

Access the autistic community in any way you prefer, by joining groups, following advocates, reading autistically authored books, or reaching out to your local community and finding autistic families. This way you can surround yourself with very knowledgeable people, but also people who see neurodivergences as a 'normality', a positive thing, and something to even be proud of. Sometimes if you find the autism community first, it can lead you in the other direction; like it did to me. I don't know about you, but I always want to view my children as competent, capable, loving, deserving, beautiful, wonderful people. I never want to be involved in another group that makes me doubt that – ever again!

Schools and Diagnoses

In Australia: In order to apply for government funding for the school; the school will need to know you if have an official diagnosis or diagnoses, and what they are. The school is the one that applies for funding, not you. You need to give them the documentation from all the therapists and sign their application form once they have completed it. Some schools do not want to apply, have no experience in applying, or think it's a waste of time; especially if they are a private school, as private schools do not receive as much funding as public in this country, but they still receive some, so it's worth pushing them to apply. The teachers can sometimes forget to apply, or they need to be nagged to do it.

Every country has their own funding and requirements for disabled children in the public school system. If you want more information look at your states or territories, countries or county's education departments website, or pick up the phone and call them. Each country also has their own requirements about plans that help to accommodate disabled children in the classroom. But most will still need an official diagnosis to consider what is needed or necessary.

Some schools will have information packs or flyers about assistance programs or supports that may help. Do your research, ask other parents and autistic adults about recommendations and available resources in your area. You can also contact one of the advocate groups mentioned throughout this book. Also read the section on Schools and Homeschooling (book 5) for more information or for alternatives to mainstream schooling.

The types of reports the school will need, will be from your OT/ Speech/ Paediatrician/ Psych/ Physio/ Chiropractor etc, to cater their education style to your child, make adjustments and accommodations, understand your child's needs better; and to come up with an Individual Learning Plan (ILP, IEP or 504 etc) – or whatever name your school prefers to use for this agreement. There are many different names for this across schools/states and countries. See the school section for more information (book 5).

Some schools will want weekly or fortnightly updates about what your child is learning in therapy sessions. They can use this information to support your child with their learning journey.

By using the same stories, books, equipment in the classroom; your child can see the link between therapy, school and home. It also helps teachers to understand what level your child is working at and achieving, and where they can fill the gaps. But in my experience, not many teachers will utilise this valuable information. Or they don't have the time to go through it or use it; but it can be used to adjust a plan over time, or to inform future decisions. If your child receives additional diagnoses throughout their schooling life, the school will need to be informed of these as well; it helps them to adjust learning plans and supports.

School Diagnosis and Advocacy

It is important to have open communication between yourself and the school, about everything, including their diagnoses, and their progress. If you find a school is being obstructive, or not helping your child in the way you had hoped, or they are using ABA tactics (which has been banned in some countries for good reason); it's either time to have a meeting with the teacher and head of the school (or take it to the school board, or to the department of education, and even possibly to the police – if necessary), or possibly. ... walk away.

I know that sounds harsh and is a privilege many don't have; but if your child is in a toxic environment, you may need to move them, or find a lawyer or an advocate that can help you find justice for your child. You wouldn't willingly stay in a job that was abusive, or bullying, you didn't feel safe attending, or that you weren't being effective, or one that made you cry daily – so why would you leave a child in a school that does the same to them. If you can't move to a different school; there are options, there are free discrimination lawyers, and there are free advocates that are willing to help and understand your position all too well.

I know there are restrictions on schools, and on parents to find suitable educational institutions for their children, and less options in country towns, and in some areas (as I have firsthand experience with this); but sometimes you just have to do **something**. I wish I had changed schools in both primary and secondary school or (preferably) been able to do homeschooling; but it was seen as wrong, or too hard, or not even discussed as an option in my day, and it's a privilege my parents didn't have. And I wish I had recognised the toxic environment that I had placed both my children into when starting their school journey. But sometimes we can't see the forest for the trees. Once I did see what was going on, I felt like a neglectful parent, I had so much guilt that I cried – a lot. My poor children (at age 3 and 4) had already experienced irreparable trauma, but it wasn't too late – it is never too late to do something, anything that will help them.

I started with advocating for them; having meetings with staff and teachers, including the inclusion co-ordinator, and I even talked to the parents of my child's bully (which turned out to be a total waste of time). I researched, and I talked to other parents who had been in similar situations. I implemented things they had tried. When I'd exhausted those options; I sought out a free discrimination lawyer, and an advocate service for advice and help. This worked for a few months, with some backlash from the assistant principal who was a little horrified by my 7-page letter which was full of legal jargon, (quoting advice from the lawyer) and demanding action. I had my key worker (an advocate) attend meetings with me at the school, to make sure I had a witness for every item brought up. I had a plan drawn up. I had therapists attend the school to see how they could help and implemented their plans as well. I had a paediatrician and a psychologist step in as well; to advocate for the school to change and make accommodations; to no avail.

I attended the school for excursions and every time I received every tiny phone call (I received a lot of phone calls). I never could've held down, even a part time job, with the amount of time I was spending at the school, and on advocating for both children. I felt like I never left the school, I was there at all times of the day, to support and help, or pick up my children when it all became too much for them. My children started their 'school can't' journey; sometimes called 'school refusal' by people who do not understand that it is definitely: 'can't'. Especially after you have exhausted all means and your child knows it. They begin to say no – rightly and justly! Everyone knows when they hit their own limit, and my kids had hit theirs. The anxiety about school became so toxic that one of them passed out on the paediatricians' desk and then woke up and threw up (major anxiety), and the other one became violent and aggressive in an attempt to not be taken to the school, and definitely not left there.

I applied to other schools, and toured many, and was rejected by a couple. But my children had had enough. They were traumatised and could not step inside another school, or face yet another bully. We had exhausted every single option. We now homeschool – and they are finally happy, feel safe and secure, and love learning. I'm not sure why it took me so long to end their torment, after all; I'd been through a similar experience in both primary and secondary schools (public and private). But I felt that I couldn't face myself, unless I'd done everything in my power to advocate, to help, to support and to fight the system. And I suppose I wanted to believe that the world could change, that people weren't truly discriminatory, or that children under the age of 6 couldn't be bullies, or that my kids deserved but could also receive the very best education I could attain for them. It turns out that homeschooling fits that bill for my kids. Not every child is the same, and not every option is right for all. You need to figure out what is right for your child, and your family.

Hopefully this gives you a small glimpse of how hard advocacy can be after receiving a diagnosis, and the process you may have to follow. Hopefully your journey will be easier, and have better outcomes, and perhaps a teacher may read this book, and hopefully take on board the suggestions; to make your child's education a happier, and more inclusive one. And hopefully a journey where advocacy is not needed at all, because all children have their needs met, and are included as part of a naturally inclusive school culture.

Therapists and Diagnoses

Therapists need to know as much about your child as possible, so they can cater their therapies to your child. Most autistic adults will tell you that your child does not necessarily **need** therapy. This is because your child is perfect as they are. What they **need** is support, to help them understand themselves and the world around them. But they do **not** need therapy to **change** them, tell them how they should act, say things, or do things, etc; like a NT person.

Money and focus is often put on 'early intervention', but we are autistic for our entire lifetimes. We will likely need specific tools and equipment throughout our entire lifetimes, to help us; stay emotionally regulated, cope with a world not built for us, cope with our co-occurring disabilities, or assist us with ongoing issues. We will possibly need therapists throughout our lives to recommend new techniques and ways to deal with pain or problems like low mobility, muscle weakness, eating disorders, mental health and accessing the community, but we do not need therapy that teaches us how to be more 'normal'. This is why ABA is redundant.

Children develop in their own time, in their own way, but sometimes we need therapies to help us attain certain skills, or to overcome difficulties. A child with low muscle tone may need a physio or OT to help build muscles for simple things, like holding their head up for long periods, or feeding themselves. A child that does not look people in the eye does not need therapy, because there is nothing wrong with this. This is what your therapist needs to know; they need to know the things your child needs help with – opposed to the things that society **thinks** we need help with.

Autistic kids may need additional help or therapy to learn certain skills. Eg: how to use an AAC device, learn certain vocal sounds, improve strength, ease or minimise toe walking (as it can lead to pain and muscle issues – and eventually often needs Achilles surgery to correct), how to use hand movements to do certain tasks (like washing hands), how to use a simple tool like a makeup sponge or pencil grip, or keyboard, or speech to text; to make writing easier and less painful etc. They could also use a therapist to learn how to calm themselves (self-regulate) and figure out what tools help them in different situations. There is also an opportunity to help a child grow muscle mass/strength/coordination or better fine or gross motor skills, or to help with tics or motor neuron responses that can prevent them from doing what their brain is asking their body to do (this can happen with DCD).

It is the way in which the therapist does this, that is extremely important. (see ABA: book three). ABA is unnecessary as it only teaches NT favoured skills, (it does not work on these above mentioned 'needed' and necessary skills – it only works on behaviours) and it is **not** performed by a trained physio, OT, speech therapist or psychologist; it is usually performed by a person who has done a short course on how to remove items from a disabled child, until the child bends to the will of the ABA'ist.

Your chosen therapist also needs to see your NDIS plan, your insurance or your funding institute (if you have one; depending on your country and financial agreements). Not all therapies are covered under insurance or under NDIS. For NDIS participants – the therapist does not need to see the dollar amounts that your child has been allocated, they just need to see your NDIS appointed goals; because they need to meet these goals in order to be paid by NDIS. Some people print out the plan and then blacken out the dollar amounts – then send it on to all relevant parties. But I've found it useful for some of my kid's therapists to understand that we have about 6 therapists (or more) and we have X dollars available – therefore, they would only have a 6th of the budget to spend, or even less. It can help them plan their schedules and the amount of therapy your child will receive per year. Therapy is often a half an hour session, per fortnight, or even once a month; depending on the type of therapy and the funds allocated to achieve the goals.

For **NDIS**: The therapist needs the plan because it will have goals in it. Each child's goals are different to the next child. The therapist is paid by NDIA to deliver a service. Every year the therapist needs to do a report; to say how they have worked on these goals, and how, and in what ways; the child worked towards them or possibly achieved them, what they still need to work on next year, and possible goals for the next year. In other words, the goals in the NDIS Plan becomes the therapists job description for your individual child.

All therapists will need to know what their limitations are. You, as the parent, have the right to demand no ABA, no PBS, and no rewards or consequences. You can set the parameters for the therapy, in the best interests of your child. You also have the right to terminate any therapy that you deem unfit or abusive (or even because you don't like them), or postpone therapy if you feel your child would benefit from a break. You are the one paying the bills, the therapist is under your employ. That being said, most fully qualified therapists (that don't use ABA) are brilliant, and flexible, and are there to help your child. They often studied the profession because they love kids, or love what they do, and are more than willing to help your child; in the way your child wants to be helped. But they need all the information and diagnoses to be able to see the whole picture and to be able to amend any sort of therapy to best suit the individual.

A full background of your child, from pregnancy to now is required. The therapist can use this information to find the reasons behind certain behaviours, or why the child is delayed in certain areas, and where the child may need specialist therapy that is outside their realm of expertise. Eg: a multidisciplinary team is used because a psychologist can work on anxiety or regulation techniques, but they will not be able to help with feeding issues, muscle strength, a co-occurring disability or certain skills development. To achieve all those goals; you would probably need a SLP, and OT, a physio, and paed and a psych. And they would all need every piece of information that you have about your child in order to help them comprehensively, competently and affirmingly.

Ableism

The definition of ableism is that of other 'ism's' (racism, sexism etc). It is the discrimination of people with disabilities; or the thinking that abled people are superior, or it is the social prejudice or bigotry against the disabled. In the case of autism or ND people, ableism is the discrimination of ND people, or the bias of NT people over ND's.

Medical News Today (https://www.medicalnewstoday.com/articles/ableism#types), Zawn Villites writes: "The definition of "disability" depends on context. For example, autism spectrum disorder (ASD) may be a disability in a world that values a neurotypical way of thinking, but in a world that values and understands neurodiversity, it might not be."

I love this quote, it speaks to the classification of autism as a disability, and whether we should question categorising all autistic people as disabled, or not. At the moment, the way the world views autism and neurodiversity, and does not support it – yes – we are disabled by society.

In my experience there's nothing my kids, or I "can't" do. There's plenty we won't do, or struggle to do without supports (mostly due to our sensory aversions, and co-occurring disabilities), but we are capable of achieving anything. All we need is a little assistance. Eg: I have APD; I need help to make connections in my brain between hearing sounds, lip reading, (or reading subtitles) processing the sounds and repeating them. As a child I needed to learn using the gestalt language processing method to learn to use mouth words (hearing language repeated in different ways and different contexts, until the meaning becomes apparent). I needed more time than some other kids, but I was capable of it, I just needed support. Some autistic kids have co-occurring disabilities, some of these disabilities can make it harder to achieve specific things. But it's never right to assume anything of a disabled person, or of anyone for that matter. That is what being ableist is all about. It is judging a person based on their ability, or inability to do, or not do something.

If we lived in a world where all disabilities were accommodated to the point where adaptions, supports and accommodations do not have to be asked for – then we wouldn't be classed as disabled. Misa on Wheels: Amanda Knightly (www.youtube.com/c/misaonwheels also available on Facebook, Instagram,

Twitter etc) is a fantastic person to follow. Misa often shows photos depicting ableism; if you'd like to understand it better, check out her page, full credit to her, she's opened my eyes and is a great advocate.

Examples of ableism, or poor treatment towards disabled people:

- Having a wheelchair lift, but putting a sign on it that says "ask reception for the key".

- Having a wheelchair ramp, but not adding a handrail, making it too steep, not adding a gutter interchange to get to it.

- Only having steps and no wheelchair access.

- Not having subtitles on video training materials.

- Not accommodating people's needs when asked.

- Assuming anything about the person or their disability.

- Offering only NT preferred play or tools in any setting.

- Asking them "what is wrong with you?"

- Assuming someone who is a part time wheelchair or AAC user is 'faking' or doesn't really need these supports.

- Limiting a disabled persons use of a support because you think it's inappropriate or you think they use it too much.

- Giving autistics a 'level' of functioning based on NT assumptions and preferences for what they think; we should or shouldn't be doing at a certain age.

- Not making things accessible to all.

- Touching people or their support tools without permission.

- Not believing a disability exists because you can't see it.

- Calling a disabled persons behaviour poor, bad or otherwise because it doesn't align with neurotypical behaviour.

- Tone policing autistic voices because you assume they are being rude, instead of it being part of their communication style.

- Putting children in ABA or behaviourism training because you want them to behave or act or talk etc – in a more neurotypically 'appropriate' way.

- Invalidating or gaslighting a disabled person when they tell you something is harmful to them, and you speak for them, or over them, or ignore them altogether.

- Movies like; 'Rainman'.

- Talking about a disabled person in front of them, instead of directly to them.

- Telling someone that their reactions and emotions are a "choice". If this was true, PTSD and cPTSD the world over would be cured or not exist in the first place.

- Making decisions for them, without them.

- Assuming disabled people need or want fixing or curing, or that there is a cure or fix for every disability.

- Changing your tone of voice or speech patterns to talk to disabled people, or assuming an intellectual disability – it is infantilising as well as ableist.

- Using offensive language about disabilities.

- Referring to non-disabled people as 'normal'. This is why I have used inverted commas when using the word 'normal' throughout the book, because it is an ableist term and is offensive to many.

- Only accepting a driver's licence as ID. Not all people can drive or want to drive.

- School policies that do not include incontinence as a supported need, and demand kids to be toilet trained and wear underwear instead of continence wear.

- A disabled toilet that does not have an automatic door or a lock on it. Or room to turn a wheelchair around, or a sink that doesn't work etc.

- Telling a disabled person how they should; play, learn, behave, what tools they should and shouldn't use to: play, learn, behave etc.

- Asking someone to prove their disability or question their disability.

- School policies that require proof of disability before accommodations can be requested or made.

- Telling a disabled person their experience isn't real, or not shared by other disabled people – so therefore it doesn't exist or is invalid.

- Avoidance of disabled people.

- Social conditioning that train the population to see one set of social behaviours and speech patterns as superior to others. Eg: if you are not like me, then you are 'bad' or 'unworthy'.

- Seeing some disabled people, or some disabilities as superior to others. Eg: seeing physical disabilities over mental health or intellectual disabilities, or temporary disability better than permanent.

- Or: Aspergers as better than autism. Or using severity, functioning labels, or levels; these literally grade disabled people against each other and cause an ableist bias for one level, label, or 'severity' over another. It literally forces the public to see a disabled person as better, worse, or more/ less 'functioning' than (not only) NT people, but comparable to other disabled people. It's probably one of the more horrible discriminatory ableist things, that people don't understand and keep using, and keep arguing to continue using them.

- 'Praying' for people with disabilities; this often sees the disabled person as evil, demonic, or 'unclean', or that disability is a sin to be ashamed of etc and it is truly offensive. It might be nicer and less offensive to pray for a kinder world that accommodates and accepts disabilities.

- Viewing a disabled person as inspirational for doing everyday tasks.

- Assuming autistic people can't hold down a job, complete high school or a university degree, get married and have children (of any neurotype), or don't have anything of value to teach about autism, or assume that they aren't the real experts on autism – of course they are – they are the only ones who can talk about it from the internal experience.

Autism is a disability, and often people treat us differently and think neurotypical brains are superior. They are not, they are just difference. But in an alternate world where autistics or ND brains are the majority, then NT people would be considered the minority and may become the group that struggles to live in an ND world.

What should you do if you encounter ableism? (if you are privileged to be able to do these things):

- Call it out. Educate and try to explain. But keep in mind that you do not owe anyone an explanation of your disability or your offence; a simple – that's offensive is sufficient. If they argue with you; this is doubling down on ableism.

- Take note of time, date, place, and people, and report it.

- Children should also be reported and educated (eg: school environments or playgrounds or in other venues). Children

329

are not exempt from ableism, and teaching the young is important.

- Seek support. Wherever that support might be, eg: support groups, psychologists, or counsellors. Ableism can severely affect mental health and other areas of your life, please seek help when/if you need it.

Internalised ableism

This is when a disabled person discriminates against themselves or other disabled people. Or they are biased towards (have a preference for, or favouritism for) non-disabled people, abilities, thoughts, speech patterns, labels, behaviour, supports, needs, and acts etc.

Internalised ableism also includes a definition of people being ashamed of their disability. This is where is gets a little tricky and a little condescending and harmful. Just because a disabled person would like one photo that does not show their disability or would like to not feel pain for a day, or would like to feel like they fit in – just once – does **not** mean they have internalised ableism, or that they should be called out or patronised for their request for assistance.

Think about a feature you have, that other people don't think is perfect, or pick on you about it, or you are self-conscious about because society doesn't value that specific feature, or it's something that causes you frustration or you need to adapt it; to feel comfortable or even get through the day. Do you occasionally think, it would be nice if it was smaller, or bigger, or rounder, or straighter etc? Are you sick of being bullied for it? Does it hinder you in any way? It doesn't mean that you would go out and change it, or that you hate it, or you want someone to fix or cure it for you, or that you think no-one in the world should have that feature. It's just that society has made you feel uncomfortable about it, or that sometimes it causes you pain or difficulty, or aggravation. You have the right to vent, and the right to feel the way you do.

No-one should patronise or tell someone off for being upset or frustrated by their disability. Calling out internalised ableism should only be done when, what is being said, advised or written etc will or is harming other disabled people.

If a disabled person asks for help to cover up their disability, because it makes them feel more confident, helps them achieve a goal, or any other reason – they should be given that help – they shouldn't be told "there's no need to cover it up, they're perfect the way they are". This is condescending, unhelpful and causes the disabled person to feel shameful for asking for help. It may cause internalised ableism, or force negative mental health issues. When we ask for help, it's for a reason. Many disabled people become **un**able to ask for help because this is the way they are treated.

Being praised constantly for doing typical things that we used to ask help with (even if it causes pain or is extremely difficult for us), sends the message that asking for help is not typical and should be avoided at all costs. We get so used to not asking for help. If we do ask for help, we are often patronised in this way; with compliments and statements about how wonderful we are, how good we are at certain things, that we should be proud and happy. But this isn't help, this isn't support, this isn't what we asked for. It's great to get compliments, but being validated is even better and serves a better and more meaningful purpose. Listening, validating, and then doing what we ask, is the ultimate support.

Telling us we have internalised ableism because we asked for that support is also not helpful and causes more harm than good. Remember that self-care is extremely important and just because you are disabled, doesn't mean you're always proud or happy – and feeling that way doesn't mean you have internalised ableism. If you are struggling with self-hatred, or can't see any positive, you may need more help and support and I hope you will seek that help. Internalised ableism can be tricky and it's hard to know the difference between wanting and needing support, and harbouring negative views of disability that may harm your inner psyche or that of other disabled people. If you are struggling to understand the difference, I definitely recommend seeking professional help from a neuroaffirming therapist, but also recommend following people like "Misa On Wheels"; where perspectives on ableism and internalised ableism are very thoroughly discussed and examined, and help to put forward the thoughts and feelings of all disabled people, and how to help us.

Minorities within Minorities

I would like to start this topic by mentioning that educating people about minorities should never be the responsibility of the minority in question; we all have a responsibility to learn as individuals (and as a majority), in order to help, support and live harmoniously as one human race.

But, I will also mention that people do not often learn from their mistakes, and more specifically – we don't learn from our own histories. History is always written by the winner, the oppressor, the majority. This skews history and causes the victor to win the spoils, and to live in ignorance of past wrongs, and to possibly repeat atrocities.

In more recent history, humanity has begun to record or collate information about both sides of the wars, or oppressions or atrocities, etc. But this is **still** often one sided and is still often written by someone who is from the majority – or from a group of oppressors. What is written is history. When we write about history, we are talking **at** people, we are **not** having a conversation **or** learning what to do in the future **or** learning how to help or do things differently. A history is just that – it's the past, it's what **has** occurred. Talking about it doesn't usually change anything.

Often talking about the history of one minority, and what happened to them, even if it happened yesterday – doesn't help. **Unless** you are going to do something about it today or tomorrow and the next day, and every day afterwards. Yes, it's important to know what happened, to discuss it and understand what went wrong so that we don't do it again. But if we don't move on from talking about the past, we will continue to live in the past. And if we don't learn directly from those minorities as to what we should be doing instead – the atrocities will continue.

I learnt this from an Aboriginal community group. They learnt that talking about the past wasn't changing their present, or their future. And they also learnt that it was making the current situation worse. They used to speak at conferences about their history and what atrocities did and do currently occur. When they did this, the feedback they received was all negative. Their own people told them they were enraged, upset, and felt powerless to fight. And the majority of other people at the conferences said they also felt powerless, but they also felt attacked, guilty, saddened, disgusted and many cried. But none knew or understood what the group were after, what they wanted or needed for the future. Nothing came out of these connections with the public. Everyone always left the conferences feeling like crap, and it didn't help anyone, it didn't achieve anything but to educate about a history and current situation that would never change unless they started to talk about different things.

Now, this group talks about the future, they talk about how things can and should change. They talk about how the majority can help; how indigenous people can help themselves, and how the majority can support and live harmoniously. How we can support and learn from each other. This group is brilliant. They are one of best groups I've ever heard of; ones that have learnt from the past and are making in-roads to change their future. Yes, the onus is **not**, and **should not** be on them, or of any minority to teach or educate anyone else. But how will the majority learn, and know how to help a minority, unless that minority speaks and advocates for what they want and need.

NOTE: When a minority says, "it's not my job to educate you", the person/people they say it to are often left in the dark.

They are left in a state of perpetuating what is already been/ being done. They asked a question and hit a brick wall. They are not directed to a source where they can learn or **should** learn from. They often then either drop the topic and ignore it forever (washing their hands of responsibility), or they do their own research, and learn from the wrong sources. This further perpetuates the issues; where the majority are learning and guessing what to do to help, or the minority are perpetuating the blame game.

Eg: if you have a child in a struggling moment, the first thing you ask is usually: "how can I help?" If the child responds with "it's not my job to educate you": you are a left to guess, or to walk away. Guessing can cause more harm than good (gaslights or invalidates as well) and walking away helps neither individual. And if either of these routes cause more harm to the child, the child is left to build more anger, resentment and continue to blame the adult – because they either did the wrong thing or did nothing. I will no longer be using the excuse of "it's not my job to educate you", or say things like "if you don't know, I'm not going to tell you". Because all it does is cause anger in me and doesn't help my situation to improve, and causes the other party to purposely ignore me, or implement the wrong things in the future. It's my fault, because I'm not willing to take responsibility for meeting them halfway and telling them what I do need and want.

This can also be seen as ableist, as some of us are unable to communicate our needs and wants. But, if I was not part of a specific minority group, but I knew one member of that group that needed support – I'd ask both the individual and the minority group they belong to – about how to help. I would not guess, and I would not walk away unless I was told to. I would go to the source and ask the group. That's what this section is about – asking you to please go to the group that relates to your loved one – and ask for help, for information and for guidance. If they say it's not their job to educate you – challenge them on it – ask them "if not you, then who, where, what, why and how?"

Guessing: Often the majority make guesses about how they should help, and this is where they get it horribly wrong and make everything so much worse. This is how ABA (conversion therapy for autistics) was born. It was born from the majority trying to help, and thinking they are helping- but it actually hinders, harms, and ends in abuse, suppression and oppression, depression, PTSD, and suicide of a minority neurotype. Now, autistics are trying to educate the majority about how abusive this type of 'help' is. If we don't educate them, who will? If the majority don't listen, and continue with conversion therapy – then yes, we can hold them accountable for their atrocities, but if no-one says anything and no-one stands up to even let them know that what they are doing is hurting us – how will they change, how will they know what to do instead (unless we give them the options), and how will they know what to do in the future?

If we don't take some ownership, some responsibility, some onus and make some action to right the wrongs of information hidden, regarding our ancestors, or ourselves, how do the majority in the present learn and change? That's what the "Nothing For Us, Without Us" Movement is about. How can the majority learn how best to help us, if we don't educate, if we don't advocate, if we don't join together to help each other. Where will the majority get this information from, how will they form their strategies to 'help'; if the minority aren't the ones at the forefront of the rhetoric?

Please stop and listen to **all** minorities when you can. But don't just listen to their past -it will help no-one. Listen to their past and what is happening now, and then **ask** – **what do we do now and tomorrow**? Get them to name **exactly** what they need, what they want, what they hope for – and then make it happen! Don't just do lip service to their words, **act**! It is the responsibility of us all, to act! Change doesn't occur when the majority aren't listening. Positive change happens when individuals turn to each other and spread the word, and lift the voices of those minorities, and then act on what the minority are asking for; in an inclusive, and mutual give and take, of mutual respect, where all parties are treated equally, and no one is left with 'less'. **Hideous** change occurs when the majority listen but then interpret in their own way, instead of involving those minorities in the decisions that are made about them and for them. Or – sometimes it goes very wrong when the majority do not consider everyone involved, and only focus on one group or individual. Everyone can get what they need and want if we work together, stop blaming each other and start taking responsibility for our own individual strengths that we all bring to humanity and to society – and especially stop oppressing or abusing any one minority.

Intersectionality of neurodivergent people

Your child is in a minority group if they are autistic. Approximately 1% - 5% of the world's population are autistic. We don't actually know the true figure – because of the stigmatism, and the extensive number of barriers to obtaining an official diagnosis. Eg: cost of diagnosis, bias of therapists, lack of knowledge about how autism presents in anyone other than white middle class cis males, and the downfalls for some people from asking for a diagnosis. (Please see the section on "hindrances to diagnoses").

If you are autistic and you also identify with another minority group, eg: female, or identify as LGBTQIA2S+ or a "Black, Indigenous or Person of Colour" (BIPOC), use a wheelchair, speak a different language to the majority in your community, or do not use mouth words, deaf or blind, have another disability, obese,, immigrant, etc, etc, etc – you are also a minority within a minority group.

This is called **Intersectionality** and was coined by Kimberle Williams Crenshaw (1989). Where two or more minority groups/ categories/distinctions collide in one person. From Oxford Dictionaries: "the network of connections between social categories such as race, class and gender, especially when this may result in additional disadvantage or discrimination". www.oxfordlearnersdictionaries.com/definition/english/ intersectionality

I am white, and I'm not trying to talk for BIPOC/ BAME, LGBTQIA2S+ or any other minorities, and I am definitely not trying to talk **over** these people either. I am trying to draw everyone's attention to the struggle they live daily and try to add a section in this book that might be helpful. (I hope is helpful). It is very important that all of these people get their time to talk, be heard and truly listened to, (not matter what their preferred medium for communication is) and valued – especially by our autistic community. Our community is trying very hard to be inclusive of **all** people, but we get it wrong too – no-one is perfect, but I hope we (as a group) can do better in the future. We (autistics, or neurodivergents) as a minority already struggle; and many of us are also intersectionalled. We need to join as one to support each other and make at least one step forward to try and ease some of the struggle for our fellow humans all over the world.

Parents are a growing group within the autistic community; mainly (I believe) due to parents realising that they are also autistic; after having their children assessed. But a diagnosis is a privilege that not all can afford. Assessments for autism are aimed at the middle-class white cis male heterosexuals from an English-speaking background without other disabilities. Diagnosis becomes even harder for those minorities within the minorities. This is just the beginning of the struggle for minorities, getting a diagnosis is hard enough, but then what to do with it? Some countries only offer certain therapies to certain people,

343

and some countries do not even recognise or understand what autism is, and what is needed. This makes it very difficult for the parents/guardians of these children to find and establish any sort of help.

There are also socioeconomical issues, demographic, lack of access to medical equipment or facilities and location issues. Think of all the things that make it difficult for you to find the right help for your child, now add to that systemic racism, sexism, or any other 'ism' to the mix.

People from all cultures can still struggle with ableism within their own communities, in their own culture and even sometimes within their own homes when it comes to raising autistic children. I've heard some very sad stories where people have been disowned or been taken from their home (and put in foster or group care by government bodies) or kicked out of their own home just because they are autistic. Sometimes their family and community do not believe autism exists and will not put up with them not acting neurotypically. Sometimes religions have described an autistic as a person "possessed".

Some cultures do not accept autistics for different reasons. I have heard of families that have abandoned or hurt their child because the child couldn't eat certain foods (due to ARFID), couldn't wear the religious outfits (due to SPD), or couldn't use mouth words (due to apraxia), and they would not and could not accept these things. They weren't willing to accommodate them or love them as they are. Their culture or religion was so important or so stringent that there was no way that these things would ever be accepted. This is their culture and the way they were brought up. You cannot change a person's culture or upbringing, but hopefully we can adapt, or perhaps influence a more positive view of autism and co-occurring disabilities to the world, so all cultures will be more willing to accept or simply understand us better.

Culture, religion, and community matter to many, and they often rely on synergy and compliance; where some autistic people will never be understood or accepted or be able to achieve the set NT standard. Please be mindful of cultural differences when speaking about autism and ways to help an autistic child; because something that works for (perhaps) a Catholic predominantly white family, - may not work for an Indian Hindu family, or a Christian African American Family, or an Atheist Chinese/Malay family. There is no rule that fits all. And no method that fits all. I hope there are enough tools and refences in this book to help anyone and everyone, from all backgrounds and walks of life. But I will get it wrong – I'm not infallible, please pick and choose from the different sections to find and adapt something that suits your individual family, and each individual within the family.

Just remember, that everyone has privilege in some way. White people will never understand the struggles of BIPOC or BAME people living in a white community. Heterosexual people with never understand what it's like to be prejudiced against for being part of the LGBTQIA2S+ community, and hearing and, or verbal people will never understand what it's like to be in a world that values hearing or mouth words over other forms of communication; and how that affects the way they live their lives and interact with it. Every single person in the world lives with some form of privilege, some have more than others, some less. What we do with that privilege, and how we treat others that do not have the same privilege as us, is what truly matters

Terms:
BIPOC: Black, Indigenous, People of Colour (mostly used in the USA)
BAME: Black, Asian, and Minority Ethnic (mostly used in the UK)

BIPOC / BAME:

Racism is still everywhere in the world, and for someone who is BIPOC/ BAME and autistic the challenges are extraordinary. Some of the stories I've read have broken my heart and ruined my faith in people. There are even videos on YouTube of these twice victimised people being abused, accosted, and even murdered. These videos are extremely hard to watch and traumatic for the viewer. How hard they must be for the individuals – I can't tell you, but it makes me sick.

Often a diagnosis for a BAME or BIPOC person is denied. They are gaslit and told they have anger issues, are sometimes arrested for what society deems inappropriate behaviour, or told that they need to 'behave' – instead if being assessed and diagnosed as autistic (or another neurotype). They are misdiagnosed with things like ODD, instead of PDA, because the therapist is seeing a horrible societal stereotype of opposition or defiance, instead of struggling, or they are not seeing the disability for what it is. And they are often treated like subhuman beings because people do not see disability in these people (for God knows what reason), they only see their skin, and correlate it with a negative. Which I've never understood, and probably never will; but that's my privilege talking.

To help these children cope and survive these (sometimes truly hideous) outcomes, and to be considered for diagnosis; we need to work together. We need to lift their voices, listen and act. We need to acknowledge that anyone in the whole world can also be autistic, and all people are deserving of respect, help support and accommodations no matter their background. Some children may need a little extra help, or specific skills training, social stories, learning to mask for safety, different aides, support people, AAC devices, tools that identify them as disabled, and even dashcams and other people videoing the incident etc can save their life. All autistics will require tools and things to help them throughout their life, but for the intersectional – these tools can become lifesaving tools, especially when trying to escape or overcome systemic racism or any of the 'isms'.

Masking is horrible for autistic people and can cause many issues, but for a twice profiled person – it may save their life. For a different perspective, please read the article by Cheyenne Thornton (18 April 2021) NeuroClastic: "ABA for Creating Masking Black Autistics" www.neuroclastic.com/aba-for-creating-masking-black-autistics/. This article is written by a Person Of Colour; who believes it is possible to stay safe without the use of masking and ABA. It also points out that it is society that should be educated and changed, not the autistic person. I agree that it is **all** people that need to be educated and stop the racism. I doubt this will happen in our lifetime, or possibly our children's lifetime, but we all still need to try and make a concerted effort. **Not masking** may still be a privilege that many can't afford and cannot take the risk to even try.

There is a Facebook advocacy/blog page called Fidgets and Fries (www.facebook.com/fidgetsandfries/), by Tiffany Hammond; which may be able to help you to understand the argument for masking from a BIPOC perspective. This advocate is also an author, you can check out their books online. Also check out the YouTube video by "Nigh Functioning Autism" (Tiffany Joseph) that explains how to navigate ABA for people who are court ordered to do ABA or have no choice in the matter: "Don't start ABA therapy for your autistic child before watching this! – Autistic Parent Insight" www.youtube.com/watch?app=desktop&v=dQ7ajs8uCiw&feature=youtu.be TW: there are flashing pictures in the background, which may be difficult or intolerable for epilepsy or eye stigmatisms, or if you have APD and trouble reading subtitles while there are flashes behind them. But it does have a great message, and she's a fantastic advocate, with many helpful videos online.

Court orders: If you are being court ordered to do ABA because of a paediatrician who has reported you for neglect (or some other reason), maybe show the paediatrician and the court this article by Dr Zate (24 September 2021) "Why are Pediatricians still Prescribing ABA?" Dr Sarah Zate: www.drzate.com/blog-posts/why-are-pediatricians-still-prescribing-aba

or try the article by the same author, but featured in the Therapist Neurodiversity Collective: Dr Sarah Zate "Medical Neglect – Physician and Court Ordered ABA for Autistic Children" www.therapistndc.org/medical-neglect-physician-and-court-ordered-aba-for-autistic-children/

A lot of paediatricians, and judges are completely unaware of what actually happens during ABA therapy sessions. Eg: they are not aware that some children are physically restrained or sprayed in the face with water sprayers, or given electric shock treatments, or that new ABA is considered by the community as abusive and a form of autistic conversion therapy – that uses positive reinforcement to convert your child to an NT person. Educating them on what happens and why autistics consider it to be the same as gay conversion therapy, and why it's considered abusive needs to come first when educating doctors, teachers, lawyers etc at university level, but until

Universities change their ways, we all need to help to get the word out about abusive therapies.

Some BIPOC/BAME and LGBTQIA2S+ autistics have also said that masking and acting NT have been vital for saving their own life, and their children's lives; and some have used ABA to teach their children how to mask; please don't berate them or tell them off. They are doing what they can, the best way they see they can. They are trying to survive. And often they are forced into ABA by courts or social services or are given no alternatives.

Some parents teach masking without the use of ABA; as ABA teaches masking as a biproduct of the therapy. Where you can teach masking without the potentially harmful techniques used in ABA. Parents teach their children (safely) how to act in certain situations (to appear more NT)- to not draw attention to themselves, and to keep themselves and their family members safe. They teach the benefits of masking; how and when to drop the mask in the safety of their own homes, often when only their safe people are surrounding them. Sometimes it is not even safe to unmask in their own homes. Eg; there was a case (in America) where a BIPOC person was killed because their grandparents felt the need to call the police; the police shot him, at his home, for being an unmasked autistic.

These parents teach their children safety techniques; ways to hide autistic behaviours that may be deemed by police as violent, menacing, threatening or weird. It is a way of teaching self-advocacy and survival tools; in a way that is safe for the autistic individual.

We all could learn something from these people. Everyone in my family has faced bullying and we have all used masking for self-preservation. Masking has helped us, but I know it has also hurt us when we didn't know when or how to drop the mask. That is the difference between masking for safety - and ABA forcing and teaching masking as a consequence of their techniques. It is a huge difference and one not to be taken lightly. ABA and other therapies often **inadvertently** teach masking; the therapists are not aware that this is the outcome of their techniques. Masking is only ever safely taught when the individual is taught when and how to use it effectively and safely **and** how and when to drop it safely.

Acting classes (if you can find any that are neuroaffirming and affordable); they may be a fantastic way to teach yourself, or your child how to mask and how to drop it when you need to. Some classes even teach about emotions and not being caught up in the role – which is one of the reasons why masking can be so dangerous. We can get carried away trying to be something else, that we lose ourselves within the role we are playing. Some actors are examples of how playing a role too much, or becoming the character completely in its entirety can end in tragedy. Eg: actors like Heath Ledger, who was thought to have dived too deeply into the depression and anger of the role of The Joker, and couldn't drop it when not in front of the camera. But this is purely speculation, as no-one can know what someone else is thinking and feeling.

Caution: Masking can be dangerous. When we mask, we are putting on an act; we think we are doing a great job, but most of us are not academy worthy in our acting abilities. People see the mask and wonder why we are 'acting'. They don't understand the need for the mask, so they profile us as hiding something or as: 'not to be trusted'. ABA teaches masking in a way that we don't even know we are doing it, so we can't explain that to people – so they can understand us and the situation better. Acting classes are better, because you are taught to know when you are acting and when you have dropped the mask – which makes you more aware of your surroundings and of yourself within those surroundings. Making it safer to mask, unmask, or be able to explain when people misinterpret your responses, actions and communication. Masking helps you fit in, but only to the degree that people believe your 'act' or 'mask' (eg: Uncanny Valley Theory). This uncanny phenomenon can cause bigger issues and create more danger for people who are being racially or sexually vilified.

Let me explain. ... If a police officer thinks you are hiding something, when you are actually masking (see the section on Uncanny Valley); it may incite them to more violence and profile you even further. Eg: perhaps your mask makes you look guilty of something, or they suspect you are hiding something (because you don't seem neurotypical, or acting 'normally' -and therefore you might be hiding something); so the police pull their gun, or arrest you, or try to restrain you.

Masking also causes massive meltdowns that you cannot control, which can be a danger to an autistic individual, but it is even worse for BIPOC/BAME/LGBTQIA2S+ autistics. If the autistic person has a meltdown in public because they'd been masking their pain/SPD or trauma etc; the bigger the meltdown will become and the bigger the reaction from the police. I know when I've been trying to hold in a meltdown, (especially for a prolonged period because I'm in public or at work), my explosion (when it finally erupts) is often catastrophic. I have alienated many people by trying to hold it in, but I can't hold it in forever.

If I had exploded with one of these catastrophic meltdowns in front of a police officer; I can bet you that I would've been arrested, and probably injured in the process. But for BIPOC and BAME autistics to have the same outburst; often police are taught to react with guns; instead of identifying a person stuck in a trauma response and finding ways of helping with non-violent tactics.

I recommend reading the sections in this book about the Uncanny Valley Theory and the section on Masking to understand the dangers more. And reading the book "Unmasking Autism" by Dr Devon Price. Or the book "Managing Meltdowns" by Deborah Lipsky and William Richards.

I have no say in the topic when it comes to other people and their families, and their decisions (especially as a privileged Caucasian), but I can add the articles, blogs, Facebook groups and other interesting reading by BIPOC/BAME/ LGBTQIA2S+ autistics – that may help you to feel less alone, more connected, and help you navigate the NT world and the struggles that may occur for you or your child.

I would ask that if you are using masking and/or acting; to help your child through racial, sexual discrimination etc - that you please talk to other BIPOC/BAME/LGBTQIA2S+ autistics, and seek support (if you are not already) to make sure you and your child are well supported in the community and stay safe – see the list and links for advocates and helpful spaces below, (and at the end of this book) for more support and where to find more information on this sensitive topic.

LGBTQIA2S+

Before talking about anything further I want to add **A NOTE on Gender**: Ask the person what **pronoun** they prefer. Gender in my opinion is not a thing we should be biased about. Clothes should be clothes – not girls' clothes or boys' clothes. Why do we assign colours and specific toys to specific children's groupings? It's ridiculous. If you watch an Episode of TV show "QI" with Stephen Fry; the colour pink was apparently originally the colour assigned to boys at birth, but somewhere along the way, it switched. Therefore, things are obviously able to change, I'm just not sure how they did it back then, or how they can now. The same with long hair for men. The romans started the tradition of short hair, to stop the enemy from being able to grab it during a fight, but most of the other cultures around the whole globe still preferred long hair to show their masculinity. These days, my boys are sometimes picked on or people assume their sex is different, just because of the length of their hair. It's wrong to assume anything based on sexual stereotypes.

A NOTE on Titles: Please be aware that not all of us use sexist or outdated titles like Miss or Mrs. Please ask what title **and** pronoun the person prefers. Why do we still use labels like Mr or Ms? This is a pet peeve of mine. The use of terms like Miss and Mrs breaks down the sexes further, by using their marital status to define themselves and their position in society (comparing their single self to their married self), and the female population as a whole. If you know the history of the title Ms – it was brought out by the Women's Rights Movement as a replacement to Mrs and Miss; to stop women being prejudiced against because of their marital status. Instead, Ms became a third alternative, and everyone continued to use marital status to identify and discriminate against women. And we are still arguing about these titles now – why can't we get rid of all titles? I know there is now the option in some places to use Mx – Why is it important for everyone to know how we identify? Why can't we just be known by our first or last names? And why do those names have to be gendered as female, male or unisex names? Why do we always say things like "let the lady pass" instead of something more neutral like "let the person pass" – we are all people, we are all human – why do we have to assign sex /titles and labels

357

to everyone. I identify as female, but I'm leaning towards using Mx as I'm fed up with titles and labels that gender us.

I personally think we shouldn't have 'titles' at all, we should just say our preferred name. But each to their own, and I will take my lead from the LGBTQIA2S+ Community, as they are the ones that are often discriminated against when these titles are used incorrectly or arbitrarily assigned based on assumptions. Titles have always been about status and do not help to break down the barriers between groups. I will always try to use them/they for everyone, until they tell me their preferred pronoun. As using they/them is not gendering, it is neutral. Once you know their preferred pronoun, it would be rude to continue using they/them (unless that is their preference).

- Please also remember that using the wrong pronoun, title or label can trigger a trauma response or add to a person's cPTSD, anxiety, depression, or existing trauma. Please be respectful, this is important for anyone at any age or life stage. This is very important for teachers and therapists working with children, tweens, and teens, and especially the intersectionalled communities who may have a higher incidence for pronoun, title, label differences. We think differently and experience life differently; it's almost redundant that we would have a different opinion from the social 'norm' on all things, including language, and how we identify.

Autistic and LGBTQIA2S+: There are many autistics that identify as LGBTQIA2S+. According to the article: "Autistic People More Likely to Identify as LGBTQ" (Marina Sarris 22 June 2022 for SPARK; www.sparkforautism.org/discover_article/autism-lgbtq-identity/#:~:text=A%20higher%20percentage%20of%20autistic%20people%20identify%20as,with%20autism%20who%20are%20gay%2C%20lesbian%2C%20or%20bisexual) – "4.5% of Americans identify as LGBTQ". Whereas somewhere closer to "15 to 35%" of autistic people identify as LGBTQ+.

I believe this figure should grow and be better researched as it is a misrepresentation of the true situation of both autistic and LGBTQ+ representation. Due to people being diagnosed as autistic as children, but not coming out as LGBTQ+ until sometimes their teens or adulthood. This accounts for only one disparity in the figures, another would be the lack of official diagnoses for self-identified autistics; that are not considered or represented in these figures, so the actual figure may be as high as 80 or 99%- we honestly have **no** idea unless barriers to diagnosis, and discrimination against minorities are stopped, and it becomes more acceptable and safer to identify as you want. These studies are sometimes used for things like eugenics, which stops and prevents many of us from contributing to them.

With more recent discrimination against ND people who also identify as LGBTQ+ (with the introduction of TERF's etc), the research into this area, and the help we give them has been stalled somewhat, or even taken a back step or retreat. Which is horrific and needs to stop, we need to help not discriminate. Please, if you have a child or family member who is intersectional, help them, validate them, and support them in any way you can. There are support groups specifically for these people, but there are also support groups for their parents. This is important for parents who need additional information about how to support their children better, and in a more gender **and** neuro affirming way.

Conversion Therapy and LGBTQIA2S+: The LGBTQIA2S+ community knows conversion therapy all too well. Thank goodness Gay Conversion Therapies are now being banned in Australia and New Zealand. This wonderful community (along with the autistic community) have also set their eyes on Autistic Conversion Therapies that also needs to be banned (otherwise known as ABA, PBS, or behaviouralism etc). Teaching a child not to be LGBTQIA2S+ is the same as training them not to be autistic; it is truly abusive to try and change a person's identity and sense of self, to make them see themselves as broken and requiring a fix or cure, or denying them gender affirming care.

Abuse: As with people of colour and other minorities, the LGBTQIA2S+ Community may fear abuse of all kinds, including physical abuse and profiling by police and authority figures. This becomes worse when the person is also autistic or identifies as a different neurotype (intersectional). The more categories of minorities you fit into, the worse it gets. Sad, and horrifying, but true. And there are many groups and organisations that are trying to help with this. If you need help, please ask groups like ASAN, Trans army or AIM for advice and help. I especially love ASAN's monthly email updates on how they are actively working on issues for intersectionalled communities and individuals.

Things that may help some minorities:
Practising a speech for when you are pulled over or questioned by police. Something like: "My name is. … I'm autistic, I don't like …… I am co-operating. … Please call ……" etc. Scripts can be problematic in that some people can't adapt them to different high stress situations when under pressure or on the middle

of a meltdown. But they do help others to prepare for these occasions – it will depend on the individual and what they prefer to use. A medical alert bracelet or necklace, a script, a letter that can be given to the emergency services staff etc can also be good options.

I suggest a tool that shows and identifies the person as autistic or 'other'; whatever the person needs to communicate in an emergency, eg: if the person is situationally non-speaking or apraxic, deaf or epileptic etc. Things such as; a key ring, wrist medical alert bracelet, Autism ID Card, or the 'Police Child ID' app was available on Apple etc. I use some of these for myself and my boys as we tend towards situational non-speaking, or meltdowns – which can be interpreted by police as a danger or threat. It's better to have these tools in an emergency than to be caught without them. They wouldn't be necessary – if we lived in a fair unbiased world, but we don't.

NOTE: Please be mindful about displaying signs where unscrupulous or nefarious people can take advantage of this information. I always remember the episode of 'Dexter' with the pictures of the family members on the car. These pictures told the killer how many people would be inside the house. Some people may use the information about a vulnerable

Minorities within Minorities

disabled person as well. But, I also know that these signs have also saved the lives of BIPOC/BAME when pulled over by police in America. So don't shame people who do use them – it is a personal choice, and you don't know those people's reasons or situations for using them. These tools have been invented for a reason, they can help.

Switching stims can also be helpful. Yes! we should all accept our kids for who they are and accept their stims as a part of who they are. But some stims can become harmful and even deadly to the individual, eg: skin picking can lead to bleeding and scaring, PICA can lead to death, and some forms of oral stimming (like Tourette's or swearing) can lead to police brutality/arrests, or gang beatings etc. In these cases, it can be a necessity to find a more appropriate stim. Autistic people still need to stim to self-regulate and cope in an NT world, so they may need your help to find a stim that helps them regulate, but won't get them killed, beaten, attacked, or arrested.

To switch a stim to something more appropriate for the individual, or to focus it positively (with their safety in mind), you will need to look at the Tools section in this book, perhaps reach out to a neuro-affirming OT, and talk to your child about options and tools they would like to try. You need to know everything about the stim and why they do it. Try explaining to them why the stim they are currently doing could put them at risk or danger, and work together to find a solution.

Unfortunately, all autistic children are at risk from bullies due to our behaviours and people seeing us as different (I haven't met an autistic person who was **never** bullied). If your child has a stim that is causing more bullying, or even physical violence, you may need to find an alternate stim. The bullies and the discrimination also need to be addressed (reported and stopped), but this is sometimes a privilege that other people do not benefit from. It has been noted that many BIPOC/BAME and other minorities feel they cannot call the police, or even report police for unfair treatment. Before you tell someone 'they should never put up with discrimination'; you might want to consider if they have the privilege to say or do anything about it, and actually be heard and helped.

See the section on Stimming for more info.

It's important to find support from people who understand your unique situation and needs. I recommend joining a **support group**, (please ask the autistic community for recommendations specific to your needs and location) but here's a few to check out, to see if you like them (also check the list at the end of the book). This is not a complete list, it's just to get you started:

The Autistic People of Color Fund: www.autismandrace.com.

Autistic Women of Colour FB Group: www.facebook.com/groups/AspieWOC/?ref=share.

AIM For The Rainbow FB Group/page: (Autistic Inclusive Meets = AIM) www.facebook.com/rainbowaim/

Trans Army: www.facebook.com/transarmy/

Educating Caregivers of Trans and Non-Binary People: www.facebook.com/groups/caregiversoftransfolk/about/

Autistic Women Support Group/ LGBTQ+ Inclusive/ Safe Place www.facebook.com/groups/1944262575825340/about/

Trans Student Educational Resources (TSER): www.transstudent.org

Mama Bears Double Rainbow Group: www.m.facebook.com/groups/MamaBearsDoubleRainbow/ or their website: www.realmamabears.org/double-rainbow

Sins Invalid: www.sinsinvalid.org a great look into disability justice and the movement in the US.

Autistics Unmasked (AU): non-profit organisation to lift autistic voices, and centre on the intersectionalled: www.autisticsunmasked.org

Please be aware when searching for any group; if they use puzzle pieces, ABA, or supports/links to Autism Speaks, NAS etc – these are **not** groups that are usually recommended by the Autistic Community. And are to be avoided if possible.

Interesting reading:

Books:

"All the Weight of Our Dream; On Living Racialized Autism" (19 June 2017) edited by: Lydia X. Z. Brown, E. Ashkenazy and Morenike Giwa Onaiwu.

Theresa Thorn "It Feels Good to Be Yourself: A Book About Gender Identity"

"Unmasking Autism" by Dr Devon Price

"Neuroqueer Heresies" by Nick Walker

BLOGS:

The Autism Wars: www.theautismwars.blogspot.com/?m=1

Black Neuroqueer Punk: www.afroautpunk.wordpress.com

One Quarter Mama: www.onequartermama.ca/?m=1

Transgender Parenting: www.facebook.com/transgenderparenting/

Lydia X.Z. Brown - Autistic Hoya www.facebook.com/Autistic.Hoya

The Black Autist: www.facebook.com/blackautist/

The Teselecta Multiverse: www.patreon.com/teselectamultiverse/comments?vanity=teselectamultiverse

Parenting through the Fog: www.parentingthroughthefog.com

The Neurodivergent Rebel (Lyric Rivera): www.neurodivergentrebel.com

Nigh Functioning Autism: www.facebook.com/Nigh.Functioning.autism/

Fidgets and Fries: www.facebook.com/fidgetsandfries/

Autistic Tyla: www.facebook.com/autistictyla

Autistic, Typing: www.facebook.com/AutisticTyping/ or www.autistictyping.com

A Link To The Spoons: www.facebook.com/ALinkToTheSpoons/

Apraxia Story: www.facebook.com/ApraxiaStory/

Thoughts From An Autistic Black Dad: www.facebook.com/BlackDadThoughts

Websites:

Autism in Black Inc: Advocacy Education and Support: www.autisminblack.com

The Black Autist: www.linktr.ee/blackautist - also available on YouTube, Website, TikTok, Twitter, and a storefront

The Source LGBT+ Center: www.thesourcelgbt.org

Neurodiversity Matters – Barking Sycamores: www.neurodiversitymatters.com/barking-sycamores-2022/

The Trevor Project: www.thetrevorproject.org – for a hotline and counselling for LGBTIQ2S+

For information about the research into how menopause affects autistics, or to contribute to their research, check out: www.autisticmenopause.com

Articles:

Suzannah Weiss (22 April 2016) Complex: "Meet the People Being Left Out Of Mainstream Conversations About Autism" www.complex.com/life/2016/04/autism-women-poc

Jackie Pilgrim (16 March 2015) The Art of Autism: "Jackie: Christian, Mom, Advocate, Entrepreneur, Artist, Poet and #Aspie" www.the-art-of-autism.com/jackie-christian-mom-advocate-entrepreneur-artist-poet-and-aspie/

Catina Burkett (21 January 2020) Spectrum News "Autistic While Black; how Autism Amplifies Stereotypes". www.spectrumnews.org/opinion/viewpoint/autistic-while-black-how-autism-amplifies-stereotypes/

Angela Weddle (28 February 2016) The Art of Autism: "The Autism Shift: The Visibly Invisible – Autistic People of Color" www.the-art-of-autism.com/the-autism-shift-the-visibly-invisible-autistic-people-of-color/

Hannah Furfaro (20 November 2017): Spectrum News: "Race, class contribute to disparities in Autism Diagnosis" www.

spectrumnews.org/news/race-class-contribute-disparities-autism-diagnoses/

Carrie Arnold (Updated 14 June 2017): Pacific Standard Magazine: "Autism's Race Problem" www.psmag.com/.amp/news/autisms-race-problem

Jason Arday has a few articles that may be of interest, he is a professor of sociology (Cambridge) that is helping the BAME community in England, some of his work is linked here: www.en.m.wikipedia.org/wiki/Jason_Arday

There are a few articles about him becoming the youngest ever black professor at Cambridge. Try this one from Sally Weale (23 February 2023) The Guardian: "Jason Arday to become youngest ever black professor at Cambridge" www.amp.theguardian.com/education/2023/feb/23/jason-arday-to-become-youngest-ever-black-professor-at-cambridge

YouTube Video: I'm Autistic, Black and Magical: www.youtube.com/watch?app=desktop&v=zk9BBL3n_hI

Join: "Ask me, I'm an AAC user! (24 Hour Rule)": great group: they have also been recognised for their work on self-advocacy.

Where to now

Book Two

Please read Book Two for information on: Co-occurring disabilities and specific topics that have more information about ADHD, PDA, Sleep disorders, Masking, AAC, Incontinence, and ARFID.

Book Three

Please read Book Three for more information on: Applied Behavioural Analysis (ABA), DIR Floortime, Alternative Ways to Help Your Child, and Elopement.

Book Four

Pease read Book Four for more information on: Useful Tools (such as sensory products), Other things you may want help with, (such as: light sensitivities, head banging, hospital visits, showering and bathing, nail trimming and clothing), and Other Topics, (such as; inflexible thinking, NDIS, and Hobby Burnout).

Book Five

Please read Book Five for more information on: Schools, Homeschooling, University or Higher Education, Workplaces, The Future, Extra Information, Where or who to go to for more information and help, References, and About the Author.

References

1. ADDitude Editors, 1 March 2022, reviewed by Dr Roberto Olivardia "What is Oppositional Defiant Disorder (ODD)?" (https://www.additudemag.com/what-is-oppositional-defiant-disorder/).

2. Tanveer Ahmed (3 May 2023) Financial Review: "NDIS has made autism label the diagnostic elephant in the room" www.afr.com/politics/federal/ndis-has-made-autism-label-the-diagnostic-elephant-in-the-room

3. Gus Alexiou (23 June 2020) Forbes "Doctors issuing Unlawful 'Do Not Resuscitate' Orders For Disabled Covid Patients 'Outrageous'". www.forbes.com/sites/gusalexiou/2020/06/23/unlawful-do-not-resuscitate-orders-for-disabled-covid-patients-outrageous

4. Apollo Behaviour (13 April 2022): "Relational Frame Theory and its Application in Autism Treatment plans" www.apollobehavior.com/what-is-relational-frame-theory/

5. Carrie Arnold (Updated 14 June 2017): Pacific Standard Magazine: "Autism's Race Problem" www.psmag.com/.amp/news/autisms-race-problem

6. ASAN (Autistic Self Advocacy Network) "Find your local Day of Mourning vigil site" (9 December 2022): www.autisticadvocacy. org/2022/12/2023-vigil-sites/?emci=7a32213d-94a8-ed11-994d-00224832eb73&emdi=39368eb2-bca8-ed11-994d-00224832eb73&ceid=26999051

7. AskAnAutistic (August 2019) Stop ABA, Support Autistics: "The Great Big ABA Opposition Resource List" www.stopabasupportautistics. home.blog/2019/08/11/the-great-big-aba-opposition-resource-list/

8. AUCADEMY (25 November 2021) "Resources supporting preference, but importantly wellbeing properties, of identity-first language: we are Autistic" www.aucademy.co.uk/2021/11/25/resources-sup porting-preference-but-importantly-wellbeing-properties-of-identity-first-language-we-are-autistic/

9. AustRoads Website: "Assessing Fitness to Drive: for Commercial and Private Vehicle Drivers 2022 edition, Medical Standards for licensing and clinical management guidelines" www.austroads. com.au/drivers-and-vehicles/assessing-fitness-to-drive (downloadable PDF)

10. Autability (7 July 2021) Disabled Living: "Screen time and autism: When are screens necessary" www.disabledliving.co.uk/blog/screens-and-autism-when-are-screens-necessary/

11. AutisticMe (14 January 2018) "Autistics Make Others Uncomfortable, Instantly" www.tameri.com/wordpress/autisticme/2018/01/13/autistics-make-others-uncomfortable-instantly/

12. Autistic Strategies Network (19 May 2023) "Non-speaking autists' experiences of ABA" www.autisticstrategies.net/nonspeaking-autistics-against-aba/

13. Awake and Mindful: "5 Best Kids Yoga Videos on YouTube" www.awakeandmindful.com/best-kids-yoga-videos-on-youtube/

14. Marquaysa Battle, Brittany Gibson Clara McMahon (9 March 2022) "19 Helpful Products for Anyone Trying to Stop Biting their Nails" BuzzFeed: www.buzzfeed.com/marquaysa/products-stop-biting-nails

15. Chris Bergman (16 July 2015) The New York Times: "Don't Limit Your Teen's Screen Time" www.nytimes.com/roomfordebate/2015/07/16/is-internet-addiction-a-health-threat-for-teenagers/dont-limit-your-teens-screen-time

16. Sarah Blunden (19 August 2022) "Is there such a thing as 'too old' to co-sleep with your child? The research may surprise you", The Conversation: www.theconversation.com/is-there-such-a-thing-as-too-old-to-co-sleep-with-your-child-the-research-might-surprise-you-188145

17. Chris Bonello: "Autistic not weird" (25 January 2021) "So, you want to teach autistic students? Here are 12 tips from an Autistic teacher" www.autisticnotweird.com/teaching/

18. Chris Bonello: Autistic Not Weird (23 March 2022) "Results and Analysis of the Autistic Not Weird 2022 Autism Survey" www.autistic notweird.com/autismsurvey/

19. Anne Borden King. Autistics for Autistics (Canada): "2020 has not been a good year for ABA: a research review" (https://a4aontario .com/wp-content/uploads/2020/12/ABA-Research-Review-2020.pdf

20. Botha, M., & Frost, D. M. (2020). "Extending the Minority Stress Model to Understand Mental Health Problems Experienced by the Autistic Population", *Society and Mental Health*, *10*(1), 20–34: www.journals.sagepub.com/doi/full/10.1177/2156869318804297

21. Monique Botha and Eilidh Cage (24 November 2022) Frontiers in Psychology: "Autism research is in crisis; A mixed method study of researcher's constructions of autistic people and autism research". www.frontiersin.org/articles/10.3389/fpsyg.2022.1050897 /full?fbclid=IwAR2YasTbvBWS1UG4TubvxR-ILH3BuTx4_9Mg9s4vyn G8X2bNa60XgVxNmwM

22. Kristen Bottema-Beutel and Shannon Crowley (5 May 2021), Frontiers in Psychology: "Pervasive Undisclosed Conflicts of Interest in Applied Behavior Analysis Autism Literature" www.frontiersin.org /articles/10.3389/fpsyg.2021.676303/full

23. Pia Bradshaw, Claire Pickett, Mieke L Van Driel, Katie Brooker and Anna Urbanowicz (Volume 50, Issue 3, March 2021) Australian Journal of General Practice "'Autistic' or 'with Autism'? Why the way general practitioners view and talk about autism matters". https://www1.racgp.org.au/ajgp/2021/march/autistic-or-with-autism?mibextid=j16qom

24. Jade Bremner (8 July 2021) The Independent: "School wins legal battle to electric shock children to 'correct behaviour'". www.independent.co.uk/news/world/americas/massachusetts-school-electric-shock-fda-b1880365.html

25. Phyllis Brown (10 June 2015) University of California "Fidgeting may help children with ADHD perform better in school" www.universityofcalifornia.edu/news/fidgeting-may-help-children-adhd-perform-better-school

26. Sarah Cassidy, Louise Bradley, Rebecca Shaw, & Simon Baron-Cohen (31 July 2018) 9,42; "Risk markers for suicidality in Autistic Adults" Molecular Autism: www.molecularautism.biomedcentral.com/articles/10.1186/s13229-018-0226-4

27. Catholic Education Commission of Victoria (CECV November 2017) "Guidelines for the Provision of Personal Care Support in Schools" www.cecv.catholic.edu.au/getmedia/56a1892e-fc3f-45f8-b057-daa8dd462dfd/CECV-Personal-Care-Support-in-Schools.aspx?ext=.pdf

28. Catina Burkett (21 January 2020) Spectrum News "Autistic While Black; how Autism Amplifies Stereotypes". www.spectrumnews.org/opinion/viewpoint/autistic-while-black-how-autism-amplifies-stereotypes/

29. Bridget Chapman (7 August 2021) WNCT News "Judge rules Wake County Schools inappropriately put student with special needs in closet 24 times" www.wnct.com/news/north-carolina/judge-rules-wake-county-schools-inappropriately-put-student-with-special-needs-in-closet-24-times/

30. Chavisory (11 May 2014) We are Like Your Child: "A Checklist for identifying sources of Aggression". http://wearelikeyourchild.blogspot.com/2014/05/a-checklist-for-identifying-sources-of.html

31. Natassia Chrysanthos (28 January 2024) The Sunday Age (Also printed in the Sydney Morning Herald) "Autism in schools gets help boost": www.smh.com.au/politics/federal/world-leading-autism-expert-joins-effort-to-reshape-australia-s-education-system

32. Natassia Chrysanthos (19 May 2023) The Age and The Sydney Morning Herald: "Sharp rise: More than 8 per cent of young school children now on NDIS" www.amp.smh.com.au/politics/federal/sharp-rise-more-than-8-per-cent-of-young-school-children-now-on-ndis

33. Cleveland Clinic: "Dopamine Deficiency" https://my.clevelandclinic.org/health/articles

34. Alex Colon and Angela Moscaritolo (28 March 2022) PC Mag: "The Best Smart Light Bulbs for 2022" (www.au.pcmag.com/lighting /30286/the-best-smart-light-bulbs).

35. Communication First: The Movie "LISTEN": www.youtube.com/watch ?v=ooKVxwVt8il ("Learn From Us"): www.communicationfirst.org).

36. Aaron Cooley (31 August 2022) Britannica "Ivan Illich" www. britannica.com/biography/Ivan-Illich#ref1221206

37. Chris Coombes (17 December 2021), DSC: "At What Cost": https:// teamdsc.com.au/resources/at-what-cost

38. E. B. Cooper, J. L. Anderson, C. Sharp, H. A. Langley and A. Venta (2/8/21) BPD and ED: Bio Med Central: "Attachment, Mentalization, and Criterion B of the Alternative *DSM-5* Model for Personality Disorders (AMPD)" www.bpded.biomedcentral.com/articles/10. 1186/s40479-021-00163-9

39. Samantha Craft (Updated May 2016) Spectrum Suite: "Samantha Craft's Autistic Traits Checklist" http://www.myspectrumsuite.com /samantha-crafts-autistic-traits-checklist/

40. Samantha Craft (10 June 2019) "Females and Autism / Asperger's: A Checklist": The Art of Autism www.the-art-of-autism.com/females -and-aspergers-a-checklist/

41. Catherine J Crompton, Danielle Ropar, Claire VM Evans-Williams, Emma G Flynn, Sue Fletcher-Watson (20 May 2020) Sage Journals: "Autistic Peer to Peer information transfer is highly effective" www. journals.sagepub.com/doi/10.1177/1362361320919286

42. Cassandra Crosman (20 March 2019), In The Loop About Neurodiversity – Wordpress: "The Ableist History of The Puzzle Piece Symbol for Autism" https://intheloopaboutneurodiversity. wordpress.com/2019/03/20/the-ableist-history-of-the-puzzle-piece-symbol-for-autism/?fbclid=

43. Herwig Czech (19 April 2018) Molecular Autism: "Hans Asperger, National Socialism, and 'race hygiene' in Nazi-era Vienna" www. molecularautism.biomedcentral.com/articles/10.1186/s13229-018-0208-6

44. Michelle Dawson, Isabelle Soulieres, Morton Ann Gernsbacher and Laurent Mottron (August 2007) "The level and nature of Autistic Intelligence" National Library of Medicine: www.pubmed.ncbi.nlm. nih.gov/17680932/

45. Diverticular Disease and Diverticulitis information from the UK Government. https://www.nidirect.gov.uk/conditions/diverticular -disease-and-diverticulitis and from the Victorian Government Australia https://www.betterhealth.vic.gov.au/health/conditions andtreatments/diverticulosis-and-diverticulitis

46. William Dodson (4 April 2022) "free resource: understanding Rejection Sensitive Dysphoria", The Additude Store: https://www. additudemag.com/download/rejection-sensitive-dysphoria-treatment-symptoms/?src=test

47. Jessica R Durling (18 June 2022) The Pointer: "ABA: Inside the controversy surrounding the most popular therapy for autistic

children in Ontario" www.thepointer.com/article/2022-06-18/aba
-inside-the-controversy-surrounding-the-most-popular-
therapy-on-autistic-children-in-ontario

48. Reece Epstein (2 September 2019) Web Archive: "How to enroll more ABA Clients by overcoming parents objections ... without being pushy or salesy" www.web.archive.org/web/20190904141632/http:// www.reputationelevation.net/how-to-enroll-more-aba-clients- by-overcoming-parent-objections-without-being-pushy-or- salesy/

49. Evidence for Learning: "Repeating a Year": (www.evidencefor learning.org.au/the-toolkits/the-teaching-and-learning-toolkit/ all-approaches/repeating-a-year/).

50. Patrick Farenga (May 2016) "The Foundations of Unschooling" www. johnholtgws.com/the-foundations-of-unschooling

51. Dr Naomi Fisher (2 November 2022) Internet Culture: "How to talk to kids about video games" www.blog.mozilla.org/en/internet-culture /how-to-talk-to-kids-about-video-games/

52. Wendy Fournier, National Autism Association of America, April 3, 2017 "New Study Highlights Mortality & Risk In Autism Wandering/ Elopement".

53. Freedom from Torture (25 November 2020) "What is Torture?" www. freedomfromtorture.org/news/what-is-torture Scott Frothingham (7 August 2019) Healthline: "Should I switch to Xylitol?" www.health

line.com/health/dental-and-oral-health/hydroxyapatite-tooth paste#where-to-buy

54. Devon Frye and Linda Karanzalis (27 April 2022), ADDitude Magazine: "What is Non Verbal Learning Disorder?" www.additude mag.com/what-is-nonverbal-learning-disorder-symptoms-and -diagnosis/

55. Hannah Furfaro (20 November 2017): Spectrum News: "Race, class contribute to disparities in Autism Diagnosis" www.spectrum news.org/news/race-class-contribute-disparities-autism-diagnoses/

56. Hollie Gabler Filce and Leslie Lavergne (2011) University of Mississippi: "Educational Needs and Accommodations for Children with Bowel and/or Bladder Dysfunction" https://files.eric.ed.gov/fulltext/EJ95 5441.pdf

57. Baden Gaeke Franz (from ASAN Winnipeg, 5 June 2017) "Help! My child is regressing!- On Autistic Burnout and How to Manage It" www.adaptmanitoba.ca/autistic-burnout/

58. Amy T Galloway, Laura M Fiorito, Lori B Francis and Leann L Birch (May 2006) National Library of Medicine (Appetite) "'Finish your soup': counterproductive effects of pressuring children to eat on intake and affect." www.ncbi.nlm.nih.gov/pmc/articles/PMC 2604806/

59. Miraca U. M. Gross, "Exceptionally Gifted Children: Long term outcomes of academic acceleration and nonacceleration". https://files.eric.ed.gov/fulltext/EJ746290.pdf

60. Dr Marcia Eckerd (31 August 2021) Psychology Today: "Are we giving Autistic children PTSD from school?" www.psychologytoday.com/us/blog/everyday-neurodiversity/202108/are-we-giving-autistic-children-ptsd-school

61. Elizabeth P Eminisor and Kelly Ezzell (April 2019), KidsHealth: "Antegrade Continence Enema (ACE)": www.kidshealth.org/en/parents/antegrade-enemas.html

62. Reece Epstein (2 September 2019) Web Archive: "How to enroll more ABA Clients by overcoming parents objections … without being pushy or salesy" www.web.archive.org/web/20190904141632/http://www.reputationelevation.net/how-to-enroll-more-aba-clients-by-overcoming-parent-objections-without-being-pushy-or-salesy/

63. Wendy Fournier, (3 April 2017) The National Autism Association: "New Study Highlights Mortality & Risk in Autism Wandering/Elopement" (https://nationalautismassociation.org/new-study-highlights-lethal-risks-of-missing-persons-with-autism/)

64. William Furey, Education Next: Teachers and Teaching VOL 20 No 3, 2022. "The Stubborn Myth of 'Learning Styles'" https://www.educationnext.org/stubborn-myth-learning-styles-state-teacher-license-prep-materials-debunked-theory/

65. Hannah Furfaro (20 November 2017): Spectrum News: "Race, class contribute to disparities in Autism Diagnosis" www.spectrumnews .org/news/race-class-contribute-disparities-autism-diagnoses/

66. Senait Gebregriorgis (8 May 2022) WESH 2 News: "Rollins College valedictorian with non-verbal autism delivers moving graduation address" (www.wesh.com/article/rollins-graduation-speech/399 38324?utm_campaign=snd-autopilot#)

67. Kenneth Goldsmith (26 August 2016) Quartz: "Why you should give your kids unlimited screen time" www.qz.com/767100/why-you-should-give-your-kids-unlimited-screen-time/

68. Maria G. Grammatikopoulou et al (Volume 11, September 2021) Science Direct: "Peeking into the Future: Transdermal patches for the delivery of micronutrient supplements" www.sciencedirect. com/science/article/pii/S2589936821000335

69. David Gray- Hammond (28 December 2022) "Spectrum 10K is back, and now they want to exploit you" Emergent Divergence: www.emergentdivergence.com/2022/12/28/spectrum-10k-is-back-and-now-they-want-to-exploit-you

70. John Greally: Autistics Worldwide: "List to identify ABA"

71. Jane Green (7 April 2022) TES Magazine: "Autism: 5 Adjustments needed in your classroom" www.tes.com/magazine/teaching-learning/general/autism-5-adjustments-needed-your-classroom

72. Kevin Gruenberg (2015) UMI Dissertation Publishing and ProQuest LLC: "Mentalization in DIR/Floortime: Facilitating Reflective Functioning in Parents of Children with Developmental Challenges" www.proquest.com/openview/64de6a6c321017f7cebaf783896fd5 d1/1?pq-origsite=gscholar&cbl=18750

73. The Guild for Human Services (29 November 2021) "Ask the Expert: 'nonspeaking' vs 'nonverbal' and why language matters" www. guildhumanservices.org/blog/ask-expert-nonspeaking-vs-nonverbal-and-why-language-matters

74. Rich Haridy (21 September 2021), New Atlas: "Large study finds potential benefits of digital screen time for children" www.new atlas.com/health-wellbeing/digital-screen-time-children-positive-self-report-problem/

75. Ciara Harte (4 June 2019) "Reframing Compliance: Exposing Violence Within Applied Behaviour Analysis" City University of Seattle CiaraHarteThesis2019.pdf (cityu.edu)

76. Harvard Health Publishing: Harvard Medical School "Anticholinergic drugs linked with dementia" (1 August 2018) https://www.health. harvard.edu/mind-and-mood/anticholinergic-drugs-linked-with-dementia

77. Luke Henriques-Gomes (11 November 2020), The Guardian: "Government called in private law firms to fight a third of NDIS cases, figures show": (https://www.theguardian.com/australia-

news/2020/nov/11/government-called-in-private-law-firms-to-fight-a-third-of-ndis-cases-figures-show

78. Aileen Herlinda Sandoval-Norton and Gary Shkedy (18 July 2019) Taylor and Francis Online (Cogent Psychology Volume , 2019): "How much compliance is too much compliance: Is long-term ABA therapy abuse?" www.tandfonline.com/doi/full/10.1080/2331 1908.2019.1641258

79. Dr Melanie Heyworth, (15 February 2019) Reframing Autism: "A Manifesto for Allies Adopting an Acceptance Approach to Autism" https://reframingautism.org.au/a-manifesto-for-allies-adopting -an-acceptance-approach-to-autism/

80. Dr Melanie Heyworth and Emma Marsh (31 January 2022) Reframing Autism: "Neurodiversity-Affirming Language: A letter to your child's support network" (www.reframingautism.org.au/ neurodiversity-affirming-language-a-letter-to-your-childs-support-network/)

81. Ansley Hill (21 November 2019) Healthline: "10 Interesting Types of Magnesium (and what to use each for)" www.healthline.com/ nutrition/magnesium-types.

82. Katie Hines (2020) "Is your Therapy Masquerading as ABA?": www. docs.google.com/document/d/1Ib7TsIgNgsqFIG5xQDXrDIoJoqht qKCTjWF7mWV-Je4/mobilebasic

83. Camille Hours, Christophe Recasens, Jean-Marc Baleyte (February 2022) Frontiers in Psychiatry "ASD and ADHD Comorbidity: What

Are We Talking About?" www.ncbi.nlm.nih.gov/pmc/articles/PMC 8918663/#B3

84. Erin Human, on EISFORERIN: "Tendril Theory" (10 August 2015) www. eisforerin.com/2015/08/10/tendril-theory/

85. Dr Michael Ryan Hunsaker: Why Haven't They Done That Yet? (16 April 2018) "PBIS is Broken: How do we fix it?" www.whyhavent theydonethatyet.wordpress.com/2018/04/16/pbis-is-broken-how-do-we-fix-it/

86. Matt Jancer (25 March 2022) Wired: "The best sunrise alarms to help you rise and shine": www.wired.com/gallery/best-sunrise-alarm-clocks/

87. Chaminda Jayanetti (10 September 2023) The Guardian "Revealed: covert deal to cut help for pupils in England with special needs" www.theguardian.com/uk-news/2023/sep/10/revealed-covert-deal-to-cut-help-for-pupils-in-england-with-special-needs

88. Michael S Jellinet (1 May 2010) Clinical Psychiatry News: "Don't Let ADHD crush Children's Self Esteem" https://www.mdedge.com/psychiatry/article/23971/pediatrics/dont-let-adhd-crush-childrens-self-esteem

89. Keeping Your Cool Parenting "Why Timeouts and The Naughty Step Doesn't Work and What To Do Instead" www.keepingyour coolparenting.com/why-timeouts-dont-work-and-what-to-do-instead/

90. Alfie Kohn (29 January 2020) National Education Policy Centre: "Alfie Kohn: Autism and Behaviorism: New Research Adds to an Already Compelling Case Against ABA" www.nepc.colorado.edu/blog/autism-and-behaviorism

91. Lily Konyn (8 February 2022) Assistive Ware: "Gestalt Language Processing and AAC" www.assistiveware.com/blog/gestalt-language-processing-aac#:~:text=Gestalt%20Language%20Processing%20(GLP)%20is,word%20to%20reach%20our%20meaning

92. Ira Kraemer, Autistic Science Person (31 March 2023) "Autism Acceptance Week and Applied Behavior Analysis" www.autistic scienceperson.com/2023/03/31/autism-acceptance-week-and-applied-behavior-analysis/

93. Henny Kupferstein (2 January 2018) Advances in Autism: Emerald Insight and Emerald Publishing Ltd: "Evidence of increased PTSD symptoms in autistics exposed to applied behavior analysis" www.emerald.com/insight/content/doi/10.1108/AIA-08-2017-0016/full/html

94. Henny Kupferstein (12 November 2019) Doogri Institute: "Why caregivers discontinue Applied Behaviour Analysis (ABA) and choose communication-based Autism Interventions" www.hennyk.com/2019/11/12/why-caregivers-discontinue-applied-behavior-analysis-aba-and-choose-communication-based-autism-interventions/

95. Henny Kupferstein (1 October 2019) Emerald Publishing Ltd: "Why caregivers discontinue applied behavior analysis (ABA) and choose communication-based autism interventions" www.emerald.com/insight/content/doi/10.1108/AIA-02-2019-0004/full/pdf

96. 'Ladysnessa', (23 August 2019) NeuroClastic: "Dialectical Behaviour Therapy & Autism: An Empowering Set of Skills" www.neuroclastic.com/dialectical-behavioral-therapy-autism-an-empowering-set-of-skills/

97. Jennifer Larson (7 April 2021) "What is Hydroxyapatite Toothpaste?" (which are all found under the same page link on the Healthline Website. www.healthline.com/health/dental-and-oral-health/hydroxyapatite-toothpaste#where-to-buy

98. Fede and Laurent, (2020) Autism Level UP!: "The Essential Guide To The Autism Level UP Levels!" https://autismlevelup.com/the-essential-guide-to-the-autism-level-up-levels/

99. Kathleen P. Levinstein (2018) „Distorting Psychology and Science at the Expense of Joy: Human Rights Violations Against Human Beings with Autism Via Applied Behavioral Analysis," Catalyst: A Social Justice Forum: *Vol. 8* : Iss. 1 , Article 5: https://trace.tennessee.edu/catalyst/vol8/iss1/5

100. Marc Lewis (19 August 2013) Psychology Today: "When the thrill is gone: reward deficiency syndrome" www.psychologytoday.

com/au/blog/addicted-brains/201308/when-the-thrill-is-gone-reward-deficiency-syndrome

101. Daniel Lin and Valsamma Eapen (10 June 2022) UNSW Sydney: "Opinion: Kids on the Autism Spectrum Experience More Bullying" www.newsroom.unsw.edu.au/news/health/kids-autism-spectrum-experience-more-bullying

102. S Long and J Goldblatt (Vol 45, Issue 4, April 2016) The Royal Australian College of General Practitioners website "MTHFR genetic testing: Controversy and Clinical implications" www.racgp.org.au/afp/2016/april/mthfr-genetic-testing-controversy-and-clinical-imp.

103. The Lovaas Centre. http://thelovaascenter.com/about-us/dr-ivar-lovaas/

104. C.L Lynch (28 March 2019) NeuroClastic: "Invisible Abuse: ABA and the things only Autistic people can see" www.neuroclastic.com/invisible-abuse-aba-and-the-things-only-autistic-people-can-see/

105. C.L Lynch (8 July 2019) NeuroClastic: "Life Skills Aren't What You Think: What Research Says About Raising Autistic Kids" www.neuroclastic.com/life-skills/

106. C.L.Lynch (23 June 2021) NeuroClastic "Justice for Xavier Hernandez: Texas School Still Practicing Illegal Restraints After Killing Young Autistic Man" www.neuroclastic.com/xavier-hernandez-fort-worth-autism-restraint-death/

107. MadAsBirdsBlog (3 April 2017) "I Abused Children For a Living": www.madasbirdsblog.wordpress.com/2017/04/03/i-abused-children-for-a-living/

108. Jane Mantzalas, Amanda L. Richdale, Achini Adikari, Jennifer Loew, and Cheryl Dissanayake (9 March 2022) Vol 4. Iss 1. "What is Autistic Burnout? A Thematic Analysis of Posts on Two Online Platforms" Autism in Adulthood www.liebertpub.com/doi/10.1089/aut.2021.0021

109. Emma Marsh and Melanie Heyworth Reframing Autism (31 January 2022) "Neurodiversity-affirming language: A letter to your child's support network" www.reframingautism.org.au/neurodiversity-affirming-language-a-letter-to-your-childs-support-network/

110. Christina Maslen, Rebecca Hodge, Kim Tie, Richard Laugharne, Kristen Lamb and Rohit Shankar (2022, Volume 72, issue 720) British Journal of General Practice: "Constipation in autistic people and people with learning disabilities" www.bjgp.org/content/72/720/348?fbclid=IwAR00wtMA1YRj6oZkyT5vDI_1BUT2Wqs7V6aRDBVjrS7zd5cH7-g9rtEnZ4Q

111. Jessica McCabe: How To ADHD: "ADHD in Women" https://www.youtube.com/watch?v=EMpt40zNK-w

112. T.A.M McDonald (11 March 2020) Liebert Publishers: "Autism Identity and the "Lost Generation": Structural Validation of the Autism Spectrum Identity Scale and Comparison of Diagnosed

and Self-Diagnosed Adults on the Autism Spectrum" www.
liebertpub.com/doi/full/10.1089/aut.2019.0069

113. Laura McGuinn (23 September 2019) HealthyChildren.org, American
Academy of Pediatrics "Should my child repeat a grade?" (www.
healthychildren.org/English/ages-stages/gradeschool/school/
Pages/Repeating-a-Grade.aspx)

114. Roger McKinney (28 September 2018) Colombia Daily Tribune
"Special Education Program Transitions Back To CPS Control"
www.columbiatribune.com/story/news/education/2020/09/28/
special-education-program-transitions-back-to-cps-
control/114159494/

115. S. A McLeod (5 February 2017) Simply Psychology *Behaviorist
approach*: www.simplypsychology.org/behaviorism.html

116. Medline Plus "Arginine: glycine amidinotransferase deficiency"
www.medlineplus.gov/genetics/condition/arginineglycine-
amidinotransferase-deficiency

117. Lyanne Melendez (20 May 2022) ABC7News: "2 UC Berkley students
make history as 1st nonspeaking autistic graduates" www.abc7
news.com/uc-berkeley-cal-graduation-nonspeaking-autism-
graduates-david-teplitz/11870714/

118. Michelle Menezes, Jim Soland, Micah Mazurek (September 2023)
Science Direct: "Screen time and diagnoses of anxiety and
depression in autistic vs neurotypical youth" Research in Autism
Spectrum Disorders (Vol 107, 102222) www.sciencedirect.com/

science/article/abs/pii/S1750946723001228?fbclid=IwAR2WSi
6noq0qBTyUL0tdGXLTdCIi0h84c1CXjsy6T_i-PeMFzSAdJ65TUOk

119. Carol Millman (27 March 2019) NeuroClastic: "Is ABA Really 'Dog Training for Children'? A Professional Dog Trainer Weighs In." www.neuroclastic.com/is-aba-really-dog-training-for-children-a-professional-dog-trainer-weighs-in/

120. Damian Milton (2014) National Library of Medicine: "Autistic expertise: A critical reflection on the production of knowledge in autism studies" www.pubmed.ncbi.nlm.nih.gov/24637428/

121. Minister of Education James Merlino (22 May 2018) "Inclusive Education Scholarships for Teachers" (https://www.jamesmerlino.com.au/media-releases/inclusive-education-scholarships-for-teachers/).

122. Christine Miserandino, (2003) www.ButYouDon'tLookSick.com , "The Spoon Theory". https://lymphoma-action.org.uk/sites/default/files/media/documents/2020-05/Spoon%20theory%20by%20Christine%20Miserandino.pdf

123. Katie Munday (29 January 2022) "Autistic Realisation and Shielding", AUCADEMY: www.aucademy.co.uk/2022/01/29/autistic-realisation-and-shielding/

124. Lisa Neilsen (20 November 2018) Tech & Learning: "Why you shouldn't limit screen time" www.techlearning.com/features/why-you-shouldnt-limit-screen-time

125. Judith Newman, 21 October 2021, National Geographic: "Here's how parks and public lands are becoming more autism-friendly" (https://www.nationalgeographic.com/travel/article/heres-how-parks-and-public-lands-are-becoming-more-autism-friendly

126. Not An Autism Mom (20 July 2020) "100-ish Books on autism and Neurodiversity": www.notanautismmom.com

127. Daniel Noyed (11 April 2022) "Best Headphones for Sleeping" from Sleep Foundation: (www.sleepfoundation.org/best-headphones-for-sleeping)

128. Lindsay Oberman, Alvaro Pascaul-Leone (17 June 2014) National Library of Medicine "Hyperplasticity in autism spectrum disorder confers protection from Alzheimer's disease" www.ncbi.nlm.nih.gov/pmc/articles/PMC4392915/

129. Occupational Therapy Helping Children: "Should my child repeat next year?" (www.occupationaltherapy.com.au/should-my-child-repeat-next-year/).

130. Corinne O'Keefe Osborn "Should you be worried about Fluoride Toothpaste?" (25 October 2019), www.healthline.com/health/dental-and-oral-health/hydroxyapatite-toothpaste#where-to-buy

131. Amy Orben & Andrew K. Przybylski (14 January 2019), Nature Human Behaviour: "The Association between adolescent wellbeing and

digital technology use" www.nature.com/articles/s41562-018-0506-1

132. Simon Parkin (9 January 2022) The Guardian "The trouble with Roblox, the video game empire built on child labour". www.theguardian.com/games/2022/jan/09/the-trouble-with-roblox-the-video-game-empire-built-on-child-labour

133. Ayesh Perera (6 September 2021) for Simply Psychology: "Uncanny Valley": www.simplypsychology.org/uncanny-valley.html

134. Physician on FIRE: "3 Years of Homeschooling & Worldschooling: What We've Learned & What's Next!" www.physicianonfire.com/three-years-of-homeschooling/

135. Jackie Pilgrim (16 March 2015) The Art of Autism: "Jackie: Christian, Mom, Advocate, Entrepreneur, Artist, Poet and #Aspie" www.the-art-of-autism.com/jackie-christian-mom-advocate-entrepreneur-artist-poet-and-aspie/

136. Ed Pilkington (10 July 2007) The Guardian "Parents sue after boy dies during autism treatment" www.theguardian.com/world/2007/jul/10/usa.edpilkington

137. Rachel Pontin (17 March 2022), Shoestring Sustainability: "Best ADHD Homeschool Resources -Australia": www.rachelpontin.com/best-adhd-homeschool-resources-australia/

138. Nicole Precel (2 May 2022) The Sydney Morning Herald: "Push for special schools to be phased out under inclusive education plan" www.smh.com.au/education/push-for-special-schools-to

-be-phased-out-under-inclusive-education-plan-20220428-p5agxd.html?utm_medium=Social&utm_source=Facebook#Echobox=1651460233

139. M. Prior, J.M.A Roberts et al. Australian DSS reports, "A Review of the Research to Identify the Most Effective Models of Practice in Early Intervention for Children with Autism Spectrum Disorders" 2011. The Australian Society for Autism Research (ASFAR) https://www.dss.gov.au/sites/default/files/documents/10_2014/review_of_the_research_report_2011_0.pdf

140. Michelle Pugle (21 July 2021) Very Well Health: "What is Glutamate" www.verywellhealth.com/what-is-glutamate-5188294

141. Yenn Purkis (18 May 2022) "'You don't speak for my child'. Actually No, I don't". (www.yennpurkis.home.blog/2022/05/18/you-dont-speak-for-my-child-actually-no-i-dont/)

142. Yenn Purkis blog (22 May 2022) Yenn Purkis Website: "Things Ableists Say" (www.yennpurkis.home.blog/2022/05/22/things-ableists-say-2/)

143. Jake Pyne (17 November 2020) Cambridge University Press: "'Building a Person': Legal and Clinical Personhood for Autistic and Trans Children in Ontario". www.cambridge.org/core/journals/canadian-journal-of-law-and-society-la-revue-canadienne-droit-et-societe/article/building-a-person-legal-and-clinical-personhood-for-autistic-and-trans-children-in-ontario

144. Meg Raby "Stimming is fun" www.neuroclastic.com/infographics /#elementor-toc__heading-anchor-51

145. Real Social Skills website (17 July 2015) "Appearing to enjoy behavior modification is not meaningful": www.realsocialskills. org/2015/07/17/appearing-to-enjoy-behavior-modificiation-is-not/

146. Reframing Autism: "Position Statement on Therapies and Interventions" (12 February, 2020) www.reframingautism.org.au/ position-statement-on-therapies-and-interventions/

147. Glenn Robertson (2 January 2019) Specialist Hypnotherapy, YouTube video: "What is ARFID?" www.youtube.com/watch?app =desktop&v=JK9r14D4d-k&feature=share

148. Danielle Romanes & Jordana Hunter (21 September 2015) Grattan Institute: "Grade Repetition: there are better ways to move kids forward than by holding them back" (www.grattan.edu.au/news /grade-repetition-there-are-better-ways-to-move-kids-forward-than-by-holding-them-back/).

149. Andrea Romano (Updated 27 April 2022) Travel and Leisure: "These 12 Famous Museums offer Virtual Tours You Can Take on Your Couch" www.travelandleisure.com/attractions/museums-galleries/museums-with-virtual-tours

150. Lucy Rome (18 January 2022) Educational App Store: "Best Apps for Parents" www.educationalappstore.com/app/category/apps -for-parents

151. Michael Samsel "Functional Models: Drives, Layers, Segments, and Character Armor": Reich and Lowen Therapy www.reichand lowentherapy.org/Content/Principles/functional_model.html

152. Erika Sanborne: Autistic PhD (7 August 2023) "What is bottom-up thinking in autism" www.autisticphd.com/theblog/what-is-bottom-up-thinking-in-autism/

153. Noah Sasson, Daniel Faso, Jack Nugent, Sarah Lovell, Daniel Kennedy, Ruth Grossman (1 February 2017) National Library of Medicine: "Neurotypical Peers are Less Willing to Interact with Those with Autism based on Thin Slice Judgments" www.ncbi. nlm.nih.gov/pmc/articles/PMC5286449/

154. Dr Elizabeth Scott (3 May 2022) Very Well Mind: "What is a Highly Sensitive Person (HSP)?" www.verywellmind.com/highly -sensitive-persons-traits-that-create-more-stress -4126393

155. Abby Sesterka and Erin Bullus, Psyche: "How to be a good friend to an Autistic person" www.psyche.co/guides/how-to-be-a-good-friend-to-an-autistic-person

156. Deb Sharpe, The University of Vermont Continence Project "Best Practice Recommendations for the Care and Management of Students with Bowel/Bladder Incontinence". https://www.uvm. edu/sites/default/files/Center-on-Disability-and-Community-Inclusion/ContinenceBestPracticeRecommendationsfortheCare andManagementofStudents.pdf

157. S C.K Shaw, M Doherty, L Carravallah, M Johnson, J O'Sullivan, N Chown, S Neilson (17 October 2023) National Library of Medicine "Barriers to healthcare and a 'triple empathy problem' may lead to adverse outcomes for autistic adults: A qualitative study" www.pubmed.ncbi.nlm.nih.gov/37846479/

158. G. Shkedy, D. Shkedy & A. H. Sandoval-Norton (6 August 2022) Springer Link: Advances in Neurodevelopmental Disorders: "Long-term ABA Therapy Is Abusive: A Response to Gorycki, Ruppel, and Zane. www.link.springer.com/article/10.1007/s41252-021-00201-1?fbclid=IwAR2d6Mq8I3B7kHvBjKPagARTyjzGimZhwvfh7LfDy_gLPTu-iuu4xwR5cIU

159. SilentlySpeakingVolumes (13 April 2020) Autistic Self-Advocates Against ABA (Wordpress): "Problematic and Traumatic: Why Nobody Needs ABA" www.autisticselfadvocatesagainstaba.wordpress.com/2020/04/13/problematic-and-traumatic-why-nobody-needs-aba/

160. Larry Silver (13 July 2022) ADDitude Magazine "ADHD Neuroscience 101" www.additudemag.com/adhd-neuroscience-101

161. Alexandria Sims, (2 July 2015), The Independent "Teenage girl dies from heart attack after not going to the toilet for eight weeks". www.independent.co.uk/life-style/health-and-families/health-news/teenage-girl-dies-of-heart-attack-after-not-going-to-the-toilet-for-eight-weeks-10357533)

162. Noelle Sinclair (11 October 2021) The Autistic Perspective: "Language Matters: The PFL v's IFL debate" www.theautisticpers pective.com/post/language-matters-the-pfl-vs-ifl-debate

163. Hannah Smith (16 January 2022) Educational App Store: "Best Homeschool Apps" www.educationalappstore.com/best-apps/best-homeschool-apps

164. Jennifer Smith Richards and Jodi S. Cohen (28 May 2021) Chicago Tribune "Illinois schools secluded and restrained children thousands of times this year despite pandemic closures" www.chicagotribune.com/investigations/ct-seclusion-restraint-illinois-schools-data-20210527-6i4hbdbfrfdzfcsr27yi7fphsy-story.html

165. Mikle South, Andreia P.Costa, Carly McMorris (12 January 2021) "Death by suicide among people with autism: beyond Zebrafish" JAMA Network: www.jamanetwork.com/journals/jamanetworkopen/full article/2774847

166. Maxfield Sparrow (Shannon Des Roches Rosa, 7 April 2017) from the Thinking Person's Guide to Autism: "If not ABA, then what?" https://thinkingautismguide.com/2017/04/if-not-aba-then-what.html

167. Shishira Sreenivas (3 December 2021) WebMD: "What is Conversion Therapy?" https://www.webmd.com/sex-relationships/what-is-conversion-therapy

168. Callum Stephen (16 February 2023) The Independent "'I speak – but I rarely feel heard': Why autistic people like me feel lonely" www.independent.co.uk/voices/ken-bruce-children-chris-packham-autistic-b2282801.html

169. Julia Sterman, Erin Gustafson, Lindsay Eisenmenger, Lizzie Hamm and Jules Edwards (17 June 2022) Sage Journals: Occupational Therapy Journal of Research: "Autistic Adult Perspectives on Occupational Therapy for Autistic Children and Youth" Volume 43, Issue 2 www.journals.sagepub.com/doi/10.1177/15394492221103850

170. Louise Sutton (27 June 2019) "Are you Worried that your child might be Allistic?" http://ablogaboutraisingmyautisticson.com/are-you-worried-that-your-child-might-be-allistic/

171. Rohan Tandon (12 February 2022) MMA Insight: "Best Reaction Training Lights" (www.mmainsight.com/guides/best-speed-and-agility-lights).

172. The Autism Wars (11 August 2017) "How My Non-Speaking Autistic Son Taught Me YouTube Speak" www.theautismwars.blogspot.com/2017/08/how-my-nonspeaking-autistic-son-taught.html?m=1

173. The Conversation (1 April 2022) "Autistic people are six times more likely to attempt suicide – poor mental health support may be to blame" www.theconversation.com/autistic-people-are-six-times-more-likely-to-attempt-suicide-poor-mental-health-support-may-be-to-blame-180266

174. The Healthline Medical Network (8 March 2019) "What Does Gamma Aminobutyric Acid (GABA) Do?" www.healthline.com/health/gamma-aminobutyric-acid

175. "The Measured Mom" (12 May 2022) "What teachers should know about Dyslexia" www.themeasuredmom.com/what-teachers-should-know-about-dyslexia/

176. Therapist Neurodiversity Collective: The Problem with Pairing: www.therapistndc.org/the-problems-with-pairing/

177. The Therapist Neurodiversity Collective (2020): "ABA is not Effective: So says the Latest Report from the Department of Defense" www.therapistndc.org/aba-is-not-effective-so-says-the-latest-report-from-the-department-of-defense/

178. Therapist Neurodiversity Collective: "Why not Positive Behaviour Support (PBS) Positive Behavioural Interventions and Supports (PBIS), or Positive Reinforcement?" www.therapistndc.org/positive-behavior-support-pbs-positive-behavioral-interventions-and-supports-pbis-or-positive-reinforcement/

179. Therapist Neurodiversity Collective, (January 2018), "IEP Makeover" (https://therapistndc.org/wp-content/uploads/2020/09/IEP-Make-overs.pdf)

180. The TLC Foundation: for body-focused repetitive behaviors: "The great big list of favorite fiddles or stimulation substitutes and behavioral blockers for BFRB's" (9 August 2021): www.bfrb.org/blog/1-blog/679-the-great-big-list-of-favorite-fiddles

181. Cheyenne Thornton (18 April 2021) NeuroClastic: "ABA for creating Masking Black Autistics" www.neuroclastic.com/aba-for-creating-masking-black-autistics/.

182. Beth Tolley, Alliance Against Seclusion and Restraint: "The problem with behaviourism" www.endseclusion.org/articles/the-problem-with-behaviourism/

183. Celi Trepanier, Crushing Tall Poppies "A gifted Child Checklist for teachers" June 9, 2014 https://crushingtallpoppies.com/2014/06/09/a-gifted-child-checklist-for-teachers/

184. Dr Patricia Turner (5 March 2022), Turners Psychology Calgary: "Gifted Adults are sensitive to light, sound, texture, and medication dosage" www.turnerpsychologycalgary.com/giftedness/gifted-adults-are-highly-sensitive/

185. University of Nottingham (21 August 2018) "New Research Sheds Light on Why Suicide is More Common in Autistic People" www.nottingham.ac.uk/news/pressreleases/2018/august/new-research-sheds-light-on-why-suicide-is-more-common-in-autistic-people.aspx

186. University of Portsmouth (26 April 2022) Medical Xpress: "Study suggests early self-awareness of Autism leads to better quality of life" www.medicalxpress.com/news/2022-04-early-self-awareness-autism-quality-life.html

187. Terra Vance, (17 August 2021), NeuroClastic: "An Interview with Soma Mukhopadhyay, Pioneer of Rapid Prompting Method (RPM)" (www.

neuroclastic.com/an-interview-with-soma-mukhopadhyay-pioneer-of-rapid-prompting-method-rpm/)

188. Terra Vance (12 April 2020) NeuroClastic: "On Autism and Intelligence: Language and Advocacy" www.neuroclastic.com/on-autism-and-intelligence-language-and-advocacy/

189. Terra Vance (2022) "When a Non-Autistic Child Is Raised by Autistic Parents, Their Experiences Are Similar to Autistics Raised by Non-Autistics" www.neuroclastic.com/having-autistic-parents-when-you-are-neurotypical/?amp#top

190. Terra Vance (22 September 2018) Psych Central: "Allism Spectrum Disorder" www.psychcentral.com/blog/aspie/2018/09/allism-spectrum-disorders-a-parody

191. Terra Vance (12 April 2020) NeuroClastic: "On Autism and Intelligence: Measuring and Understanding IQ" www.neuroclastic.com/on-autism-and-intelligence-measuring-understanding-iq/

192. J.M.J van der Meer, A. M Oerlemans, D. J van Steijn, M. G. A Lappenschaar, L. M. J de Sonneville, J. K Buitelaar, and N. N. J Rommelse (2012) Pub Med (American Academy of Child and Adolescent Psychiatry. Published by Elsevier Inc.) "Are autism spectrum disorder and attention-deficit/hyperactivity disorder different manifestations of one overarching disorder? Cognitive and symptom evidence from a clinical and population-based sample" www.pubmed.ncbi.nlm.nih.gov/23101742/

193. VicRoads website: www.vicroads.vic.gov.au "Learning to Drive with a Disability, Road Safety and Medical Review" Factsheet (April 2019).

194. Victorian Department of Education "Repeating a Year Level": https://www2.education.vic.gov.au/pal/repeating-year-level/resources

195. Frances Vidakovic 'Is Santa Real'; (https://pin.it/6IuOTpP) (www.InspiringlifeDreams.com)

196. Zawn Villines and reviewed by Heidi Moawad (8 February 2023) Medical News Today: "Serotonin Deficiency: Symptoms and Treatment" www.medicalnewstoday.com/articles/serotonin-deficiency

197. Zawn Villines, Medical News Today "What is ableism, and what is its impact?" November 7 2021 https://www.medicalnewstoday.com/articles/ableism#types

198. Alvin Ward (14 October 2019) Mental Floss: "This 'smart' bed accessory will rock you to sleep" www.mentalfloss.com/article/602877/smart-bed-accessory-will-rock-you-sleep

199. Sally Weale (23 February 2023) The Guardian: "Jason Arday to become youngest ever black professor at Cambridge" www.amp.theguardian.com/education/2023/feb/23/jason-arday-to-become-youngest-ever-black-professor-at-cambridge

200. Angela Weddle (28 February 2016) The Art of Autism: "The Autism Shift: The Visibly Invisible – Autistic People of Color" www.the-art-of

-autism.com/the-autism-shift-the-visibly-invisible-autistic-people-of-color/

201. Suzannah Weiss (22 April 2016) Complex: "Meet the People Being Left Out Of Mainstream Conversations About Autism" www.complex.com/life/2016/04/autism-women-poc

202. Ashley Welch (19 January 2021) Healthline "Rate of Suicide 3 Times Higher for Autistic People" www.healthline.com/health-news/rate-of-suicide-3-times-higher-for-autistic-people

203. Rose Weldon (14 February 2023) Healio: "Video games not harmful to kids' cognitive abilities, exploratory study finds" www.healio.com/news/primary-care/20230214/video-games-not-harmful-to-kids-cognitive-abilities-exploratory-study-finds

204. Dr Gemma Wheeler (22 December 2021), Electric Teeth: "Best non-mint Toothpaste options for Adults" www.electricteeth.com/au/best-non-mint-toothpaste/

205. Evaleen Whelton, (14 March 2022), Konfident Kidz Ltd: "Autism and Behaviours- Why are we not looking at people pleasing in Autistic kids?" (https://konfidentkidz.ie/blog-2/)

206. Evaleen Whelton (22 March 2022) AUsome Training: "Why Charlie Doesn't Go To School" (22 March 2022) www.ausometraining.com/why-charlie-doesnt-go-to-school/ and YouTube Video: www.youtube.com/watch?v=UlBD5_-CemM

207. Evaleen Whelton, (14 March 2022), Konfident Kidz Ltd: "Autism and Behaviours- Why are we not looking at people pleasing in Autistic kids?" (https://konfidentkidz.ie/blog-2/)

208. Signe Whitson, Psychology Today, March 25, 2012; "What parents can do when bullying is downplayed at school" https://www.psychologytoday.com/au/blog/passive-aggressive-diaries/201203/what-parents-can-do-when-bullying-is-downplayed-school

209. Daniel A. Wilkenfeld and Allison M. McCarthy (March 2020, Pages 31-69) Kennedy Institute of Ethics Journal (Volume 30, Number 1): "Ethical Concerns with Applied Behaviour Analysis for Autism Spectrum 'Disorder'". www.learningkeystones.com/wp-content/uploads/2021/02/Uploads/Ethical%20Concerns%20with%20ABA%20for%20Autism%20Spectrum%20Disorder.pdf

210. Dr Albert Wong (7 December 2022) Osomatopia "The Art Of Letting Go: Why Reichian Character Armor Is Worth Dismantling" www.somatopia.com/blog/the-art-of-letting-go-why-reichian-character-armor-is-worth-dismantling

211. Maya Yang (19 April 2022) The Guardian "US Man gets $450,000 after unwanted work birthday party triggered panic attack" www.theguardian.com/us-news/2022/apr/18/unwanted-office-birthday-party-lawsuit-panic-attack

212. Benjamin Zablotsky, Matthew Bramlett, and Stephen J Blumberg (20 March 2015) National Library of Medicine: "Factors

associated with parental ratings of condition severity for children with Autism Spectrum Disorder" www.ncbi.nlm.nih.gov/pmc/articles/PMC4652641/

213. Rachel Zamzow (14 April 2022) "Why Autism Therapies Have an Evidence Problem" from Spectrum News: www.spectrumnews.org/news/why-autism-therapies-have-an-evidence-problem/

214. Dr Sarah Zate: Therapist Neurodiversity Collective "Medical Neglect – Physician and Court Ordered ABA for Autistic Children": www.therapistndc.org/medical-neglect-physician-and-court-ordered-aba-for-autistic-children/

215. Jordyn Zimmerman "This is not about me" This Is Not About Me | A story about growing up non-speaking

Books

1. Fay Angelo, Rose Stewart, Heather Anderson (1 August 2011) "Secret boys Business: This Book is About Important Boys' Business".

2. Fay Angelo, Rose Stewart, Heather Pritchard (1 May 2004) "Secret Girls' Business"

3. Dr Elaine N. Aron "The Highly Sensitive Person" (26 May 2020 – 25th Anniversary Edition)

4. Dr Luke Beardon "Avoiding Anxiety in Autistic Adults: A Guide for Autistic Wellbeing". (2021).

5. Compiled by Sally Cat "PDA by PDAers: From Anxiety to Avoidance and Masking to Meltdowns"

6.   Dr Sharie Coombes: Complete series of Books at: www.drsharie.com/published-books/

7.   Anthony Cohn, (2007), Jessica Kingsley Publishers, (London, UK and Philadelphia, USA): "Constipation, Withholding and Your Child: A family guide to soiling and wetting".

8.   KC Davis "How to keep house while drowning".

9.   Julia Cook: "Decibella, and her 6 inch voice" (March 2014).

10. Amanda Diekman "Low-Demand Parenting: Dropping Demands, Restoring Calm and Finding Connection with your Uniquely Wired Child".

11. Dr Thomas R. Duhamel: "The Ins and Outs of Poop".

12. Dr Thomas R. Duhamel (2015): "Softy the Poop: Helping Families talk about Poop".

13. Sophia. J. Ferguson, (2015), Macnaughtan Books, (London, UK): "Stool Withholding: what to do when your child won't poo!"

14. Ruth Fidler and Julia Daunt "Being Julia – A Personal Account of Living with Pathological Demand Avoidance"

15. Carrie Finison (26 January 2021) "Don't Hug Doug: (He Doesn't Like it)"

16. Naomi Fisher "Changing Our Minds: How children can take control of their own learning". (2021)

17. Naomi Fisher "A Different Way To Learn: Neurodiversity and Self-Directed Education". (2023).

18. Eliza Fricker "School Can't Not Won't"

19. Dr Ross W Greene (17 August 2021): "The Explosive Child" 6ᵗʰ Edition.

20. Dr Ross Greene (September 2014) "Lost at School"

21. Dr Ross W. Greene (released 2016): "Raising Human Beings: Creating a Collaborative Partnership With your Child"

22. Dr Edward M. Hallowell & Dr John J. Ratey (2021) "ADHD 2.0: New Science and Essential Strategies for Thriving with Distraction – Childhood through Adulthood"

23. Jules Edwards and Meghan Ashburn (19 January 2023): "I will die on this hill"

24. Gillian Harris and Elizabeth Shea (15 July 2018): "Food Refusal and Avoidant Eating in Children, including those with Autism Spectrum Conditions: A Practical Guide for Parents and Professionals".

25. Naoki Higashida "The Reason I Jump"

26. John Holt (1964) "How Children Fail"

27. Thomas W Iland & Emily Doyle Iland (15 September 2017) "Come to Life! Your Guide to Self-Discovery"

28. Ivan Illich (1971) "Deschooling Society" and *Medical Nemesis: The Expropriation of Health*" – 1975

29. Sarah Joubert (24 December 2015) "Daily Life Skills Big Book" from Classroom Complete Press. www.classroomcompletepress. com/products/ccp5793

30. Fiona Katauskas: "The Amazing True Story of How Babies Are Made"

31. Ido Kedar: (16 July 2018) "In Two Worlds"

32. Ido Kedar: (25 October 2012) Create Space Publishers: "Ido in Autismland: Climbing out of Autism's Silent Prison".

33. David A Kilpatrick (1 October 2016) "Equipped for Reading Success".

34. Cynthia Kim (10 August 2013) "I think I might be Autistic: A guide to Autism Spectrum Disorder Diagnosis and Self Discovery for Adults"

35. Alfie Kohn (28 March 2006): "Unconditional Parenting: Moving from Rewards and Punishments to Love and Reason" www.alfiekohn.org/UP/

36. Alfie Kohn "Punished by Rewards"

37. David Koppenhaver & Karen A. Erikson (17 December 2019) "Comprehensive Literacy For All: Teaching Students with Significant Disabilities to Read and Write"

38. Deborah Lipsky and Will Richards (15 February 2009): "Managing Meltdowns: using the S.C.A.R.E.D Calming Technique with Children and Adults with Autism".

39. Angus Maguire (13 January 2016) Interaction Institute for Social Change: "Illustrating Equality Vs Equity" www.actioninstitute.org

40. Jenara Nerenberg (16 February 2021) "Divergent Mind: Thriving in a World that Wasn't Designed for You".

41. Tabitha J Page (20 February 2021): "I'm a Type One Kid"

42. Allan Pease (1981) "Body Language".

43. Dr Devon Price (12 April 2022) "Unmasking Autism: The Power of Embracing Our Hidden Neurodiversity"

44. Yenn Purkis "The Awesome Autistic Go-To Guide: A Practical Handbook for Autistic Teens and Tweens" (www.yennpurkis.com/books/)

45. Meg Raby: (19 March 2019) "My Brother Otto".

46. Kate E. Reynolds (21 August 2014) Jessica Kingsley Publishers: "Things Tom Likes: A Book about sexuality and masturbation for boys and young men with autism and related conditions".

47. Kate E. Reynolds (15 August 2014): "What's happening to Tom"

48. Kate E Reynolds (15 January 2015): "What's happening to Ellie"

49. Lyric Rivera: "Workplace Neurodiversity Rising" (Nov 2022).

50. Janeen Sanders (10 November 2017) "Let's Talk About Body Boundaries, Consent and Respect: Teach children about body ownership, respect, feelings, choices and recognising bullying behaviours".

51. Dr Sally Shaywitz (2014) "Overcoming Dyslexia".

52. Edith Sheffer (2018) "Asperger's Children: The origins of autism in nazi Vienna".

53. Steve Silberman (2015) "Neurotribes: The Legacy of Autism And How To Think Smarter About People Who Think Differently"

54. Rachel E. Simon "The Every Body Book: The LGBTQ+ Inclusive Guide for Kids about Sex, Gender, Bodies and Families". (2020).

55. Nelly Thomas (3 March 2020): Some Brains: A book celebrating Neurodiversity"

56. Sandra Thom-Jones "Growing in to Autism" (2022).

57. Gregory C Tino: "The Autistic Boy in the Unruly Body: Autism and I Series Paperback" (27 July 2022).

58. Sun Tzu "The Art Of War" – written 5th century BC.

59. Elizabeth Verdick: "Calm-Down Time" (toddler tools)"

60. Tracey J. Vessillo: "I Can't, I Won't No Way! A book for children who refuse to poop".

61. Dr Nick Walker (2021) "Neuroqueer Heresies"?

62. Evaleen Whelton "Standing Up For Myself" from AUsome Training.

63. Sonny Jane Wise (12 February 2022) "The Neurodivergent Friendly Workbook of DBT Skills"

64. Rebecca Wood, Laura Crane, Francesca Happe, Alan Morrison, and Ruth Moyse (April 2022) "Learning from Autistic Teachers: How to be a Neurodiversity-Inclusive School".

65. Melanie Yergeau (2018) "Authoring Autism: On Rhetoric and Neurological Queerness"